SUZO

EMBRACING THE HARD + HOLY ROAD
TO WHOLENESS IN A QUICK-FIX WORLD

JOY MCMILLAN

DEDICATION

Dedicated to the women who have walked
with me on the road to wholeness.

To Christine, who saw me and sought me out as an
awkward tween, and ignited a life-long passion
in me for health and fitness.

To Cindra, who tended faithfully to my weary
adult soul, and was instrumental in my journey
to learning to live as the beloved.

And to my mother, who modeled what it looks like
to truly love and follow Jesus, and who continues
to shape and stretch my spiritual life.

UBUNTU

"I am because we are"

CONTENTS

INTRODUCTION

Earth's crammed with heaven, and every common bush afire
with God, but only he who sees takes off his shoes;
the rest sit round and pluck blackberries.

Elizabeth Barrett Browning

Our daughter, Alathea, was just shy of 3 years old when we moved into our house out in the country. I had painted a large tree - complete with potato stamp leaves and glitter-eyed owls - onto her already butter yellow walls. She had loved it then, and very sweetly embraced it as her bedroom reality for over seven years. In an effort to modernize and mature her living quarters with minimal effort, when she turned eight, I painted an adjacent wall sky blue. When she hit ten years old, I could stand the tree no longer. This may have had something to do with the fact that her bedroom is the first one down the hall, and the 'owl wall' stares at you as you sit on the loo - as one does multiple times a day, with the

1

door open, when you live here. In an attempt to procure more blue walls, while protecting her mother's work of art (and feelings) in the process, she'd kindly suggested I simply "paint blue around the tree". I may have blown tea out of my nostrils in response. Ain't nobody got time for that. No, it was time to bid farewell to my 8 year old mural, and to usher in the uncluttered coolness of a big girl's room.

With a long weekend upon us, I kicked Alathea out of her room (moving her in with her little brother), and picked up two gorgeous shades of blue paint; aqua and teal. With my hubby working long hours on a big case and my kids occupied with books, Lego and MineCraft, I clicked play on a new audio book and powered through the long-awaited makeover, pausing only to feed and smooch said children. By Sunday afternoon it was time for the big reveal. I'm not sure who was more excited; her or me.

Her walls, decked out in stunning new shades of Caribbean blue, made the sheer white curtains, comforter and princess (aka. mosquito) canopy, hanging from the ceiling, stand out. I mounted a beautiful silver-rimmed mirror on the far wall, adding a flurry of little white 3D butterflies behind the canopy for effect. A mini gallery wall, complete with family photos from our recent trip to South Africa, adorned her desk wall, and I brought in the two teal-based lamps from my own bedside tables. Finding a pretty planter, I took a fun faux tree - with plenty of personality - from my studio and placed it in the far corner, adding a touch of green to the sea of blue and white.

When I had sufficiently faffed with the finishing touches, I gave her the Fixer Upper spiel; pulling up the unimpressive 'before' photos on my phone, and then swinging the door open to dramatically reveal her bright new space. She just stood there, mouth-agape, in her doorway...and then spent the next half hour sitting cross-legged on her bed - under her princess net - taking it all in. It was one of my favorite decorating projects to date - and it still makes me smile every time I sit on that loo across the hall.

When my husband came home from work, I gave him the whirlwind tour - highlighting some of my favorite details and deals (like the mirror I'd searched for, and scored in the clearance section of Dollar General for $7.50). He loved the color and overall look, but almost immediately zoomed in on a wall. The one I'd hoped he wouldn't notice.

"Did you spackle this, Babe?".

"Of course I did ... and I sanded it", I scoffed. Because apparently this fact wasn't obvious.

"How many times did you spackle ... and which sandpaper did you use?"

Insert awkward silence here.

"Once ... and the one in my studio".

We moved from wall to wall, as he traced the outline of the embossed tree branches and owl's eyes, still staring uncomfortably at us through the Aqua Fiesta 053, pointing out divots and holes as if I hadn't seen them and intentionally ignored them in my scurry to move into the more exhilarating portion of my projects. In his defense, that may have happened. But I'd sanded that tree into what felt like oblivion. I'd slapped on that spackle, waited until it had turned from a Pepto-Bismol shade of pink to a pasty white, and then sanded it off. I'd been aware of the small patches of drywall that had sort of, slightly been ripped off over the years, and had filled and smoothed them enough to make them look better than they had. After all, teal covers a multitude of sins, no?

Apparently we have differing opinions on what spackle is capable of, which sandpaper grit is best for smooth walls, and what a wall should look and feel like before being covered with color. I'd heard something, at some point, about needing to let spackle 'cure' for a full 24 hours before

3

painting over it, but I had a makeover to pull off and that pink paste turning white was like a red light turning green for this painting freak. There may have been a little, well 'puckering', over the filled holes, but nothing another layer of paint couldn't fix. Surely people would be so enamored by the gorgeous color and shiny new accessories that they wouldn't even notice the minor blemishes and woodland outlines on the wall.

About that.

As it turns out, I like to fill holes. My husband prefers to mend walls.

༺༻

As I worked on my own bedroom walls a few weekends later, carefully spackling and sanding imperfections with a fresh sense of purpose, I sensed the Lord whisper to my heart. "I'm much more like Joe when it comes to dealing with the brokenness in humanity. I don't just fill in holes and then cover them up. I mend them."

I've been aware of this unfortunate tendency in myself for some time now. If life had a Staples 'easy' button, I confess I'd use it frequently. Even when writing a book, I want to design the cover and format the chapters with pretty headers - before I've even put pen to paper, or fingers to keys. If it were possible to decorate a house before building it, I would find a way. I'm all about getting the grunt work over as fast as humanly possible so we can get to the good stuff. Make it look good - even if it isn't. And I'd hazard a guess that I'm not alone in my partiality to fast, minimally invasive results too. Unless you're a 1 on the enneagram, in which case you're dying right now (more about that later). The deeper issue, of course, lies in the reality that **speedy fixes often result in a compromised process.** And process is what this life is all about. There are no shortcuts, despite our dogged determination to keep finding them. What is it about humans that makes us resistant to the process - to the work, discomfort and time involved in doing things the best way. We settle for fast, flashy, highly-processed counterfeits when we were created for deeply satisfying, life-giving nourishment. This is as true in our diet as it is in our spiritual life. As evident in our communication with our loved ones as it is in the quality of media we consume.

We've bought into the lie that well-packaged and convenient is worth the sacrifice of real and authentic. But we've paid a high price for this exchange, and we're paying for it in our bodies, in our mental and emotional health (our soul health), and in our faith journeys. But beloved, hope is not lost. It never is. It's right where we let go of it, waiting for us to look back up and take a wobbly first step toward it.

> *I wish to do something great and wonderful,*
> *but I must start by doing the little things like*
> *they were great and wonderful.*
> *Albert Einstein*

If you're looking for a book that will teach you how to rock at life in five easy steps, written by an expert life-rocker, keep looking. This is not it. I am not she. I'm simply a fellow sojourner, a garden-variety grace practitioner, learning to take brave steps toward health and wholeness, failing extravagantly, and then getting back up again. A little faster every time.

I'm learning to rely more on God, and the people he's placed in my life, and less on my ability to single-handedly nail it or do #allthethings. I'm learning to be as honest with my failures as I am with my successes. And I'm learning to find Him – and His kindness - in the midst of said failures. And I'm learning to focus more on incorporating good things into

5

my life than obsessing over eliminating the bad.

Please hear me: I didn't write my first book because I was an authority on the topic of sex and marital bliss, but because I had a messy story and wanted to invite people on my journey to healing. I didn't write Penduka because comparison, focus, and fear of failure weren't issues for me - but because they were. The same holds true here. I'm writing honestly about health and wholeness - spiritual, emotional and physical - because I have struggled so much in all of these areas for much of my adult life. And because I've become unabashedly obsessed with the process of restoration and renewal.

ALL THINGS NEW

You see, God is in the process of making all things new (Revelation 21:5). The word "all", in the original Greek, doesn't translate to some reduced version of the word. It remains all encompassing. God is literally - right now - in the process of making all things new. That means you, and me - and every other thing He has created - are in process. He is actively renewing, redeeming and restoring this broken world to its original glory. Yes, God is outside of time and has already made us new in Christ, and also yes, much of the renewal won't be completed this side of eternity, but it is still very much in process. The more we are aware of this stunning reality, and are willing to lean into it, the more we will get to experience it. We get to choose: to participate in renewal, or to resist it. To lean into this grand restoration plan, with all of its unknowns and discomforts, or to run from it. To surrender to the process, or to keep opting for temporary quick fixes. God doesn't violate our choice to fix things the easy way, but He does invite us to co-labor with Him in a better way. The truth is ... God is *always* present and at work in us, whether we believe it and acknowledge it, or not.

6

While I've historically chosen the easy way over the best way - I'm slowly discovering the irrefutable value of wholeness over convenience. And it is dismantling, rearranging and completely transforming my life.

It isn't easy, nor is it always comfortable (or I suppose we would all be living this way already), but it is so life-giving and liberating and good.

⁓⦿⁓

So welcome, sweet friend. I am so grateful that you've found yourself here, with these pages in your hands. It is my prayer that they become for you both scalpel and balm.

What follows is the messy story of my unraveling, and the long road home to wholeness. A road I still very much traverse. A journey that is slowly taking me from masked to naked, from guarded to open, from broken to whole. Part memoir and part coach, Sozo is also about physical health, soul care, and authentic spirituality. Yes, all three - because I don't believe they exist, in their truest and fullest form, apart from each other. They belong together. They, like the Trinity, make up three distinct, and yet inseparable, parts of a whole. And wholeness is, after all, why we're here. We can no longer afford to separate what we consider to be the sacred from the secular aspects in our lives. We are spirits and souls, with bodies, and if His spirit dwells within us - He is in it all.

This book may feel messy and disjointed at times. As I've wrestled with how to accurately communicate both the ethereal and the elemental, I've had to lay down my vision of a fancy, seamless work of art in favor of a collection of honest trail notes. Some parts may irritate you, bore you, or ruffle your feathers - and I'm okay with that. I'm finding new freedom in challenging unhealthy social constructs and dualistic church rhetoric in favor of embracing a more Jesus-centric posture. In the words of Mike Yaconelli, this is "not a book of answers from someone who has arrived; it is merely glimpses from someone who is still stumbling around yet hot on God's trail". It's a simple offering of obedience from a wide-eyed wanderer. Besides, aren't we all just walking each other home?

I invite you to join me on this hard and holy road to wholeness. It is my hope that as we replace our old patterns of convenience with new rhythms of grace, that we will lose our appetite for the quick-fix and find new life in the cultivation of healthier souls, bodies and spirits.

We must be careful with our lives, for Christ's sake, because it would seem that they are the only lives we are going to have in this puzzling and perilous world, and so they are very precious and what we do with them matters enormously.

Frederick Buechner

CHAPTER ONE

HOLY + WHOLE

*Long before he laid down earth's foundations, he had
us in mind, had settled on us as the focus of his love,
to be made whole and holy by his love.*

Ephesians 1:4

This book has been brewing quietly for almost a decade. It was conceived as a breakout session, called 'Temple Care 101', that I had taught three times in one day at a large annual Ladies Day event. Due to the response, I was asked to return the following year and lead the same workshop (come to think of it, though, it may have been watching me twirl a six-pound hula hoop around my pregnant body that wowed them). I ended up giving that same talk to multiple groups over the next few years, toting my hefty stack of handouts and visuals with me. I was wildly passionate about the intersection of emotional, spiritual and physical health and I took every opportunity to share what I'd learned.

And then life, as it tends to, took some interesting twists and turns, and the topic just sort of slipped off the radar for several years. It bubbled to the surface again in 2017 when three different organizations invited me to speak, and requested 'Temple Care 101' as their topic of choice. I discovered, much to my surprise, that my passion for the subject still burned quietly in my bones. Mid-way through that year I knew it was time to write a book. I already had a framework, had discovered additional information and resources along the way, and felt - in a rather presumptuous manner - qualified to speak to these issues. Surely my training as a fitness instructor and personal trainer, along with the nutrition information I'd gathered over the years, equipped me to speak on the subject of physical health? My years of coaching and mentoring offered me some helpful tools to speak into the emotional and mental sphere, and I assumed my role as a preacher girl earned me some street cred in the spiritual realm? I was passionate, armed with piles of information, and ready to write. Only I couldn't. Like trying to wring water from a dry sponge, there was nothing there. If there's one thing I've learned through writing books, it's that you can't push a book baby out before it's ready. What I establish as the delivery date, and what the actual timeline of full formation is, don't always coincide. Feeling a little defeated, I put the idea back on the shelf and left my embryonic book to develop quietly, out of sight and in many ways, out of mind.

It wasn't until the Spring of 2018, as I started to emerge from the rubble of what had turned out to be a complete and utter meltdown, that I felt the first tremors of labor. It was finally time to bring this book baby out into the world. Not because I knew a thing or two, but because everything I had thought I'd known had come crashing down. It has only been in the slow restoration process that I've realized I had to *flesh* it out *before* I could write it out. It seems so obvious, I know, but knowing something intellectually simply isn't enough. I had to *own* this stuff before I could give it away.

As someone who's worked hard over the years to establish a platform for the spoken and written word, communicating the insight and revelation God drops into my heart has become a fluid process. The problem, however, is that too often I gift-wrap and give away truth before I've allowed myself enough time to embrace, absorb and assimilate it. Granted, these nuggets aren't passed along in hot-potato fashion because they're too uncomfortable to hold for any length of time, but because it gives me life to bring others along on the journey. It is in my nature to want to give a good thing away. But it's also in my nature to take shortcuts. And as it turns out, it's my own restoration process I've been short cutting all this time.

Rather than chewing on and owning a truth first, allowing what I share with others to be a natural overflow of what God is doing in my own life, I short-circuit work that needs to be done in my heart. I rush the process. I pass out treasure to the masses, extracting budding revelations from my soul before they have had a chance to take root. While I've been declaring truth over you - and believing it for you wholeheartedly - I haven't always owned that truth for myself. Much of the freedom and hope I've distilled over the years has somehow bypassed my own heart. And just like that, my ministry became no longer a gift, but a costly offering.

While it may be admirable to passionately speak life over others - and should always be a rule-of-thumb when it comes to what emerges from our lips - what has gurgled beneath my eagerness to speak it hasn't always been life-giving. If I'm painfully honest about some of the underlying motives behind why I love what I do, it's that my identity and worth have always been directly connected to the value I bring to the table. What has driven me at times, so stealthily that it has taken a while to identify, is a bent toward habitual people pleasing and approval addiction.

Awkward, I know. And I promise we'll dig more into that uncomfortable confession later. But here's the bottom line: **it'll always be easier to pass along a profound thought to the masses, and revel in the accolades it brings, than do the hard work of sitting with it quietly and allowing it to rearrange your inner-world first.**

ROOTED

A seed unfolds when it's ready, her emergence consulting no one's calendar. There is no shortcut to growth, no quick three step plan to maturity. Only when nurtured and actively taking ground do roots offer stability. Only once established does a tree produce healthy fruit. Root systems will always be the least acknowledged portion of a plant, and yet without them, there is no hope of survival. Humans will always be more impressed with fruit than roots. Roots and dirt aren't sexy. We love the stuff we can see and taste and track. Root systems, on the other hand, do their thing beneath the surface where we can neither applaud nor measure. And so our focus shifts off of what truly matters - the roots that anchor our very essence - and settle on what the world can 'ooh' and 'aah' over. How very backwards - and yet commonplace - this is.

The subject of roots has long been a theme in my life, showing up repeatedly in my writing and speaking (even inspiring an anchor tattoo on my left foot in 2014), and continues to call my attention away from outward, external achievement toward eternal, hidden inner places.

♋

So why does this all matter? How do spackle and roots pertain to a healthy mind, body or spirit? And what does "sozo" mean anyway? I'm so glad you asked! Let me unpack this a little more practically. If I had to whittle the message of SOZO down to two words, they would be 'wellness' and 'wholeness'.

WELLNESS

While *wellness* has become somewhat of a buzzword over the past several years, there doesn't seem to be a universally accepted definition for it. Merriam-Webster gives it a whirl with: "*the quality or state of being in good health especially as an actively sought goal*". The Oxford Dictionary adds a little depth with this definition: "*the state or condition of being in good physical and mental health*". Much like with the concept of mindfulness, the westernized evangelical church seems to have backed away from this terminology and written it off as worldly or new-agey. So I'd like to bridge the gap and offer this definition of wellness: "*The synergistic effect created by the soul, body and spirit becoming healthy and whole*"

There are a few great words here, and seeing I love a good word, allow me to unpack this loaded statement. "*Synergy*" is the cooperation of two or more things that produce a greater *combined* effect than the sum of their separate effects. I think a healthy marriage or business partnership is the perfect example of synergy; when you and your partner each bring your unique skills and offerings to the

13

table, the impact of your collaboration is far greater than the sum of what you'd be able to accomplish on your own. In much the same way, when our souls (which encompasses our mind, will and emotions), bodies and spirits are growing and becoming healthy and whole, the synergy of their combined vitality has a tremendous ripple effect in our families, communities and circles of influence.

I intentionally used the word 'becoming' because I believe **wellness is a *journey* we navigate, not a *destination* we suddenly arrive at**. It is a fluid, ever-evolving adventure that changes and shifts as we do. And lastly, I added the word 'whole' alongside healthy, because it's central to our journey toward the heart of God. Which leads me to the next keyword:

WHOLENESS

Despite the advances made in both medicine and technology, we are more overweight, addicted and medicated than we've ever been. We live in a hurting, sin-stained world, and we are averse to pain and discomfort, so we are constantly looking for silver bullets – or new numbing techniques – to deal with the pain we feel - emotionally, physically, relationally, sexually, mentally and spiritually. We are in desperate need of rescue and restoration.

The word 'save' that we find woven so frequently into the New Testament (as in "the son of man came to seek and save the lost" in Luke 19:10) seems to have lost much of its richness and beauty in translation. The original Greek word is 'sozo'. While sozo does indeed translate as "save" in English, it also carries with it this expansive meaning: to tend to, to care for, to heal, to rescue, to preserve, to deliver, to be made well, and to be made whole.

You see, Jesus didn't come just to give us a free ticket to

heaven. He didn't orchestrate a divine escape so that one day, if we behave just right, we'll get whisked away from this broken world. In saving us, He actually came to start the process of making us whole. In fact, He came to make *all* things new. He came with *restoration* and *renewal* on his heart, and I believe wholeheartedly that He longs to restore us, not just spiritually, but also emotionally and mentally, physically, sexually, and relationally.

Sure, we won't realize the *full extent* of wellness or wholeness this side of eternity, but I certainly don't want to miss the restoration He *does* have for me now because I've settled for status quo, because health is taking longer than I think it should, or because I'm hustling so hard trying to fix things myself that I keep crashing and burning in the process.

We see a stunning example of God's desire to make His most beloved creation whole in Acts 3 when Peter heals a lame man. If you grew up in the church, you probably grew up singing about this little encounter.

Peter and John are headed up to the temple when a man, who has been lame since birth, calls out to them for monetary assistance. This has been his daily reality for as long as he can recall: being carried to the temple each morning to beg for scraps from anyone who'll take a second to pity him in order to help keep him alive. Peter sees an opportunity here, not to give him a hand-out, but to give him a hand-*up*. He hollers back about his lack of silver and gold, and mentions he has something even better he can give him: Jesus and the sozo he brings.

"Taking him by the right hand, he helped him up, and instantly the man's feet and ankles became strong. He jumped to his feet and began to walk. Then he went with them into the temple courts, walking and jumping, and praising God. When all the people saw him walking and praising God, they recognized him as the same man who used to sit begging at the temple gate called Beautiful, and

15

they were filled with wonder and amazement at what had happened to him." Acts 3:7-10

I'd like to propose that this story is sozo in action. That more than a physical miracle, which on its own is extraordinary, this man received the trifecta of wholeness. God had no intention of simply filling his physical wounds with religious spackle and slapping a band-aid on the extraordinary emotional pain that must have come with living as a crippled outcast his entire life. No, He intended to restore him fully. The lame man suddenly being able to walk revealed a physical healing, but could his leaping have indicated that he'd been emotionally restored, and might his praising of God been a delightful display of his spiritual transformation?

Jesus is called the 'Prince of Peace' for good reason. While the word we read in scripture has been translated to 'peace', the original 'shalom', was a far more holistic word. According to Strong's Concordance 7965, shalom means *completeness, wholeness, health, welfare, safety, soundness, tranquility, prosperity, perfectness, fullness, rest, harmony, the absence of agitation or discord*. This is the Jesus we follow, friend. And this represents the good work God is doing in all of us.

⌒⌯⌒

If wellness is *the synergistic effect created by our souls, bodies and spirits becoming healthy and whole,* and sozo reminds us that wholeness is a part of this grand redemption plan, I think it is our responsibility - even more so as followers of Jesus - to steward our souls, our bodies and our spiritual lives well. Rather than writing the pursuit of wellness and wholeness off as some cultural fad, or worse yet - some self-indulgent, new-age quest - I'd like to suggest we start viewing it as an essential part of our charge here on earth.

The thing is, we aren't living beings with separate little compartments for our souls, bodies and spirits. Rather, we are divinely created, integrated beings with souls, bodies and spirits intermingled. We cannot neglect one area and not expect the deterioration to show up in the other areas too. A breakdown in one always leaks over into the others eventually. The good news is that if we can understand the way in which our soul, body and spirit work together, it can work the other way too. Vibrant health and intentional growth in one area can have a beautiful ripple effect into the others - inspiring greater overall life and vitality.

While I believe these three topics shouldn't be plucked off, removed from the whole, and unpacked in isolation, I've dedicated a chapter (a long, meaty and extensive chapter) to each. This way we can look at the characteristics and expressions of soul, body and spirit health independently, examining the unique struggles and experiences we face in each area, while still honoring their relationship and influence on each other.

HEAVEN TO EARTH

I refuse to believe that the abundant life Jesus talks about in John 10:10 refers exclusively to post-death eternal life. I don't believe that once we choose to follow Jesus we just have to hold on for dear life, enduring this hell on earth, so we can make it to heaven and only then finally live. We've missed the beauty and power of the cross if we don't eagerly anticipate and expect transformation in the here and now. Even the word 'atonement' speaks to wholeness and restoration: at-ONE-ment. Defined as the reconciliation of mankind and God through the sacrifice of Jesus, we see a picture of broken becoming whole again. As we cooperate with our Creator in this restoration project, we get to choose:

integration or disintegration. While disintegration may not sound like a choice anyone would make, by not creating space for (and intentionally working toward) integration, by default we have chosen to allow ourselves to disintegrate.

We are called to be *holy* (1 Peter 1:16), which at its core means to be set-apart, sacred and dedicated. But this isn't just about good behavior, it's also very much about relationship. We are holy *because* we *belong* to God.

I believe we're called to live fully alive in the *now* - while we're being made whole and holy - bringing heaven to earth, and stirring up greater life in those around us. And in order for us to do that, and really maximize our influence and impact, we've got to cultivate a healthy soul, body and spirit.

And yes, cultivate implies *work* ... because, much like gardening, it *is*. There's just no getting around the necessity of getting our hands dirty and doing the work.

When I started putting pen to paper for this book last summer, we were growing our first vegetable garden in years. I swore I'd never garden again, after discovering my disdain for it a few years earlier, but I should probably know better than to swear such things.

When we first moved out into the country, several years ago, we jumped in with both feet and started a large garden. We tried growing every vegetable I could pronounce in a section of land larger than our entire little city yard had been. It was only natural, now that I was a country girl, that I grow my food and *love* doing it - only, as it turns out, I didn't. By the end of the first summer I was over it. I loved getting my hands dirty in the spring, digging and planting and watering, but as the satisfying hours of nurturing saplings became hot, sweaty, mosquito-bitten hours of weeding and watering - only to lose entire harvests to bugs and blight, I grew to loathe it. Just looking out at the garden, from the comfort of my air-conditioned house, triggered anxiety in me. Clearly, I wasn't the horticulturally-savvy country gal I'd hoped to be. It felt like a massive failure.

It took me a few years to say it out loud, but I finally confessed it: *I don't like gardening*. I didn't like the dailiness of the labor, and I didn't like the high chance of disappointment. So, after a couple years of resent-laden plant tending, I threw in the towel altogether. Our garden lay void of edible life, overgrown with everything else for a few years until last spring when my husband pronounced one morning, *"I want to grow something!". Responding to the terror on my face, I think the rest of the conversation went something like this,*

"Just some peppers and tomatoes, nothing much ... breathe, honey, it's going to be alright!".
"Okay, fine, but they're *your* babies and *you're* keeping them alive, right?".

And there we were, getting our hands dirty again, digging holes and sinking roots. And while I'm hesitant to admit it, I *liked* it (but don't tell anyone, okay?).

What excites me most about gardening again, apart from the promise of fresh peppers, tomatoes and herbs, is that God speaks to my heart so vividly about spiritual and emotional growth when I'm wrist deep in dirt. As a visual person who loves a good illustration, it's like Disney World for my metaphor-making mind. I've learned a lot about life - and myself - here. How creating an environment where growth can happen centers on my willingness to get messy and comfortable in the dirt. How I need to keep showing up and doing my thing, even when the bugs are out to get me and my harvest, and when crop loss threatens to derail the whole thing. I've realized how appearances can be deceptive, and that what looks big and healthy on the outside can be bitter on the inside. How important it is that we nourish and tend to what it is we want to grow more of, and that we remove - at root level - the things we need to eliminate from our lives. I've come to appreciate cultivating a Christ-centric life that thrives in the midst of struggle, rather than barely survives at the first hint of opposition. Nature will always be my favorite classroom.

While out watering and weeding early one morning, before my kiddos had even risen for the day, I was trying to figure out why this time around felt so different from the last attempts. Our children are older, yes, but that wasn't it. I wasn't blogging (aka. photo-documenting and waxing poetic) about the entire process, which certainly removes a significant amount of pressure from the experience. But I think the biggest difference was that this time we started *small*, kept it *simple and sustainable*, and by doing so, *set ourselves up to succeed*.

If we'll apply this to our lives, in the cultivation of a healthy soul, body and spirit - acknowledging that it *does* take work and dedication, and that getting our hands dirty tending to the unseen root systems of our lives is essential to wellness - we'll reap a fruitful harvest and learn to thrive in every season. And we can do this by keeping it simple, trusting God to do His part, while we take small daily steps in the right direction.

Listen to your life. See it for the fathomless mystery it is. In the boredom and pain of it, no less than in the excitement and gladness: touch, taste, smell your way to the holy and hidden heart of it, because in the last analysis all moments are key moments, and life itself is grace.

Frederick Buechner

CHAPTER TWO

THE GLORIOUS UNRAVELING

For a seed to achieve its greatest expression, it must come completely undone. The shell cracks, its insides come out and everything changes. To someone who doesn't understand growth, it would look like complete destruction.

Cynthia Occelli

If we're being honest, most of us would admit to wanting the medal without having to run the marathon. We want the *promise*, without the *process*. We don't particularly like enduring anything unpleasant, or developing patience and resilience through struggle. We'd far rather search out comfort and pleasure, and take up residence there. But we weren't created to play it safe - we were made to do hard things, and to grow and develop through difficulty. After all, God is more interested in our growth and character than He is in our comfort. He wouldn't have sent "the comforter" (the Holy Spirit) if we weren't going to need Him.

James puts it this way (James 1:2-4), "Consider it a sheer gift, friends, when tests and challenges come at you from all sides. You know that under pressure, your faith-life is forced into the open and shows its true colors. So don't try to get out of anything prematurely. Let it do its work so you become mature and well-developed, not deficient in any way."

Struggle is so necessary for development, in fact, that when we short-circuit it in nature - by assisting a butterfly in its emergence from its chrysalis, or a baby bird from its shell - we end up crippling their ability to thrive, and sometimes even survive. In order to mature and grow, our lives require some level of resistance and struggle, forcing us to grow in strength and resilience. Thankfully we can cling to the fact that we will never walk alone through these hard seasons. Sure, we'd prefer an epidural savior who simply removes all pain and discomfort from this life, handing us our prize at the end, but we have a God who, like a midwife, holds our hand and cheers us on. He champions us, reminding us why we're here in the first place and that it's all going to be worth it in the end. To keep going, to lean into the pain, and to breathe. This is the God who lovingly unfolds and undoes us when life has wounded our souls.

It's hard to put into words what you're working through when those words will be read by others. But disclosure is even harder to avoid when what seems to have been building in you for a while finally spills out and breaches the barrier of your well-manicured front. Judgment and rejection feel especially sharp when you're still split wide open.

Part of my inability to clearly articulate what I'm still in the thick of is because, well, I'm still in the thick of it. There has been no emergency clean-up squad to put me nicely back together. Little hindsight to wisely articulate - because it hasn't quite shifted into the rear-view mirror yet. The somewhat disorganized, messy bundle of questions and quibbles I've been sorting through is still very much my reality. And so, unlike my other books, portions of this were written while still very broken and bruised. It is not neatly packaged; rather it's uncomfortably honest and raw. And much like growth, it isn't as linear as I might prefer. It's downright bumbling and awkward at times. And yet - *and yet* - I wouldn't change it for the world.

❧

The anxiety began rearing its head more regularly in 2017, and the depressive funks I'd battled for years growing up seemed to be returning in spades. A master at maintaining my composure, I kept smiling and pressed onward. Having grown up in the church with a name like "Joy", I was accustomed to living up to my name. I was the happy one that people could depend on for daily doses of hope and encouragement. I had found my place in life, and I was not about to let my people down.

Because I didn't feel the pain of my past any more, I assumed I was fixed. I'd been thrust from the dark into the light so fast it was dizzying, but as the years progressed, I couldn't seem to understand why my inner world didn't line up with my outer world. Something was stirring in me, deep and furious, and I knew it.

In August 2017, the dam wall broke and I was gripped by my first panic attack in years. Joe and I were prepping to head to Washington D.C. the following day, but between crying and raging at my kids, I was falling apart. When the growing tightness in my chest and the spinning in my head didn't stop, I found my husband in the driveway and, hyperventilating, buried my face in his chest. Quite certain I was coming out of my skin, I was desperate enough to admit that I was *not* okay. I retreated back to our bedroom, weeping, and collapsed face-first on the bed. I informed God that, in case He missed it, I might be losing my 'effing' mind. This melt down revealed the first significant crack in my mask, and was the beginning of the undoing.

COMING UNDONE

I've been asked multiple times what triggered the upheaval, and I have no simple answer. I believe that God, in His infinite wisdom, lovingly sabotages our self-destructive habits. So, I suspect God has been working behind the scenes for years now, plotting the complete overturn of my apple cart, bringing everything into alignment for such a time as this.

The inner turbulence bubbled up and over after we returned from South Africa in January of last year (2018). It was as if Jehovah Sneaky tossed a sacred Mentos into the soda storm of my internal world.

Looking back, I can see that this storm had been brewing for years. I'd grown increasingly unsettled, feeling restless and dissatisfied in what seemed like every area of my life. In my attempt to verbalize what was brewing beneath the surface to those closest to me, when the deep rumbling got especially loud, I could only describe it as feeling as though I was pressed up against a glass ceiling; able to see freedom, but unsure of how to break through and grab hold of it.

As someone who is incredibly self-aware, I regularly weed my soul. I search out things that have no business growing there, and try to plant truth in their place. I remember sharing with a mentor and dear friend that it seemed as if I was repeatedly tripping over a massive root that I'd discovered while digging around in the soil of my heart. I couldn't unearth it enough to identify it, nor get my hands around it firmly enough to uproot it, no matter how deeply I dug or hard I tugged. And Lord knows, you can't fight a foe you can't see. This conversation is the one that led me into counseling in 2015.

As I've grown increasingly good at doing over the years, I wrote and spoke my way through the turbulence. In fact my book, Penduka, emerged during this season. As it turns out, you can write a book about purpose, and still feel utterly lost. Much like I managed to write a book about sex while nursing deep body image wounds. What keeps one securely in performance mode is the little tape that plays on repeat in the background: "don't let them see you flounder, they need you to be a rock. You'll lose your credibility and your platform will crumble if you're not the poster child for what you preach". A serious case of imposter syndrome kept me in performance mode while simultaneously heaping on the shame. This trap simply reinforced the chasm between my head knowledge and any experiential knowledge I had. **The sad reality is that our performance doesn't say we believe Jesus can heal us and use us, it says we have to pretend to be squeaky clean in order to be accepted into his club.**

In my desire to practice brave truth-telling and radical vulnerability over the past several months, I've peeled back layers of my life to expose a substantial lack of healthy roots. It's one thing to know *about* something intellectually and another thing entirely to know it deep in the soil of your soul. We live out of what we believe, so what emerges on the surface will always be a byproduct of what we believe at our core. Unless, of course, we're experts at pretending and performing – and then we can make whatever shows up on the surface look exactly the way it "should". We know how to curate our image to keep the crowd happy, even if it's quietly killing us.

What amazes me the most is how well I managed to convince *myself* of my health and okayness. Picture a nice array of potted plants shoved in the ground. It looks good on the surface, and there is certainly some life growing there, but there's a distinct lack of depth and freedom to grow and take root, or ever produce any sort of healthy fruit. This type of superficial growth isn't healthy or sustainable. While it hasn't been an intentional charade, it's been a performance nonetheless. One that satisfies the itch to self-preserve and hide, while still feeding my desperate need for validation. But one can only keep up appearances for so long before our edges begin to fray, before something unexpected comes along, snags a loose thread, and unravels us entirely. For me that thing was the enneagram.

SPLIT OPEN

Having stumbled upon the ancient typology tool of the enneagram[1] in the summer of 2017, I was passionately - albeit reluctantly - navigating a wild and mildly terrifying journey of self-discovery by late fall. The enneagram had caught me off guard and had subsequently split me wide open. After sticking my head back in the sand for a few weeks, attempting to hide from the hot shame it stirred up, I went back for more. I devoured books and podcasts on the subject, utterly obsessed with the new depth of personal development I had stumbled upon. As I worked through the initial shame and embarrassment of having dimensions of my inner life emblazoned in black and white for all to read, I began tasting a freedom I'd longed for, for years. This freedom I had seen through the glass, but for the life of me, couldn't access. Suddenly the giant root I'd been tripping over for years, but couldn't identify or get my hands around, had handles.

I should note here, if you're new to the soul-mapping wisdom of the enneagram - or have never heard of it before - that one typically knows which of the nine basic personality types they're dominant in by the description (motivations, core fears and tendencies) that leaves them feeling the most exposed and uncomfortable. Sounds warm and fuzzy, doesn't it? While most typology grids or personality assessments evaluate and deal with our external world, the enneagram is unique in that it deals with the 'why' behind what we do. The book, *The Road Back to You* by Ian Cron and Suzanne Stabile, is a great introduction to the nine types and was my 'gateway drug' introduction to this powerful self-discovery and spiritual development tool.

I had walked into my ennea-experience with somewhat of a smug assumption; I, Joy McMillan, am most assuredly a 7 - the *Enthusiast*. It was a no-brainer. Only ... I *wasn't*. I couldn't relate to many of the motivations or struggles of the 7. I felt indifferent about this system, until I got to the 2 - the *Helper*. The name alone made me want to gag. Don't put me behind the scenes, people. I don't want to quietly mop floors or make soup for the bedridden. I want a microphone, give me a stage, let me be *visible*, for the love of Pete. And yet, as I read on, I discovered why when all I'd done was hide for the first half of my life - suddenly the spotlight had become a feast for my soul. It's because I still hide, only now it's in ministry and a whirlwind of good activity. I find my value in doing for others, in adding value to others' lives. I feel my greatest worth when needed by others. My greatest fear is being unwanted or unworthy of love. So you better believe I work hard to earn it. I perform for validation; giving affection so I might receive it. An unhealthy enneagram 2, I learned, is overly concerned with image, desperately wants to be liked, loves the idea of being indispensable, and will resort to flattery and manipulation to satisfy their desperate need to feel appreciated and loved. Enneagram 2s are also referred to as the 'befriender' and the 'giver', go figure.

Ugh. Letting these revelations sink in was like getting a gut punch wrapped in a hug. This discovery coincided with my panic attack, and set the unraveling of my soul into motion. After the initial flood of shame that accompanied feeling completely and utterly exposed, came the sweet relief and comfort of not having to hide anymore. **The light that felt so harsh and cruel at first, became a friend.** Only *after* the infection was revealed for what it was, would the wound have a chance to heal. It took months of fighting these uncomfortable revelations to finally embrace them for the soul-mirror they were. And I had to start by admitting that, contrary to everything I'd become a master of portraying, I was *not* okay.

Beloved, the truth can be a jagged little pill to swallow, but if we're not willing to consume it, we can't mend what's broken in us. There can be no freedom and growth without first knowing where we are, and identifying what it is that holds us captive. The face of this massive, inconveniently-placed root in the garden of my heart was my desperate search for significance – and my willingness to do whatever it took to lessen the ache it had created.

SHADOW OF SHAME

I came into 2018 committing to practice two things: radical self-compassion and brave truth-telling. And they couldn't have been better companions on this rocky road to wholeness. While still in the early, uncomfortable stages of this upheaval - over Christmas and New Year of 2017 - we took a much-anticipated trip to my home country of South Africa.

And by 'much-anticipated' I mean: *years in the making*. It was beautiful and thrilling and *exhausting*. Add to the vulnerability of an enneagram-hangover and my mounting anxiety, the utter exhaustion of five weeks of non-stop travel (including 80 hours of international travel alone with my children). Then throw into that toxic cocktail the aching void of a just-going-through-the-motions spiritual life, and an obscene amount of unhealthy food for good measure, and you have yourself a fine recipe for personal disaster. *A perfect storm of busyness, emptiness, and unhealthy coping mechanisms.*

This set the stage for the unraveling that took place in January 2018. We returned from an amazing time with family and friends in South Africa mid-January, and I promptly fell apart. I cried every single day for two weeks straight, unable to articulate what was going on inside me, but quite certain I was being turned inside out. I wanted to blame it on jet-lag, and while I was physically exhausted, it wasn't that. I wanted to blame it on loneliness, going from people I love in my face for five weeks straight, to complete isolation (with hubby back to work, kids back to school, and me back in the studio)...but it was more than that. I wanted to blame it on the weather, transitioning suddenly from southern summer to northern winter, and for someone who battles with Seasonal Affective Disorder, I'm sure it factored in...but it was deeper still.

I desperately wanted to attach blame to something so that I could fix the problem, alleviate the pain, and get on with my life. Fighting to maintain my composure, I tried to tame the turbulence I felt inside, but all of my efforts fell flat. It felt like being dismantled from the inside-out. While I was unsure of how it would play out, life as I knew it was unraveling. The restlessness that had started as a gentle whisper had swollen into a screaming frenzy. I'd felt it in the pit of my stomach while we were still in South Africa, but drowned it out with fun and food. It had shown up again a few weeks in as a gnawing fear of returning to my life in the States, a life I'd worked hard to build and maintain. I somehow knew I couldn't sustain the pace at which I'd learned to function; always chasing, always striving, always creating, always competing, always saying yes, always proving myself worthy of people's time and attention. Fierce insecurity hidden in plain sight. Something inside me was clawing to get out, desperate for air, and once the cries reached a fever-pitch, I couldn't keep it together any longer. Once we returned and I couldn't hide anymore, I came unglued. I shed more tears in those five weeks than I had in the five years leading up to them, maybe because that amount of time and tears is what it took to dismantle my facade of strength and put-togetherness. God was beginning to undo things in me that were so deeply embedded that it required open heart surgery, and a total surrender to the process.

Self-knowledge is tied with inner work, which is both demanding and painful. Change occurs amid birth pangs. It takes courage to walk such a path. Many avoid the path of self-knowledge because they are afraid of being swallowed up in their own abysses. But Christians have confidence that Christ has lived through all the abysses of human life and that he goes with us when we dare to engage in such confrontation with ourselves.

Andreas Ebert

RAW + UNFILTERED

In this process of learning to live true-faced and pretense-free, the filing cabinet of my internal world got dumped out on the floor. I'm pretty sure Jehovah Sneaky was behind this upheaval too. This cabinet is where our belief systems reside. Where everything we learn about life and justice and faith and fitting in are neatly filed away in well-labeled compartments. There are overflowing file folders and empty ones, some that contain folders I'm not allowed to touch, and others that boast thickly laminated guide sheets. I've spent the past several months slowly wading through the chaos; sorting fact from fiction, sifting truth from lie, and tracking down foggy origins of default practices hard-wired in. I'm slowly reorganizing and refiling things, and reveling in my newfound freedom to burn some of it. I couldn't continue going through the motions. I didn't just want to know a lot about, or write and speak about, God. I needed to intimately experience Him. **The hard questions we're willing to ask ourselves will always be more important than the answers we think we know.** God can never be bigger than the boxes we've put Him in, and beloved, we box Him in. What sort of faith journey are we on if we don't ever have to exercise any faith? This deep soul work is not unlike Michigan road construction; time-consuming, messy, and mind-blowingly inconvenient. It throws off our routines, slows us down, and makes us want to climb out of our skin in frustration. But the disruption is essential if we want to be made whole.

Part of the struggle during those first months home was the internal war between hope and fear. I was desperate for change, but terrified of the unknown. These were unchartered waters and I felt torn between my obvious need for greater depth and my desire to return to the safety of the shore. My theology had been repeatedly shaken over the years, and I was trying to find a solid place to rest my feet. I knew God was inviting me in over my head, but I had to decide whether I wanted Him more than I wanted my reputation and image intact. I was terrified to let go, to fully trust Him with my heart and dreams, and my questions and doubts - was I willing to risk losing the lovely sand castles I'd fashioned for myself on the sand? Slowly, finger by finger, I loosened my grip and bid farewell to my comfort zone. I can't say I'll ever not feel overwhelmed by life in the depths, or ever stop feeling a tug toward the comfort of sand beneath my feet, but I am all in and I cannot go back. I have felt His presence so sweetly and tangibly in this season of sorrow and searching because He is faithful to meet us most fully right where we really are. Psalm 23 says that He walks with us and comforts us in the valley of the shadow of death. That He sets a table before us and nourishes us in the presence of our enemies, and that his goodness and mercy will follow us all the days of our lives. Yes, this is the God I know and love.

BE:LOVED

If you read my first book, *XES: Why Church Girls Tend To Get It Backwards...And How To Get It Right*, then you know I walked into marriage pretty banged up. I've added the 'Journey of Joy' chapter from XES at the end of this book for context, as it'll give you a clearer understanding of the sexual baggage and deep identity wounds I've been working through over the past 15 years. Go ahead and dog-ear this page, read chapter ten, and return after you've read my initial story in the back.

So, you know that part where a cute boy scooped me up off a bathroom floor, got down on his knee, and then asked me to marry him...again? It was August 2003, and it was the first time in my adult life I could recall feeling truly seen and known...and still wanted. I was undone. This was the Gospel playing out before my very eyes. It marked me in such a stunning way that it literally changed the trajectory of my life. Because of this one radical act of grace, I was thrust out into the open and within a matter of months I'd shared what had become 'my story' with everyone from my parents to youth at a purity conference. The crazy thing is that after several years of self-protective lies and pain-filled hiding, I just assumed that this was it; sweet *freedom*. Badda boom, badda bing! Coming out of hiding felt so deliciously foreign to me that I assumed I'd taken a direct flight from Egypt's captivity to the Promised Land.

The only problem was, I completely forgot about the wilderness. I was so eager to leap from broken to beautiful that I applied my own spiritual kintsugi[2] and shared my story with the world. I desperately wanted to trade in the messy shame for the pretty, presentable outcome that I short-circuited the healing process. I stuffed any negative emotions that emerged, edited out anything that might make me less enjoyable to be around, and pressed on with a smile. I successfully made myself a conduit, hollowing out my insides to make room for the healing and freedom of others, without realizing I'd robbed myself of those very things. The ache of loneliness drove me outward toward people, to speaking and writing and noise. When what I needed most was silence and solitude within. I fashioned a persona that helped meet my need to be wanted and valued. I plowed through, finding busyness to be the perfect distraction from the grieving that kept inviting me in. When I stopped producing, the hum of the ache got louder. I was comfortable with the distance a public platform provided me. If people don't *really* know me, then they can't reject me. I was more concerned with being usable than being lovable. How can one possibly feel loved if they don't feel known, and how do we allow ourselves to be known if we refuse to let our guard down? The walls I'd built to protect myself were the very thing that now imprisoned me. While I gave people unfettered access to my time and talent - a considerable upgrade from unrestricted access to my body, circa 1990s - I struggled to allow people access to my heart.

The beginning of love is to let those we love be perfectly themselves, and not to twist them to fit our own image. Otherwise we love only the reflection of ourselves we find in them.

Thomas Merton

A few years ago, in 2015, I sensed God inviting me on a journey to mend my identity. A rescue mission of sorts. The word I sensed He'd given me on my birthday, as a theme the year before, was 'beloved'. This was all about me learning to live as the beloved, as one radically loved by her God. As I sat with this, and prayed over what this might look like, the Father spoke to my heart. *Joy, you've stepped out of your rags, you have stripped off the shame of your old life, but you refuse to step into the dress I've made for you. You're standing there, naked and vulnerable to any item of clothing the world throws at you, clinging to their offerings in the hopes that they'll validate you and cover your nakedness, but their material doesn't last long and then there you stand, shrinking smaller in an effort to protect yourself. But here, here is your dress...will you step into it?* These words were accompanied by a scene that played out in my minds-eye, of me standing in my daughter's room, excitedly showing her the exquisite gown I had hand-made just for her, only to have her turn it down, sheepishly insisting it was far too beautiful and precious for her. My heart hurt because I knew that she represented me, but more so because I just couldn't step into the dress. It wasn't out of reach, just out of the question.

I got a tattoo on my right shoulder that year of a mandala

that capped my upper arm, representing the lace of a bridal gown that I was determined to don, one way or another, with the word 'beloved' in small script across my upper back. Friends and mentor figures occasionally asked that year whether I'd put on the dress yet, but I could never offer a confident 'yes'. It was always a 'well, I'm slowly stepping into it' or an awkward 'I'm trying'. But no, I hadn't. And I didn't...until this year.

YES TO THE DRESS

With that blasted dress hanging in the corner of my heart and the enneagram having spilled my inner-workings out into the open, I was ripe for breakthrough. My dear friend, Melissa and her hubby Dan, had been raving about a particular ministry for a couple of years. In a way that my husband unabashedly described as annoying. They kept inviting us to participate in the marriage weekend that transformed their own, and to make time for what they called a "Story Weekend". After months of them badgering us, as dear friends who are passionate about something tend to do, we signed up.

While we signed up in late 2017 (before going to South Africa), our independent weekends fell on the first and second weekend of March 2018. While I was excited to finally find out for myself what these people were raving about, I was admittedly reluctant to drop the hundreds of dollars on something I feared might be useless to me. We relinquished in part to shut them up. A Story Weekend is for people who haven't faced and unpacked their story yet, I reasoned. I *know* my story. I've shared my story for 15 years now. I've *published* my story, for goodness sake. But as January turned into February, and my Story Weekend got closer, a great anticipation began to build in me. There was no mistake that our getaways weren't the previous year, or that mine fell smack-dab in the middle of my unraveling. I have yet to live through a 'coincidence' that doesn't have Jehovah Sneaky written all over it.

So, there I was, sharing my journey with a small group of women, with the raw emotion of someone who'd freshly dug her hands into the dirt of her story. There was no poise or eloquence. No pretty bows to tie it up with or lessons to take away from it. No churchy platitudes or pithy one-liners to make it less heart-wrenching than it actually was. It was the first time in 15 years I'd said "rape" without quantifiers or qualifiers. There were no attempts to soften the blow or frame it neatly in a more palatable way. I'd silenced a cry for fifteen long years and the lump in my throat finally broke free. I sobbed through the entire thing, and then took a two-hour nap.

In my journaling and reflection time, after all our stories had been told, God spoke directly to the pain and tended to my open wounds. It was during this weekend that my wilderness epiphany hit. I hadn't miraculously jumped from Egypt to the Promised Land in that little Haslett apartment. I had, through a flood of tears, emerged through the Red Sea into - ta-da - the *Wilderness*. And I've been navigating it ever since. You read that correctly. I've been moving and breathing and growing and failing and learning and building resilience in the wilderness...for the past fifteen years.

It is here that the Israelites learned to trust God for their sustenance (the sweet water, manna & quail), to be led by his presence (by the cloud by day and the pillar of fire by night), and to depend on Him alone for their deliverance. There was no denying God's relentless pursuit of His people's hearts, or His desire to dwell in their midst, despite their constant rejection of His efforts. It was also here that, despite having been extracted from Egypt, God extracted Egypt from them. As I laid on my bed, jotting down thoughts and looking up scripture, I was reminded that the weeks leading up to this weekend had been drenched with tears. God whispered to my heart in that moment, "*You've come through the River Jordan, you've battled the giants of approval addiction and fear of man, and you're ready to take up residence in the land I've promised you. Oh, and you just zipped up your dress*".

Oh, friend. Seriously. How does one even attempt to put into readable words what a revelation like this - after all this time - does to one's heart? I was undone. As it turns out, I hadn't publicly shared my whole story before the 'Story Weekend'. I'd been repeating the same well-edited, Hallmark version I'd come to know so well; relatively void of emotion, with the chasm between story and soul virtually undetectable.

It dawned on me, as I soaked in the extraordinary beauty of that retreat, that I suddenly had an answer for Abby, a sweet newly married gal I've been mentoring. She'd been standing near my kitchen sink while I was making us tea one Friday morning, and had asked about the meaning behind my two little stacks of yellow pebbles erected in my kitchen window. I explained the story behind keeping an 'ebenezer', named after the commemorative stone Samuel set up as a reminder to the people of God's divine rescue (find the story in 1 Samuel 7). I mentioned that while the presence of two stacks in my window was significant, symbolic of the way God had rescued me, I couldn't yet pinpoint what they represented. Until now. As Joshua led the people through the Jordan River, he instructed men (one from each of the twelve tribes) to take a stone from the bed of the river, where the priests had stood with the ark, and create a memorial on the west bank of the Jordan. I smiled at the thought of these two little stacks of Lake Huron pebbles, daily reminding me of the two tear-filled rivers God has tenderly led me through on the road to freedom. A breath-taking exit from captivity through one river, and the brave entrance into the Promised Land through another.

Yes, I know you can only take a metaphor so far, and yes, I realize old testament narrative only overlaps our own stories to a point, so if you find yourself shaking your head ever so slightly, don't read too much into my words. Resist the urge to pick my experience apart. I too struggle with when to let a good analogy fizzle out, but am also learning to delight in the nuggets and insights God shares with me - in ways that are uniquely meaningful to me - without allowing external analysis to diminish it. I'm getting more comfortable with the reality that God speaks to us all differently. The small and simple things that move me deeply, might annoy you. What delights your heart to no end, might not do a thing for me. That's the beauty of an extraordinarily personal God. He knows how to connect with our innermost parts - and how to expose them when need be - because He made us and intentionally knit us together this way. Rest in the knowledge that He knows you intimately, leads you uniquely, and communes with you in a way that will delight and gently convict your specific spirit and soul.

Our faith is not meant to get us out of a hard place or change our painful condition. Rather, it is meant to reveal God's faithfulness to us in the midst of our dire situation.

David Wilkerson

CHAPTER THREE

HARD + HOLY WORK

*A wound that goes unacknowledged and
unwept is a wound that cannot heal.*

John Eldredge

As I look back, I can identify a myriad of childhood experiences that told me it wasn't safe to be me in this world. I was too sensitive, too tall, too needy, too inquisitive, too emotional, too large, too softly-spoken, too sensual, too detail-oriented, too awkward, too talkative, too competitive. Too much, and yet somehow, never enough.

Repeatedly I allowed the broken record lies about my

worth or identity to drive me into hiding. "Oh, that's not popular? You don't like that about me? I can change that!". Rejection and the sense that I never quite fitted in drew their sharp nails over the creases of my heart, reinforcing my need to fold up, to hide, and to only show up just so. I learned at a young age that I could adapt easily to make myself more palatable for the masses, charming my way into people's hearts. Desperate for acceptance, and driven to perform in exchange for affection, meant unfolding and refolding myself into new shapes, morphing the origami of my soul to satisfy others. By 35, despite the continual rescue efforts for my soul, pieces of me remained tightly closed up. I was completely unaware that the little paper shape I'd come to know was but a small, crumpled version of who I was created to be. I had become such an effortless shape-shifter that I was barely aware of the shift. Nor was I awake to the fact that I'd lost myself in the pursuit of belonging.

FOLDED UP + FINE

When God invited me out of hiding 15 years ago, much of me unfolded to let in the light. It was scary and liberating and extraordinary. But self-preservation was so deeply ingrained in me that the deepest recesses of my soul remained tucked away, hidden even from me. Over time those creases that had become so natural to embrace, meant I simply folded back in for a new crowd. But one can only perform and self-adjust for so long before the exhaustion of curating your every move escorts you to the brink of insanity. While - thank God - there have been multiple, gradual unfoldings over the years, each experience exposing more little pockets or intricate flaps I didn't know were folded into my story, it wasn't until I was willing to face my crippling fear of failure and conflict, and wean myself off of the approval of others, that I would fully open up.

It's astounding, really, when I think about how well I've avoided conflict in my adult life. From my masterful shut-down at the first sign of turbulence in my marriage, to my uncanny ability to quietly own all responsibility for disturbance in my friendships, I've internalized it all. The record plays on repeat: *always be the nice girl - don't ruin your witness with silly feelings and irrelevant opinions - don't offend a soul - and don't rock the boat.* In essence: *shut up, sit down, and keep smiling.*

I can't tell you the number of times, growing up in the church, I heard well-meaning people take it upon themselves to educate me on what my names stood for. JOY, Jesus, others, and then yourself. Cute, isn't it? With a serious inferiority complex already spreading like cancer in my soul, I simply heard: *you don't actually matter*. Your feelings don't matter, your opinions don't matter, your hurts don't matter, your voice doesn't matter. Making myself invisible was a skill I mastered during my teenage years in an attempt to blend in with the ever-changing crowd. When you're tall and have an accent, it's a tricky gig to pull off - but an insecure kid can only move across the world so many times before they tire of the new kid label and ache to disappear. I became a chronic apologizer. If something went wrong, no matter how disconnected I was from the matter, I owned it. A need didn't get met; my fault. I should have done more. Someone's feelings were hurt; my fault. I wasn't sensitive enough to what he needed. A friendship fizzled; my fault. I wasn't engaged enough. No matter the issue, no matter the person, if something went down, I carried the weight of failure. I was always the weakest link. I worked hard to not be an inconvenience or imposition to anyone. I even remember, in the early months of marriage, trying to control my breathing at night so I wouldn't annoy my husband ✳

41

(which, while it might make him sound wickedly irritable, only speaks to my intense fear of being an irritation). Other enneagram 2's will be able to relate to this tendency to over apologize. You could spill hot soup in my lap, bump into me with your car, or ride over my foot with your grocery cart...and I'd be the first to say sorry.

With my ear tuned ever to the health of my friendships, when there's an issue, I'll own it – even if only internally. Relational connection is so essential in my core that when something is off, it feels heavy and overwhelming. If I get the impression that someone is disappointed in me or doesn't like me, for whatever reason, I'll hunt them down and try to make amends. My approval addiction has been so deeply embedded that to say feeling disliked felt unbearable would not be an understatement. In a biblically-backwards fashion, I would leave the ninety-nine who liked me in pursuit of the one who didn't, in an effort to charm them back into the fold. So when a friend made it very clear to me that she was disenchanted with my friendship in the summer of 2017, I was wrecked. For six months I apologized for whatever harm I may have done, trying desperately to get to the root of my failure, in order to restore what I had broken. To no avail. I wore her disdain for me like a cloak of shame. I had managed to walk on eggshells so well that offending or hurting people in my life was rare. In what felt like a freak storm of relational turbulence, I had two other friends confront me about my apparent inability to be a good friend. One graciously called me out on my constant need to fix problems and people, and shared that she'd started to feel "like a ministry project". The other one just wondered where I'd been as she navigated a crisis months earlier. The one felt like a tender reprimand from the spirit, and the other served as a subversive reminder that I wasn't enough. These two situations unfolded so differently and stretched me far outside of my comfort zone. They drove me to my knees, where God exposed the magnitude of what scripture calls 'the fear of man'.

People pleasing had silently ruled my life, fueling and directing much of my behavior and decision-making. It had been the driving force behind my need to curate my image, and the glue that had held my mask in place. These relational rifts had afforded me the opportunity to weather storms I had avoided, and served to fortify my backbone. With a newfound sense of freedom and confidence, I stopped fighting for a friendship that no longer needed to exist. I stopped apologizing, recognizing that restoration wasn't on the menu, and that I'd simply served as a conveniently placed emotional punching bag for six months. As I processed the loss, and embraced anew the reality of not being everyone's cup of tea, something shifted deeply inside me. This fallout and breakthrough occurred right before the Story Weekend, and served to represent the giants I had to fight in order to take the Promised Land.

In a podcast episode I listened to a while back, Kris Vallotton mentioned that fear has become one of the most socially acceptable sins in the church. The problem is **we don't acknowledge our fear because we don't *feel* our fear, and we don't feel our fear because we've *reduced* ourselves to *accommodate* it**. He went on to say that if someone is afraid of flying, they deal with that fear by simply choosing not to fly. Boom, quick fix = no fear. We, in the same way, reduce our lives to alleviate our fears. His words sucker punched and kissed me at the same time. I'm quite certain I stopped whatever I was doing and replayed that snippet several times over. It was exactly what I'd done, and how I'd learned to live, my entire life. Folded up and small.

Those creases and lines, scored deeply into the fabric of my soul, have become well-worn paths in my brain - a set of unconscious, visceral coping skills - that I have to work especially hard to stay out of. I have had to check in regularly to make sure I haven't folded back in, even just a little. Habit and survival have a way of embedding behavioral patterns so subtly beneath our radar that if we're not looking for them, we will not see them. Maybe that's one of the reasons we're called to guard our hearts and minds so vigilantly (Proverbs 4:23). Because God knows our tendencies and self-preservation mechanisms, and He wants us to fight to protect the freedom - the sozo - that He paid such a high price for.

I am wise enough to know the fight isn't over, and that my journey isn't complete. But I'm a thousand steps closer to wholeness than I was a few years ago, and I'm all in for the road ahead. There will be more unfolding, there will be more wilderness, there will be more struggle. But like the joy that comes with each Winter's thaw, and the hope that bubbles up with the unfurling of every spring blossom's petals, I will choose to celebrate the radical transformation that has taken place, and embrace the seasons of change yet to come.

DOING THE WORK

The interesting thing about this journey is that I would have told you that I was *relatively* whole and healthy last year. And the year before. And in contrast to where I was five, ten or fifteen years ago, that would not have been entirely false. I hadn't become noticeably *less* healthy – unless you count the fifteen pounds I'd picked up along the way. Or the nagging back pain. Or the lackluster spiritual life. Or the growing cynicism and low-grade anger boiling beneath the surface. In truth, I had grown so accustomed to the subtle chank of chains around my ankles and the low hum of turbulence in my soul that it had become the norm. When years of wrestling and aching to break free of things that quietly hold us captive just stretch on and on, sometimes we give up the fight and make our prison cells more comfortable instead.

If there wasn't flat-out chaos or sickness in my world, then I just assumed I was doing okay. After all, I wasn't living in blatant deceit and rebellion like I had been before I got married. I wasn't slowing down physically. And I wasn't off rocking in a corner somewhere. I was out making things happen and teaching other women how to step out of shame and lean into their God-born passions and purpose. Surely that meant I had my poop in a group. I was a constant whirlwind of activity. Cranking things out in part because when I slow my roll and stop making things happen, the ache in my spirit gets louder. And then I don't want to get out of bed. And because that really scares me, I find something new to start.

It's just easier to hide the limp and drown out the niggling feeling that I'm still somehow wearing a mask if I'm going a hundred miles a minute. You know the canary[3] in the coal mine analogy people use to monitor the pulse of their souls? If it's no longer singing, it's no longer alive. Well, friend, if you'd pulled back the curtain on my well-choreographed routine, you'd have noticed the singing parrot replacement - and a canary on its 12th year of life-support.

⚬⚬

It is a beautiful and brutal journey, this long road home, and I've been a big, blubbering mess for much of it lately. That inner filing cabinet God upended, remains tipped over. I've spent hours sitting on the floor, the contents of my soul strewn all around me, and I am finally at peace with the wildness of it all. In the middle of the mess, there has been an abiding hope that has hung in the air. So thick I can taste it. I could feel the weight of brokenness in one hand, and the promise of restoration in the other, and I am learning to hold them closely together. They're not opposites, in fact the embrace of the one leads to the other.

The reality is, God has been inviting me into freedom and wholeness for years now, I've just not fully accepted His invitation. It wasn't until I started to come apart at the seams that I stopped running. I've had to be willing to take brave steps off the beaten path and onto the hard and holy journey home. Home to the One who loves me completely, and home to the truest self He created me to be, before the world convinced me of all the things I wasn't.

I've started to ask hard questions, to push back on things I've never felt the freedom to wrestle with. In fact, I have more questions than answers these days, and I wouldn't have it any other way. I've allowed myself to get angry over injustices that had been buried alive. I started to mourn things I'd never given myself space to fully unpack and grieve. I had simply wrapped tragedies up, tied a bow around them, and given them away in the hopes of helping another through their pain. Unaware that my own wounds lay open, draped only with the crowd-pleasing Band-Aid of service.

I've started speaking more kindly to myself, being patient with myself when I fail or flounder, and catching myself when criticism creeps in. I'm learning to smile at my reflection - even when I don't particularly like what I see. I'm finding as I compare myself to others less, and choose rather to celebrate the unique way in which my soft and strong body has been made, that I am less critical of my form. And seeing I didn't make it, nor do I have other viable substitutes to live inside, I find this to be a wise move.

I've started examining the concentric circles in my social framework, shifting my energy and attention from the outliers to my inner-circle people. My heart has returned home, to the simplicity of unseen service to my family, after years of chasing success and achievement on a stage. I've realized anew where my influence matters most. Why would I want to win the hearts of the masses if it meant losing my children's hearts in the process?

I've started the slow process of untangling my worth and value from my work and ministry, effectively unplugging the umbilical cord of my identity from the opinions of others. It has meant being willing to face the hard truth about my tendency to want to make myself indispensable to people in my life, at times keeping them stuck in their struggle simply so I can sweep in and rescue them. It has meant apologizing for rescue efforts gone wrong, to those friends who were made to feel like ministry projects.

I've started to admit that I don't actually know how to just be a friend. That small groups scare me when I'm not speaking or coaching or serving in some way. That I've preferred people's admiration from a distance, over the risk of being known up close. It has meant being quick to recognize when I'm slipping into helper mode, not out of love for others, but to earn their affection. It has meant learning to let people in, so they can know me and love me, just because I'm me - without a song or dance to earn it.

I've started to confess that vulnerability might be easy for me to talk about from a stage, but that it's excruciating for me to put into practice face-to-face. It has meant learning to be more authentic - in the middle of a mess - rather than waiting until there's a safe distance between me and the struggle, which also means admitting that I'm scared to let people see me flounder for fear of losing credibility or respect.

I've started owning my voice, unapologetically taking up space, and being kinder to myself. I've stopped apologizing for being me. Which has meant being brave enough to not run from conflict, choosing rather to show up and speak my piece. It has meant facing relational struggles, even when standing up for myself has meant stepping away from the relationship.

I've started digging into the treasure of our rich spiritual history, adopting heart postures and prayer practices from the Christian contemplatives and mystics, and - for the first time in my adult life - not feeling sheepish or fearful over what others might think of my interest in the more liturgical and monastic practices of those who walked with Jesus before us. I've started to celebrate the uniqueness of my relationship with the Trinity, embracing all the delights and quirks of the way they express love for me. Which has meant I've started to grasp the life-changing realization that God not only loves me, but that He takes great delight in me…*and* my questions.

I've started creating regular space for silence, solitude and stillness in my life. I acknowledge my tendency to drown out the ache of loneliness with noise and the hum of insecurity with busyness, and I'm learning to take these things to Jesus instead. To sit with them, as uncomfortable as they might be, and allow Him to speak truth to my soul. I'm choosing freedom over comfort.

I've started practicing brave truth-telling, which for a recovering people-pleaser is no small feat. I'm learning to celebrate small and treasure slow, to not be paralyzed by down-times in business or resent my lack of ministry productivity. Alongside my equally burned-out, fed-up husband - who's been on his own journey to health and wholeness - we're learning to say "yes" to the right things, in order to make saying "no" to the lesser things easier. And we've taken to sabbathing like a boss.

I've started creating more space for awkward silences in conversations, resisting the urge to fill the void with helpful hints or offerings of help. I'm learning to let God be God, which enables me to just be me. I'm also learning to not always be the first to offer help, and the last to ask for it. This has been harder than heck, but oh so refreshing.

I've started to recognize my visceral tendencies, catching myself more quickly when I walk into a room and "take the temperature". I'm doing better at guarding myself against always feeling other people's feelings, and using that as an excuse to morph into what I think they need me to be, carefully presenting the most palatable version of myself, and curating my words just so. It means too that I'm able to spot the telltale signs of anxiety, resentment and rage brewing beneath the surface, and rather than allowing shame to invite them in, I can use healthy strategies or adjustments to diffuse them - and make changes when need be.

I've started practicing radical self-care, without guilt. And it has meant fueling my body with healthy food, not because it's trendy to do so, but because my body deserves to be nourished well, and because it transforms the way I feel when I do. It has also meant pushing myself more physically, not to punish myself for eating badly or as a desperate attempt to shed the pounds I've slowly packed on over the past few years, but because strength, endurance and flexibility are what my miraculous body is capable of.

I'm learning to surround myself with a colorful bunch of folk who foster in me a genuine love for Jesus, rather than simply hanging with the safe crowd and learning how to 'play church' better. I'm reminded that doing life together is a full-contact sport, and that being both resilient and unoffendable is vital to our survival.

I'm learning to think critically, without becoming critical. To choose empathy over sympathy, and to find His reflection in every good gift - even when it doesn't look the way I think it should. I want to use the rubble around me to build bridges instead of walls, and I'm learning to live with open hands and always, always defer to the ways of Jesus over the rules of an institution.

Beloved, I worked so hard for so long to earn my way in - to be loved and admired - and it cost me greatly. Learning to accept love, just for being me, is a radical, surprisingly difficult way to live. It isn't my default setting. But if we will allow God to do deep work in us, resetting our defaults and teaching us to live as his beloved, we'll discover that the most beautiful part of this whole journey is that our freedom releases others. Because we tend to project our own hoops onto other people's obstacle courses, when we hold ourselves to unattainable standards, we will measure others in the same way. **But me being fully myself gives you permission to be fully yourself.** As we allow ourselves to be loved, we can love. As we accept grace, we can extend it. As we live boldly in our freedom, we become freedom fighters for others. That's how it works in the body, after all. When one part is unhealthy, we all suffer. And when one part gets healed up, we all get a little more whole.

Nobody escapes being wounded. We are all wounded people, whether physically, emotionally, mentally, or spiritually. The main question is not, 'How can we hide our wounds?' so we don't have to be embarrassed, but 'How can we put our woundedness in the service of others?' When our wounds cease to be a source of shame, and become a source of healing, we have become wounded healers.

Henri Nouwen

OUT OF HIDING

Right in the middle of this vulnerable truth-telling journey, my family headed out of town for an event and I forgot my clothes for a speaking engagement I had the next day. Mind you, it wasn't just my clothes. It was my outfit, my hair brush and products, my deodorant, my make-up...my entire bag of tricks. As my mind raced through all the possible solutions to what could be a very stinky situation, I sensed an invitation wrapped into the mix. An opportunity to put into action what I'd been learning; to flesh out what I now believed to be true. That my pretense doesn't serve anyone. The world doesn't need to see our strength on display, but our humanity. I no longer wanted to live fearful of being a liability to God. I wanted to know - in my marrow - that my imperfect, messy life was simply a vessel for Him to fill. Scripture quoting holy-rollers were never people I was drawn to when I was hurting - so why would I want to pretend to be that for others. So would you believe it... I rocked up at that event in the very same clothes I'd worn for the entire day before, without touching my hair (miraculously my curls didn't budge overnight), having applied the deodorant I found in my car on the way, and with only a fresh layer of lipgloss on my kisser. It was scary and liberating, and a hilariously awkward step toward learning to be real.

෧෧

Today I feel more myself than I ever have. Even my face feels different, in the sense that I'm not constantly morphing to portray the expression I think is expected of me at any given moment. It is content to just be my face. The mask is off and the gig is up. I'm no longer interested in performing for the approval of others. Fear has held me captive for long enough and I refuse to give it another day of my life. I feel, for once, at home in my body. There is a stillness in my soul and a fire in my spirit that I don't want to live another day without. There is a clarity and peace of mind that I'm not sure I've ever really felt, even with all the questions and unknowns I'm surrounded by. I suppose I'm learning to rest in the mystery of not having it all figured out, while walking hand-in-hand with the One who does. There's a rhythm of grace that comes with being in step with the Spirit, even when it seems out of sync with the cadence all around us.

Over the summer my nature-loving son and I were pouring over his animal encyclopedia - which, as it often does, inspired a series of insect videos on YouTube. As is the norm, we flittered from one nature snippet to the next, based on the recommendations made down the right side of the screen. Next up: The Caddisfly. What started off as a banana slug research operation for my son turned into a mask-shattering epiphany for me. Assuming you're as clueless about this little creature as I was, allow me to rock your world. Because caddisfly females lay their eggs on vegetation just above bodies of water, the larvae drop into the water when they hatch. Almost immediately these little guys get to work constructing protective cases around their bodies. Using sand, stones, pieces of leaves and sticks, fragments of shell and other debris, they literally build cocoons to protect what the narrator refers to in the video as their "very sensitive butts". This morsel of information was greatly appreciated by my 8-year-old. Fascinated by this resourceful little insect, we clicked on another video to learn more. Much to our surprise, some unorthodox artisans have noticed the creative skills of the caddisfly and have taken it upon themselves to curate the insect's environment. Providing the larvae with ample gold nuggets, fragments of pearls and precious stones, they enable them to craft beautifully bedazzled butt coverings which eventually get turned into jewelry. Never mind the absurdity of wearing a bug's rump art around your neck, I sensed the Lord put his finger on my heart and whisper, "This is what you've done. You shed your old hiding place, but instead of remaining free and vulnerable, you fashioned for yourself a new protective shield out of your new, carefully curated church environment". Sigh. He gets me every time.

I'd become so good at hiding behind my finely edited, carefully curated existence that I couldn't see it for what it was; a second act. Only a more sparkly, church version.

Call it protection, call it a coping-mechanism, or call it survival.

But survival isn't enough, and I know that as well as you do. Sure, **clinging to survival for a season is par for the course in this sin-stained world, but it cannot be our way of life**. It isn't the wild freedom and radical vulnerability we were created for. Remember the Garden of Eden? Adam and Eve walked with God, naked and unashamed, before their sin destroyed their innocence and ushered them into hiding. We've been re-enacting that same shame inspired move ever since. We choose to believe the lie that God is holding out on us and we take matters into our own hands. We get banged up, our brokenness causes us to feel shame, and shame drives us into - and keeps us in - hiding. It plays on repeat. But God. Our kind Creator invited the first humans out of shame and out of hiding by offering up the first sacrifice, covering them with animal skin, and foreshadowing the sin-covering sacrifice that Jesus would ultimately make for all of humanity.

God continues to call our names, inviting us out of hiding - out of shame and brokenness - and into the light, into communion and intimacy. He had made a way for us to walk once again in complete vulnerability and trust with the Lover of our souls. He promises to cover us, and to never leave us or abandon us, as He walks us home on this hard and holy road to wholeness.

Therefore, since we have such a hope, we are very bold...And we all, who with unveiled faces contemplate the Lord's glory, are being transformed into his image with ever-increasing glory, which comes from the Lord, who is the Spirit.

2 Corinthians 3:12 & 18

CHAPTER FOUR

DUST + BREATH

*To be great, be whole; Exclude nothing, exaggerate
nothing that is not you. Be whole in everything. Put all
you are into the smallest thing you do.*

Fernando Pessoa

A man walking down a cobblestone street in Rome paused
for a moment to watch a group of workers laying bricks. He
zeroed in on a small cluster of men working close by. Walking
up to the first one, he inquired as to what the man was doing.
"I'm laying bricks", was his lifeless response. Walking over to
the second man, he asked the very same question. "I'm
building a wall", he replied rather flatly. Very well, thought

55

the man, moving on to the third worker who seemed to be caught up in his own world. There was a bounce in his step and what appeared to be a twinkle in his eye. "What are you doing, sir?", asked the curious man. "Why, Signore, I'm building a cathedral!", he crooned, dramatically sweeping his arms to the sky as if to paint with his fingertips the shape of the eventual structure. Of course he was. He could see it. Now he was simply adding flesh to the bones he'd already constructed in his mind's eye.

What I love most about the picture this story paints, apart from the hilariously awkward brick laying actions I cannot help but make when sharing this in person (also good for "playing hot potato" in a game of charades), is that it so clearly illustrates the difference *vision* makes in our lives. And it most certainly does take vision and a sense of purpose to build a cathedral, or in our case, a temple (1 Corinthians 6:19). It also takes a continued sense of mission and intentionality to maintain.

Sadly, many of us are day by day, decision after decision, brick by brick, unknowingly deconstructing our temples and leaving them in disrepair. Because here's the thing: **we don't tend to *care for what* we don't value, and we don't usually cherish or invest in things we don't believe actually matter.** Let alone matter to God.

Because I believe there's incredible power in sharing our very real, very imperfect stories with each other, I wanted you to know the road I've walked before I share practical insight and ideas with you. I don't know about you, but I tend to be more receptive to encouragement or advice from people who've not only got some wisdom and training, but who've also got some personal experience. I want to know they've been in the thick of it, that they've walked through the valleys I feel stuck in, and that they've emerged on the other side (with scenic routes and favorite rest stops starred on their map). While I love to read heady books from experts, sometimes I just need a sister for the journey. I trust you'll find that here.

⤜⤛

You and I, we're dust and breath. When God created humanity, He took the dust of the earth and breathed into it His breath. For us to be people who are fully and truly alive means that we must live in the reality of being the dust of the earth and, at the very same time, carrying the breath of God within us. We live in this tension of being both dirt and divine, in being both flesh and spirit.

In the next few chapters I want to unpack what it means for us to live as moving, breathing temples, because according to 1 Corinthians 6:19, our bodies are the perambulating temples God chose to deposit His spirit into. As we dig more into the subjects of health and wholeness, I hope to provide you with some helpful nuggets and fresh insight, along with some practical tools so together we can cultivate healthy souls, bodies and spirits...even when this quick-fix world keeps serving up wildly appealing cheap counterfeits.

Think of this journey as a holistic approach to the abundant life Jesus talks about in John 10:10. While the enemy of our souls has most certainly come to steal from us, to kill our hope, our peace and our joy, and ultimately to destroy us, this verse reminds us that Jesus came so that we might have life - and have it in its fullest measure. I don't believe this scripture is speaking only to post-death eternal life - for someday, way over there in the distance. Jesus came, as is stunningly portrayed through the word 'sozo', to give us vibrant life now. So much life, in fact, that it leaks over into a world so hungry for the genuine love and true belonging that can only found in the Kingdom. No, it won't be perfect life, or a full restoration of all that is broken in us or in the world, this side of heaven, but the truth remains: we settle for so much less than what has been offered to us. But, sweet one, we can change that.

I knew when I started speaking about this topic almost a decade ago, mostly to church groups, that I might run into some uncomfortable 'word wars'. Because if there's something sweet old church ladies do well, beyond potlucks, it's reminding you what words are permissible (read: good, Christian ones) and which ones are dangerous (read: risky, new age ones). And "holistic" and "wellness" were two hot button words back then. At least in more conservative circles, where congregants still balked at the idea of 'holy yoga' taking place in a church basement. But then again, I was also the one talking about sex in church fellowship halls, so I was ready for the push-back. I am, admittedly, thankful that we're getting better about not throwing babies out in their bathwater. Or maybe I'm just spending less time in those churches. But I digress.

THE TRIFECTA

We were made in the image of a brilliant Trinitarian God (Father, Son + Holy Spirit), lovingly fashioned as interconnected, triune beings (mind, body and spirit). While we tend to compartmentalize these dimensions into neat little boxes we can label and organize - enabling us to focus on the area we feel we have the most control over and neglecting the areas we're not too fond of - they are not mutually exclusive.

When I was little, my mom was the queen of the cheap meal. We grew up eating fish sticks and chicken livers. Thank you, Lord Jesus, not together. Chicken livers, because they were high in iron, and cheap. And fish sticks, because they were high in protein, and cheap. Fast discovering a distaste for all things 'meaty' and cheap, but being raised in the 'if it's on your plate, you're eating it' era, my older sister and I discovered a genius way to get them down. We found that if we pinched our noses shut with one hand, and forked mouthfuls of food in with the other, we couldn't really taste the food. We were thrilled to have beaten the system. The trick, of course, was in chasing each gulp of food with water and holding your nose for long enough to let the flavors dissipate. You've probably noticed this oddity when eating a flavorful meal while nursing a cold. Your stuffy nose diminishes your sense of taste, and if you happen to blow your schnoz in the middle of the meal, you'll notice your mouth floods with flavor. *Oh...so that's what dinner tastes like!*

While our mouth and our nose are two different body parts, and our sense of smell and our sense of taste are two unique experiences, they are undeniably connected. Like our bodies, souls and spirits - while they are exquisitely unique in form, expression and purpose, they are undeniably intertwined. As I mentioned in chapter one, when there is unhealth in one area, it eventually impacts the others.

I'm sure you can think of someone who is the picture of physical strength, but who lacks soul stability. She's got the body of Superwoman; buns of steel, chiseled arms that don't continue to wave long after her hands stop, and tight washboard abs. She eats green and she trains mean, but her relationships are in shambles, she's an emotional train wreck, and her walk with God is stale at best. Fitness is no longer a joy, it is an obsessive outlet for her pain.

 Maybe you can think of someone's who's spiritually mature, and yet physically defeated. She's the prayer warrior people call in crisis, but she's quietly losing the battle of the bulge that she's been fighting since childhood. She wrestles with shame and discouragement daily. Of course she loves Jesus more than pasta, but she's just so darn tired all the time.

Her blood pressure is dangerously high, and while her sedentary lifestyle works for prayer, it serves little else. Hospitality is no longer energizing, it simply drains her reserves.

While we'll dig into the unique ways unhealth in one area shows up in the others as we unpack each individual space, I think we can agree that - try as we might - we cannot isolate or insulate one part from the whole. A lack of vitality in body, soul or spirit will eventually spread to the rest.

While this might feel like a heavy truth to drive home, remember that the opposite is also true. When we're intentionally cultivating health in one area, the ripple effect can be tremendous. It's hard to feel more alive physically, and not have it influence your spirit. Just like it's natural for a spiritual awakening to spill over into your body and soul. It's a package deal, this miraculous being of ours, and when all areas are actively moving toward and slowly growing in health, they create a beautiful synergistic effect. And let me tell you, *this* sort of vibrancy and vitality is what makes people say, "I'll have what she's having!". It is absolutely contagious, and more needed than ever in our broken, hurting world.

For a long time, it seems as though the western church has written off the soul and body as being just the sin-prone, fleshy parts of us – with the spirit being the only dimension worth nurturing and preserving - but beloved, that isn't God's heart at all. He made it *all*, and He loves, values and delights in each dimension. In Deuteronomy 6:5 we find the greatest commandment: "*Love the Lord your God with all your heart and all our soul and all our strength*". Hundreds of years later (as recorded in the New Testament) we find Jesus being asked about it. He words it slightly differently, but it echoes the same mission: "*Love the Lord your God with all your heart and with all your soul and with all your mind*". It's not a suggestion. We are literally commanded to love God with our whole being - with our emotions, our relationships, our movement, our nutrition, our sexuality, our minds, our intellect, and our energy - and it's really hard to do that well when we don't realize how valuable and central each is to the experience.

⟶⟨⟶

One of the ways we honor our Creator in and through our daily lives is by acknowledging God-given appetites in each area, and then choosing to meet them in nourishing ways.

The spirit has needs, we need *worship* and *prayer* and *intimacy*, like the body needs *food* and *light* and *oxygen*, and like the soul needs *affection* and *significance* and *belonging*. How we go about satisfying these deep needs means the difference between delight and disaster. Because these appetites are hard-wired into the fabric of who we are, when they don't get met in healthy ways, we will quite literally do whatever it takes to get them met. This makes us incredibly vulnerable to the world's cheap imitations.

One of my favorite definitions of sin is 'meeting a *legitimate* need in an *illegitimate* way'. In other words, valid desires gone astray. We see this playing out repeatedly in our own lives and in the lives of those around us. God-given 'voids' aching to be filled, crammed with cheap counterfeits that slowly chip away at our bodies and souls, wreaking havoc in the human spirit.

HOUSING THE FULLNESS

I think it's high time for the larger body of Christ to start *behaving* like the body of Christ. For us to stop warming pews and playing church, and begin grasping the depth of beauty we've been born into. This is a wild and winsome adventure we've been invited on, but we seem to have lost the wonder. We've traded mystery for certainty, and a living organism for

61

organization.

When Jesus first called the disciples, He didn't say, "Yo, Pete! Andy! Stop and drop your nets for a moment and repeat after me...". He simply said 'follow me'. And it's an invitation He's been extending ever since. It's called being a disciple, and it requires a level of discipline and an embrace of accountability. Not the 'rap-on-the-knuckles, you're-a-disappointment' style policing we understandably shy away from. That's not what we're called to. I'm talking about the type of accountability where we lovingly speak truth and destiny over each other, in the context of community, lifting each other up, and holding each other on account of our ability. That is the heart of account-ability. Reminiscent of the way in which John of Kronstadt, a 19th century orthodox priest, would lift the drunk men out the gutters each morning, reminding them gently, "This is beneath your dignity. You were designed to house the fullness of God". That is what we've been called to.

This faith journey we're doing here isn't a one-and-done gig where we pray a prayer and then hold on to what we've got because Lord knows, life sucks but one day we'll go to heaven. Nope. It's an active, daily journey in which we keep showing up, we keep growing up, and as we abide in Him like our life depends on it - because it actually does - He keeps molding us into the likeness of Christ. Beloved, **the Christian life is a full-contact sport that requires a boatload of trust, faith and endurance.** A refusal to be easily offended helps too.

You see it's not just about salvation. It's also very much about transformation. The Christian life has been whittled down to list of do's and don'ts', when it was intended to be a divine romance. When did it become more about convincing minds than captivating hearts? (We'll dig into that much deeper in chapter seven.)

Just as our bodies are the temples of His spirit, they also happen to be the vessels many folk will have their first God encounter with. Before most people develop a *vertical* connection with God, they have a *horizontal* encounter with His kids. So is the way we care for our bodies, which are made in the image of our beautiful God and carrying His Spirit, important? And does the way we show up in the world matter? *Heck yeah.*

What God wired into our personalities and intellect enables us to think brilliant thoughts and feel powerful emotions that move and compel and change the world. Do our minds and emotions, where God placed a piece of His heart and a unique expression of His character into the wet cement of our souls, matter in the big picture of eternity? *You better believe it, sister.*

These things should matter to us, because they matter to God. We are His beloved, His masterpiece. A work of art He called good and holy and worth dying for, and it's time we started living like we believed it, wouldn't you say?

FROM GARDEN TO GHOST

So where does the whole concept of the "temple" come from in the first place? I'm so glad you asked. Let's go back in history to the beginning of the story and find out.

In Genesis we find the Trinity getting their craft on. Having a blast with creation, they place the cherry on top of their handiwork by making Adam in their image. This means that Adam - now, brace yourself - embodied both male *and* female at first. Our God does, so if mankind was made in His image, then Adam did too. He was complete. But, like the Trinity, we are made for connection and intimacy, and none of the animals had the ability to satisfy the deep desire Adam had to commune and share life with another. So God puts

Adam into a deep sleep and takes Eve - the feminine essence - from his body. And just like that, we have man and woman, who together - beautifully and equally - represent the image of God. Extraordinary, isn't it?

We know from scripture that Adam and Eve walked closely with the Lord. They shared a sweet communion that was raw and pure and tangible – and despite having it all, they threw it away because they believed the lie that God was holding out on them[4]. Sin stained their innocence and they traded abundance in for scarcity, and vulnerability for shame, losing their face-to-face, shoulder-to-shoulder intimacy with their Creator.

Flash forward to the book of Exodus. It's been 400 years since Joseph's miraculous reign in Egypt and the powers that be have all but forgotten his name. Actually, I think they *did* forget his name. The Hebrew people have grown so vast that they're getting under Pharaoh's skin, so he keeps his thumb on them by forcing them into slavery. Through a wild series of interventions, God orchestrates their escape - with Moses and Aaron at the helm, and the Israelite nation is born. As my mom pointed out to me a while ago (because this is the sort of stuff we talk about over cups of tea), this birth came complete with blood and water. The blood was placed over the lintels of their doors, during Passover, and they emerged through the waters of the Red Sea. Huzzah, God's people emerge from a ridiculously long gestation period, and spend the next forty years wandering in the desert. Stick with me, I'm going somewhere with this, I promise. About three months after leaving Egypt, we have God showing up in smoke and clouds while delivering the ten commandments, and the people decide it's just a little too intense for them and they'd rather have Moses be their middle man (Exodus 20:19-21). They don't want to go direct, because God is too scary, and so now we have the instructions for the building of the Tabernacle and the Ark of the Covenant so God can do what God's always wanted to do: dwell with His people (Exodus 25:8). Another 400+ years go by and finally, as recorded in 1 Kings 5-9, we have King Solomon building the Temple his father had dreamed of.

The progression of God's dwelling presence goes from the garden to the ark and tabernacle, to the temple. We have a picture of a limitless God, unconstrained by time and space, who will stop at nothing to redeem His people, and who chooses to reach down into our limitations to dwell among us.

Once Jesus shows up on the scene, He royally offends the chief priests by saying that once destroyed, He would rebuild the temple in 3 days. Not because he's got mad construction skills, but because he's bringing an entirely new paradigm: He is the temple. He was the living presence of God on the earth. And sweet sister, now we are. You and I, we are the body of Christ. We're the temple. The sacred place the Holy Ghost has chosen to indwell. We literally carry the glory of God in us. What a deliciously mind-blowing thought!

In ancient days, only one priest once a year encountered the presence of God in the Holy of Holies. But because His body was broken and the curtain was torn, we now get to live with that presence vibrating in our very bones, day in and day out. "Don't you know that you yourselves are God's temple and that God's Spirit dwells in your midst?" Paul writes in 1 Corinthians 3:16. If we really tried to understand this, it would still be too wondrous to wrap our little human minds around. God; around us, about us, within us. And for us.

The intimacy and identity God had always wanted for his people – in the garden, back in the desert during the exodus, and through the sacred encounters in the temple - has come to pass. As Peter so beautifully puts it, "You are a chosen people, a royal priesthood, a holy nation, God's special possession, that you may declare the praises of him who called you out of darkness into his wonderful light." (1 Peter

2:9)

> *...Didn't you realize that your body is a sacred place,*
> *the place of the Holy Spirit? Don't you see that you can't*
> *live however you please, squandering what God paid*
> *such a high price for? The physical part of you is not some*
> *piece of property belonging to the spiritual part of you.*
> *God owns the whole works. So let people see*
> *God in and through your body.*
> *1 Corinthians 6:19-20*

WHY IT MATTERS

Okay, awesome! So we've got that hammered out. Now what does that actually mean for us today – realistically and practically in our ordinary, already full-to-the-brim lives? Because we are officially more sick and tired, anxious and depressed than we've ever been. We are averse to pain and discomfort, and we fight a fear so pervasive it cripples us, so we're constantly on the hunt for silver bullets – or new numbing techniques – to deal with the ache we feel; emotionally, physically, sexually, mentally or spiritually.

...It means that we need to acknowledge the appetites of our body, soul and spirit, and be honest about the counterfeits we keep trying to stuff into the spaces only God can fill and satisfy. We'll dig into each area's appetite, and the most common counterfeits, in the following chapters.

...It means we were created for more, and that we need to stop settling for less.

...It means that we've got to stop playing small and hiding from our pain. We will only unfold and get free when we've uprooted the lies, confronted the pain and allowed God to heal our wounds.

...It means that when we're called to love our Lord with all our heart and all our soul and all our strength and all our mind...we're actually supposed to love Him that way.

...It means that Jesus didn't come so we could score a free ticket to heaven and get the heck out of dodge someday. In saving us, He came to make us whole, so we in turn could help bring heaven – and wholeness - to earth in our everyday lives.

...It means that if we're to effectively and sustainably be the hands and feet of Jesus, that we're in serious need of a *mani* and a *pedi*. And it starts with understanding who God is in us and through us and for us. And it involves us not treating the term "self-care" as a *cuss word*.

...And it means that as we get healthy and whole individually, and healthier collectively as the body, we can be actively engaged in shaping culture, rather than being shaped by it.

With that, let's dig into the nitty-gritty of our amazing multifaceted beings in the next three chapters (complete with titles that further reveal my love of Greek and Hebrew root words). In *Neshama* we'll explore the cravings and characteristics of our souls (minds, wills and emotions), in *Soma* we'll unpack the building blocks of physical health (from nutrition to movement), and finally in *Pneuma* we'll delve into the hunger and mystery of our spirits. Let's do this!

I'm discovering that a spiritual journey Is a lot like a poem.
You don't merely recite a poem or analyze it intellectually.
You dance it, sing it, cry it, feel it on your skin and in your
bones. You move with it and feel its caress. It falls on you like
a teardrop or wraps around you like a smile. It lives in the
heart and the body as well as the spirit and the head.

Sue Monk Kidd

CHAPTER FIVE

NESHAMA | SOUL

*Diseases of the soul are more dangerous and
more numerous than those of the body.*

Cicero

Born in Milan, Ohio, in 1847 and raised in Port Huron, Michigan, Thomas Alva Edison was the youngest of 7 children. He struggled with hearing loss from a young age, attributing it to the time a train conductor struck him on the ears when he blew up a boxcar with the little chemical laboratory he had set up, but scarlet fever and multiple ear infections - a far less exciting cause - were most likely to blame.

One day young Thomas came home from school with a note from the teacher with strict instructions to hand the unopened note to his mother. Tearful, she read the note to him, "Your son is a genius. This school is too small for him and doesn't have enough good teachers for training him. Please teach him yourself." And teach him she did. While he grew up to be a prolific inventor with over 1,000 patents in his name, we know him as the man behind the light bulb - the inventor and businessman who played an instrumental role in the development of this revolutionary technology. We also know him as the man who didn't fail, but who found 10,000 different ways that didn't work. And we love him for it. As the story goes, one day, long after his mother had passed away, he was going through old family things when he stumbled upon a folded-up note in the far corner of a desk drawer. It was the note from his school teacher, and it read: "Your son is addled. We won't let him come to school any more". Addled, if you're wondering, means 'befuddled' or 'gone'. Edison, after a good cry, went on to write in his diary, "Thomas Alva Edison was an addled child that, by a hero mother, became the genius of the century."

Our thoughts matter. They become our belief systems, and what we believe to be true shapes our lens. The lens through which we see gives birth to words and actions and habits, directing our decisions, and ultimately fashioning and shaping our lives.

Our words matter. What we speak over other people and what we believe about them carries tremendous power. People have a way of living up to what those in positions of authority say about them; toward destiny or detriment. And what we speak over ourselves - what we believe to be true about who we are, what we're worth and why we're alive - will impact every part of our lives and influence every single thing we do or say. Our words matter because they set things in motion. We literally speak things into being. Proverbs 18:21

says that we have the power of life and death in our tongues. If the divine power that dwells within us spoke the world into existence, shouldn't we more carefully choose what emerges from our lips? It would seem that our mouths, with all their brilliant sensory and communicative capabilities, are where our internal, intangible souls collide with our external, palpable world. What extraordinary superpowers we carry, and seem, largely, to be unaware of.

RESTORING THE SOUL

One of the areas that has been neglected in western religious circles is the soul. This could be, in part, because we've wrongfully assumed that the soul is what scripture refers to as the 'sinful nature'. While we've been trying to put them to death, our weary souls have been crying out for the attention and care God intended we give them.

The human soul, often referred to as the heart, is an essential part of who we are; intricate and unique imprints of the Imago Dei (image of God) on creation. Our soul includes our mind, will and emotions. John Eldredge writes in *Waking the Dead*, "Most Christians are still living with an Old Testament view of their heart. Jeremiah 17:9 says, 'My heart is deceitfully wicked.' No, it's not. Not after the work of Christ, because the promise of the new covenant is a new heart." If what Paul writes in 2 Corinthians 5:17 is true - "Therefore, if anyone is in Christ, the new creation has come: The old has gone, the new is here!" - then that means our hearts and souls have been made new. Yes, of course we need to deal with our old habits and tendencies (which the Holy Spirit helps us with as we grow and mature), but trying to silence the soul in an attempt to rid our lives of worldliness is about as ridiculous as lopping off an arm in an attempt to lose weight. For too long our mental health and emotional needs have been

71

minimized within the four walls of the church, in the name of "being more spiritual", and it's time for the Christians to wake up and tend to the *whole* person. Our hearts are nestled in the apex of our soul, and matters of the heart are *central* to our faith.

In the same way our body needs food, water and oxygen, our soul needs affection, attention, and a sense of significance and belonging. Not 'might benefit from', but '*needs*'. If someone was drowning, we wouldn't stand around and quietly judge their need for air. "Pshhh, they're just looking for oxygen. How *selfish*." Nor would we quickly call the prayer chain, proclaiming our faith that God will somehow miraculously save them and supernaturally infuse them with oxygen. No, we would get in the water as fast as our bodies could carry us and we would pull them out. And if you've ever attempted to rescue another person, or have had any type of lifeguard training, you know this gig ain't for sissies. They don't smile and say, "Gosh, thank you so much for taking time out of your busy schedule to come reconnect me with a ready source of oxygen, you're so kind and thoughtful." Not a chance. They will claw their way to rescue, over your head if need be, like a zombie in search of brains. And yet, when someone's heart is hurting and they're in desperate need of soul food, we shame people into thinking that they shouldn't need a sense of purpose, or attention, or affection. They're just being needy. Goodness, lady, sign up for another Bible study and get over your bad self.

When we look at this topic through the lens of need and deprivation, it is sad how little we've done to tend to people's souls, isn't it? Not to mention our own. Repeat after me: soul-care is not a dirty word.

Why are so many people struggling with depression and discouragement? They've lost heart. Why can't we seem able to break free of our addictions? Because somewhere along the way, in a moment of carelessness or desperation, we gave our heart away, and now we can't get it back.

John Eldredge

Because God created us with a soul appetite, when people's hungry hearts don't get their needs met in healthy ways - the way God created them to be met - we will do whatever it takes to fill up those tanks. Even if it ends up destroying us. We quickly become masters at numbing ourselves with relationships and substances, desperate to fill the void. As Brené Brown describes it, we're like turtles without a shell in a briar patch. What we need isn't another shell, but to get *out* of the briar patch. When the body of Christ doesn't welcome people with open arms, generously creating space for God to tend to our wounds, the world is waiting in the wings to numb the pain with counterfeits. **And because we regularly forget that the church was intended to be a hospital for the sick, not a museum of the saints, we will continue to enable society to stick band-aids on broken hearts.**

People tend to follow in the footsteps of those who extend love to them. We will show up for those who make us feel like we matter and we will grow roots where we know we belong. This is why gangs, groups and movements continue to grow and thrive. They become a hub that attracts those hungry for validation, meaning and connection to something bigger than themselves, that also provides them a place to belong alongside others who look, feel, behave and identify similarly. It's unity over a shared pain, passion or position, and a drive for this type of connectedness is wired into the fabric of who we are. Love, significance and belonging will *always* be central to what it means to be human. They are at the heart of our soul's appetite; the God-given hunger of our hearts.

※

Despite my shortage of affection for fiction, last year I read C.S. Lewis's Screwtape Letters and loved it. This witty and poignant satire records the correspondence between Screwtape, a senior tempter in the service of "Our Father Below", and his nephew Wormwood, a demon still quite wet behind the ears. In their attempt to secure the damnation of a rather ordinary young man, distracting him from any genuine pursuit of God (the "Enemy"), Screwtape offers these words of guidance: "Of course I know that the Enemy also wants to detach men from themselves, but in a different way. Remember always, that He really likes the little vermin, and sets an absurd value on the distinctness of every one of them. When He talks of their losing their selves, He only means abandoning the clamour of self-will; once they have done that, He really gives them back all their personality, and boast (I am afraid, sincerely) that when they are wholly His they will be more themselves than ever. Hence, while He is delighted to see them sacrificing even their innocent wills to His, He hates to see them drifting away from their nature for any other reason. And we should always encourage them to do so." I love how Lewis so brilliantly reminds us that when we are wholly His, we are more ourselves than ever. This seems to fly in the face of the seeming anti self-awareness and personal-development rhetoric ingrained in some church philosophies.

Because of the tri-dimensional way in which we've been created, unhealth in our souls, much like in our bodies, manifests in the other areas. It shows up physically in obsessive behavior, chronic pain, addiction and eating disorders, and it emerges spiritually through apathy, passivity, and legalism. Known as a psychosomatic response, reactions in our minds can actually create physical conditions, simply based on our belief systems. We can think ourselves into sickness and feel ourselves into insanity. Our mind, will and emotions are just that powerful. And for good reason. Now we just need to learn how to use them for restoration and renewal.

THE MESS OF MENDING

Soul health is particularly dear to my heart because it's an area of my life that was neglected for so long, and an area where God has done a tremendous amount of work and healing in me over the past twenty years. While I, by all outward appearances, seemed like a healthy, sparkly church girl, my sick soul was silently destroying me from the inside out. I was going through the motions, numbing the pain and drowning the fear I'd become so accustomed to battling, with good works, boldly proclaiming truths I hadn't actually claimed for myself. I was losing the fight on the battlefield of my mind. My spiritual life felt stale and dry, my body wouldn't cooperate no matter how hard I tried to beat it into submission, while my heart continued to quietly fold in on itself. It has taken years upon years of God peeling the layers back, countless hours of mentoring and counseling, and the faithful pursuit of good friends who have loved me through the pretense and called me out of hiding.

There were seasons where, in the thick of loneliness and depression, I begged God to fix me faster. I was so tired of dealing with the same old lies and battling the same issues I'd struggled with since childhood. I was desperate for freedom, exhausted from what felt like a never-ending fight with fear, anxiety and self-loathing. I knew God could snap His fingers and make it all right in an instant. I had no doubt He could fix me. But it seems He rarely works that way. I remember lying in bed late one night after another hard day, crying out for Him to please deliver me from all the stuff I felt so stuck in, when I felt His gentle whisper. "I won't deliver you *from* it, but I will deliver you *through* it. I will walk with you through this so that one day you'll be able to walk with others through their own brokenness and healing." How encouraging would we be, after all, if our only response to another person's pain was, "I don't know, sorry, I just can't relate. God completely healed all my wounds back on August 10th, 1995." No, beloved, it is a long road home. A hard and holy journey to wholeness, with Him by our side.

Last summer, after two tall poplar trees in our back yard had become sick and clearly started dying, we knew it was time to cut them down. I was devastated. Not because I have an affinity for poplars - I most assuredly do not - but because we have so few trees on our property to begin with. One of them sat directly outside our dining room window and deck, offering us a much-needed reprieve from the summer sun. Once I'd come to terms with this unavoidable loss, however, I started to get excited about open lawn and an unblocked view of the little lake out back. My husband gathered the men in our small group, promising them the opportunity to get their hands on power tools and cold beer, and the tree cutting began. Within hours the trunk and limbs were horizontal, arranged in chunks and pieces across the lawn like a massive disassembled toy.

It took days to clear the debris, as we split and stacked what would become heat for our house for winters to come. Only the stumps remained. I suggested an artsy table or giant bird bath, neither of which gained any traction with my hubby, and the stump grinding company was called. I had visions of a little tractor-looking contraption coming in and drilling down neatly into the stump. They would flatten out the ground so we could sow grass seed and move on with our lives. But no, I had clearly not read Stump Grinding for Dummies. It was wide, it was deep, and it was messy. We returned to find our lawn completely chewed up, 8 feet in every direction from what had been two small, unassuming stumps. What looked to be a completely unnecessary upheaval of ground (and desecration of my 'lake' view), was a necessary and strategic move to eliminate all possibility of regrowth. This is true for us too. Deep healing requires deep work. And rarely is it not messy, inconvenient, uncomfortable and time-consuming. But it is necessary if we are to live free, healthy and unhindered lives.

ॐ

God cares about our souls because this part of us carries a unique imprint of His heart. Jesus sunk His hands into the wet soil of our humanity and wove personalities, strengths, gifts and passions into us, wiring us to express His heart for the world in a specific way, in our unique circles of influence. This is at the heart of what God came to do, through this sacred romance and the radical offering of sozo.

Remember the beautiful illustration of sozo we find in Acts 3 where Jesus heals a man, tending to his body, soul and spirit with such compassion? This isn't a rare occurrence, it's just how Jesus does ministry. It's what He came to do; mend us and make us whole. He was always renewing the spirit while healing the body. Tenderly restoring the soul while confronting the sin in people's lives. **Could it be that He knew our attempts to manage our sin, without dealing with the pain and personal suffering that leads us to sin, would be fruitless?** It only leads to more spiritual striving and slavery. As Richard Rohr has said, "if you don't transform your pain, you will transmit it." In other words, if we don't heal what hurt us, we'll bleed on people who didn't cut us. Jesus, throughout his earthly ministry, modeled for his followers a grace-drenched, holistic salvation experience for the lost and hurting. It's up to us to fully embrace the restoration process.

∞

In ancient culture, spiritual suspicion and superstition ran high. Religious folk had - and still have - a way of connecting dots Jesus never did. If you were blind, it was because of sin. If you had leprosy, it was because you were cursed. If you were infertile, it was because you were unworthy. Any opportunity to increase the outcast population and further separate the spiritual elites from the riff-raff. But it's in the midst of the riff-raff that we always find Jesus.

In John 9, Jesus has just slipped away from the temple grounds, escaping a stoning after being accused by the Jews of being possessed. As they walk, He and the disciples notice a man, blind from birth, and the usual questions begin. "Rabbi, who sinned, this man or his parents, that he was born blind?". It wasn't an unusual question, seeing blindness was a scarlet letter of sorts. But Jesus' response is everything. "Neither this man nor his parents sinned, but this happened so that the works of God might be displayed in him." This poor man, labeled an outcast from birth, was shunned and spat upon by the very people who should have loved him and helped his family care for his needs. And then into his small world walks the Savior of the world. We know Jesus could have touched him, breathed on him, or simply spoken one word and the blind man would have been healed. But no, Jesus chooses to use the very thing that has been a source of shame and a stamp of disapproval for the entirety of his life: spit.

Imagine being that blind man, hearing the excited whispers of Jesus' proximity, and hoping that this might be the day your life changes. What if Jesus sees you, notices you, and chooses to set you free from your darkness. And as you sit taller, and breathe quicker, heart racing with anticipation, you hear that familiar, heart-wrenching sound. He's clearing his throat and spitting. The ache and loss hits you like a blow to the stomach; even Jesus has dismissed you as a lost cause, cursed and unworthy. Only He doesn't spit *on* you, He kneels down beside you and you can feel the warmth of his smile. His touch is tender and his presence reassuring even as He wipes mud, a blend of his own spit and the dust from which He fashioned you, on your vilified eyes. And then you hear it. His star-flinging, storm-stopping, life-giving voice: "Go, wash in the Pool of Siloam," and life as you've known it comes to a screeching halt. **Jesus has *chosen* you and *nothing* will ever be the same. Not because you begged or performed or worshiped your way into his good grace. But because Jesus does what He always came to do; make his beloved whole.** And the very substance that has shamed you all of these years becomes the unlikely fluid that restores you to health: saliva. Only Jesus would do something as unorthodox, extravagant and redemptive as this!

This same boundary-pushing, paradigm-shifting God-man chose to reach out and physically *touch* the untouchables. Hebrew law made it clear that touching those who were 'unclean' was forbidden, but in Matthew 8:3, we find Jesus touching a leper. We know a word would have done the trick. Heck, the fringe of his outer garment healed the woman[5] who had hemorrhaged for years. Through this scandalous encounter, Jesus doesn't just eliminate the infection that had ravaged the leper's body for years, He reaches out and touches his soul by reaching out and touching his *skin*. He satisfied this outcast's ravenous skin hunger, and ministered to the very depths of his being.

This is the Jesus I love and follow. The one who walks alongside us on the harrowing road to wholeness, making right what has gone wrong, mending our frayed edges, binding up our broken hearts, setting us free, and restoring our

souls.

Whether it's his kindness or his creativity, God is constantly teaching us about ourselves, and our unseen, internal world through the seen, external world. He uses the tangible to teach us about the intangible. And most likely because I think and speak in metaphor, He speaks to me in gardening illustrations, through weeds, seeds and roots. And *seasons*.

In the same way our earth experiences seasons, consistently and without fail, we walk through seasons in our own lives; spiritually speaking, in our marriages, physically, and as soul beings.

I heard a story a few years ago about a father who wanted to teach his four sons an important lesson about life by sending them off, individually, to observe a large pear tree a great distance away. He sent the oldest son in winter, the second son in spring, the third in summer, and the youngest son in autumn. At the end of the year, once they had all gone and returned, he gathered them together and asked what they had noticed about the tree. The oldest son observed that the tree was ugly, bent and twisted, with little signs of life. Oh no, the 2nd son contested. It was laden with little green buds and full of promise! The third son disagreed with them both, it was dripping with blossoms that smelled so sweet and looked utterly breathtaking, it was the most beautiful thing he'd ever seen. No, no, no, the last son hushed them, disagreeing with them all; it was drooping with fruit, ripe and lush, full of life and fulfillment. The father smiled as the 4 boys bantered. "Sons, you've seen the same tree and you are all correct. But you've each seen a single season in its life." He went on to explain that you cannot judge a tree, or a person, through the lens of one season. The essence of who they are - their joy, pleasure, purpose and love - can only be measured at the end, when all the seasons are fulfilled. "If you give up in your winter, you'll miss the promise of your spring, the beauty of your summer, and the fulfillment of your autumn," the father continued. "Please don't let the pain or struggle of one season rob you of the rest."

We live in a broken world and we're going to experience heartache, loneliness, rejection and struggle. Trouble is to be expected. We are going to navigate hard seasons. We're going to endure our fair share of winters and wildernesses, and while they're never easy or pleasant, if we have eyes to see it, there is goodness and gold to be found here.

Choosing to follow Jesus doesn't guarantee us a trouble-free life - in fact, choosing to walk with Him can sometimes feel like it makes life even harder. But we can cling to the fact that we will never walk alone. We will never have to navigate the seasons of our lives without His presence. God wastes nothing. He will somehow work all things for our good (Romans 8:28), so if it isn't good, then it isn't over.

SCIENCE + SCRIPTURE

For the longest time, it seemed people thought the Bible and science were at war. As though one couldn't embrace them both, but had to side with either one or the other. But scientists are discovering things the gospel has been telling us for years.

With all the mind-blowing information emerging about neuroplasticity, neural pathways and the brain's ability to literally rewire itself, I can just hear the writers of scripture whispering a unified "*Finally*!". We're urged in Philippians 4:8 to think on what is true, noble, right, pure, lovely, admirable, excellent or praiseworthy. Why? Because what we think about actually leaves its fingerprints on our brain and what we dwell on takes root in our being. In a day and age where we have locks on everything from our homes and cars to our computers and phones, why on earth aren't we guarding the epicenter of our lives more effectively? Why aren't we more careful about what we allow to slip in and take root in our hearts and minds? Proverbs 4:23 reminds us to "Above all else, guard your heart, for everything you do flows from it." If everything flows out from this place, might it be wise to more vigilantly guard our inner world? In speaking about guarding the heart, Solomon is referring to the inner core of a person, essentially their soul. The thoughts, feelings, will and desires that make that person who they are, and as the New Living Translation says, "Determines the course of your life". The Living Bible uses the word "affections" instead of heart. If we were more careful about what we gave our hearts to (our energy, attention and time), we'd notice a profound change in our lives because at the end of the day, we become like that which we behold. In other words, we resemble the things we love. Our wills - with their intentions, inclinations and choices - are shaped then, by default, by that which captivates our hearts.

Scripture tells us that our thoughts influence who we become (Proverbs 23:7 and 27:19). Dr. Caroline Leaf is a cognitive neuroscientist from South Africa who talks and writes extensively on the power of the mind and the brain's extraordinary capacity to rewire itself. She explains that our thoughts aren't just little vapors, but rather tangible things that take up physical real estate in our brains. Thoughts cause neurons to fire, triggering emotions and causing a release of chemicals across the neural network, that directly influence our physical chemistry - for better or worse. As Dr. Hebb coined it in 1949, "neurons that fire together wire together". When we think something, our thoughts create little tree-like branches that grow and connect, reinforcing and strengthening as we repeat the thought pattern and build belief systems. Changing the way we think literally changes the landscape of our brains. Scripture and science are together proclaiming that *what* we think about matters. Our thoughts influence how we feel, which shapes our will and determines how we behave, and how we behave impacts everything in our lives from our relationships to our legal standing. In other words, what goes on internally, behind the scenes, will always eventually show up externally, on display.

With our uncanny ability to pretend and perform, and our propensity to hide behind masks, it's not always easy to know people as they truly are. In fact, we're not even certain we know who we are. This is part of what makes the enneagram so unique. While other typologies unpack our behavior and explains the way in which we interact externally with the world, the enneagram revolves around motives, instincts, childhood wounds and core fears. It's a soul map of sorts, exposing our inner worlds. And it's only once we've *named* something that we can *tame* it.

While society reinforces superficial, skin-deep connection, God looks past the fluff and examines our hearts (1 Samuel 16:7). God is all about our roots (underground, unseen and uncelebrated), while we're obsessed with fruit (showy, attractive and measurable). This is why we're invited to pray honestly and simply, without religious pomp and circumstance (Matthew 6:5). This is why we're told to focus more attention on getting our inner world in order, rather than just looking the part (Luke 11:39). This is why we're told to take every thought captive (2 Corinthians 10:5). This is why we're told to resist conformity and instead renew our minds (Romans 12:2). Because God knows how He made us and what matters most; our internal world isn't just some complicated, hidden extra part of us, it's the real deal. It's the *eternal*, truest part of us. Paul writes in his second letter to the Corinthians, "Therefore we do not lose heart. Though outwardly we are wasting away, yet inwardly we are being renewed day by day" (4:16).

Let's be honest; life can be hard. It can be confusing,

83

exhausting, gut-wrenching, and downright devastating at times. As long as we put on our plastic church smiles and deny this reality, or carelessly throw Bible verses at people's pain, we will continue to alienate them and sprinkle salt in their wounds. Mental health needs to be acknowledged as a very real and present issue right now, especially within the church, where we tend to dismiss it as the symptoms of poor theology or lack of faith, or simply write it off as demonic. According to The American Foundation for Suicide Prevention[6], more Americans suffer from depression than coronary heart disease, cancer, and HIV/AIDS. Considering untreated depression is the leading cause of suicide, it's high time we start creating space for helpful conversations around this tender subject. Suicide is the second leading cause of death for people between the ages of 10 and 34 years in the United States, claiming approximately 123 lives every day[7].

Now don't get me wrong, I wholeheartedly believe we live in a world at war, and the sinister presence of evil is active and undeniable. And yes, I also believe that, as Dr. Leaf points out, over 75% of mental and physical illnesses can be traced back to a toxic thought life. I get this. But mental illness is just that, an illness, and until we acknowledge it as such, we'll just keep sticking cross-shaped band-aids on a life-sucking cancer.

We wouldn't even consider withholding insulin from a diabetic child in order to hold a prayer meeting for their healing, so why would we add shame to the healing journey of the mentally ill by demonizing medical assistance options? Jamie Tworkowski is the founder of TWLOHA (To Write Love On Her Arms), a nonprofit movement dedicated to presenting hope and finding help for people struggling with depression, addiction, self-injury, and suicide. In an interview[8] with Relevant Magazine, he said that "Christians are known for really liking their answers. We're known for telling people how to live and think and vote. What if Christians were known for meeting people in their questions, for being willing to meet people in their pain, willing to show up and sit in silence, willing to cry with someone?". Imagine how different our churches would be if we stopped treating them like museums and instead viewed them as hospitals. More mending, less performing. Psalm 34:18 says that "The Lord is close to the brokenhearted and saves those who are crushed in spirit." **If we claim to be followers of Christ, then we should be walking in His footsteps...which we'll find puts us precariously close to the brokenhearted**. We carry light and love within us, and have been called to be brokers of hope. What would it look like for us to carry that light out into a dark, hurting world, starving for the love we've been given, desperate for the hope we deal in.

We have a habit, in western religious circles, of elevating those with more public gifts and talents to celebrity status. The unrealistic expectations that accompany this feed the drive to perform, pretend and hide, which is the perfect incubator for soul sickness. Why do we think so many pastors burn out and go off the deep end? Why are we so surprised upon the discovery of their imperfect humanity? We've denied them of the freedom to be fully human and broken, and have diminished the importance of soul care in faith circles.

Jack Deere, a pastor and theologian, bared his heart recently in a profoundly beautifully written memoir, *Even In Our Darkness*. His story captured my attention and left an indelible mark on my heart because his candor seems to be rare in church leadership today. He shares, with gut-wrenching honesty and raw vulnerability, his experience of losing his father to suicide at age 12, his life with an angry, bitter mom, his own struggle with pride and anger, being asked to leave Dallas Theological Seminary because of his love of the Holy Spirit, then losing his 23-year-old son, Scott, to suicide. Deere goes on to share about his wife's painful battle with alcoholism and drug abuse after their son's death, and their long road to recovery. In a book review I read in Christianity Today, about Deere's book, the author wrote, "*In a world where, all too often, leaders present themselves as one-dimensional characters (primarily speakers, teachers, pastors, musicians, or writers), Deere shows us we are irreducibly complex beings. Our bodies matter. Our souls matter. Our minds matter. Our emotions matter. Our histories matter. These together form the whole of who we are, and any true ministry we do out of the whole is going to be wholly complex. Otherwise, it will be anemic, one-dimensional, and devoid of power. Deere recognizes this now. But it took hell to get him there. I haven't even mentioned the half of it in this review.*" She goes on to share a quote from A.W. Tozer from his book, *The Pursuit of God*, that brilliantly hits the nail on the head. "*Christian literature, to be accepted and approved by evangelical leaders of our times, must follow very closely the same train of thought, a kind of 'party line' of which it is scarcely safe to depart. A half-century of this in America has made us smug and content. We imitate each other with slavish devotion.*"

I wonder what it would take for leaders in the church arena to be invited off of their pedestals and encouraged to be more real and honest with their people. Might the ripple effect of true vulnerability 'up top' create more space for more genuine growth and transformation in all of us?

∞

Our friends, Dan and Melissa, who've been on a similar spiritual journey as we have over the past few years, have been unpacking their stories and leaning more into a holistic approach to life. Dan and I are constantly sharing books, quotes and podcasts we love, and our spouses just laugh at us. After discovering the impact that stress and neglect left upon the inner lives of those in ministry, Dan left his position as a Young Life leader and shifted into more of a soul care coach and mentor for the other area leaders. We've marveled at the growth and maturity we've seen in this friend as he's tended to his own soul, and now tends to the souls of others.

Empathy is seeing with the eyes of another, listening with the ears of another and feeling with the heart of another.

Alfred Adler

Let's start creating safe spaces in our communities of faith to dialog about depression, addiction, anxiety and burnout. Let's celebrate healthy boundaries and sabbatical, and the need to create more space for rest and retreat. And for the love of all that is good, let's stop pretending to be shiny, happy people when we feel like we're dying inside. Christians are especially guilty of manufacturing plastic positivity, possibly as a well-meaning front to more effectively represent our faith. But false positivity isn't only damaging to our own souls, it sets an inauthentic tone that only feeds people's skepticism of people of faith. Let's be real and raw and vulnerable. Let's welcome people to voice their fears and doubts and struggles. Let's stop giving people the squinty eye when they mention their appreciation for Prozac or Xanax. Let's stop shaming people who legitimately need medical intervention. Sometimes you just have to get your head above water long enough so you can actually breathe while trying to uproot the lies you've believed all your life. In order to effectively embrace this hard and holy road to wholeness, sometimes you've got to find some solid ground to stand on first.

Hear me, friend: while it is not wise to broadly numb pain

with medication and avoid the real root of a problem, it is *not* a lack of faith to pray for healing *while* medically treating an issue. Depression is an equal opportunity destroyer. Anxiety is a life-sucking beast. And my hubby and I have battled them both for seasons throughout our lives. In fact, we've talked extensively about exploring something to take the edge off the secondary trauma and low-grade, persistent PTSD that accompanies his work in law enforcement. We've had to put healthy practices in place, and hold each other accountable, or else old unhealthy coping mechanisms simply kick right back in.

At no point in your life, or spiritual journey, do you become completely immune to the temptation to numb, avoid or hide. But there is good news. As we mature and move toward wholeness, and as we intentionally equip ourselves with healthy tools, the easier it becomes to resist those visceral responses and turn instead toward health. And the quicker we bounce back when we do fail.

A HOLISTIC APPROACH

There's a significant chasm between clinical depression and the rollercoaster of blues so many of us ride. But in both cases, it's incredibly important that we work to heal and restore the *whole* person, and avoid simply throwing pills at a problem. Because of our magnificent tri-dimensional beings, every recovery effort should nourish all dimensions. I've found that when I'm in the thick of a depressive season, riddled with anxiety, and fighting emotional overwhelm, there are a few things that have proven to be very helpful.

Friends + family: Surrounding yourself with great people is essential for just about everything in life. These are your inner-circle folk. The ones you can be raw, real and vulnerable with, and those who know they can be the same around you.

They're the friends you call when you're excited about something, and when you're broken. When you're angry. When you have no words. They're kind and compassionate, but aren't afraid to call you on your crap. These are people who won't swoop in to fix you with cheap DIY advice, but who will sit with you in the darkness and offer the gift of their presence. Friends who will listen before they speak, who will cry with you, and stand in the gap for you. People whose company speaks louder than their wise, carefully-timed words. Friends who have earned the right to speak truth, even when it's hard to swallow. It was Jim Rohn who pointed out that we're the average of the five people we spend the most time with. Because, well... monkey see, monkey do. If we become like the company we keep, make sure those people in your inner circle are moving toward health and wholeness too. Are they working toward a more vibrant life in their marriage, their physical health, their parenting, their spiritual walk, their jobs, etc? We're not looking for perfection, but we are looking for friends whose influence in our lives will build us up and not break us down. It's important to note that in order to start and maintain friendships of this caliber, we have to be this type of person for others.

Mentoring + Counseling: we've sought out older, wiser people for as long as we can recall. In part, because it seemed like the smart thing to do, and partly because both my husband and I are "old souls". When I was 18, one of closest friends was 40. I think we've always been drawn to the wisdom, experience and maturity of those further along on the road than us, but over the past several years, we seek them out more intentionally. We find people who look more like Jesus than we do, and then we pay attention. We sit at the feet of those we admire and respect. We position ourselves to glean everything we can from them. Why on earth wouldn't we? This means scheduling regular times to meet with our mentor figures (who become like spiritual mothers and fathers to us), and being consistent in honoring those dates like our lives depend on it. Because in some ways, they do. We've also been intentional about seeking out professional counsel, individually, and staying in the loop with them on an 'as needed' basis. Determined to destroy the stigma associated with going to counseling, we're very comfortable talking about our love of (and need for) counseling and frequently refer people to our favorite practice. We would recommend finding a counselor whose core values align with your own, but who will also draw you out of your comfort zone. Do they tend to the *whole* person, honor and encourage an intimate faith experience, and are they trained in the areas you might need additional help in (sexual trauma recovery, EMDR therapy and/or inner-healing ministry, etc.)?

Move + refuel: as we'll discover in the body section, what we put in our bodies hugely impacts how we feel. When I don't want to get out of bed and am feeling sluggish and unmotivated, I ask myself: how long has it been since I exercised, have I been fueling my body wisely, and when last did I take my vitamins? Both my husband and I can tell when we haven't taken our vitamins for a few days (specifically the 5 HTP, maca root and ashwagandha, which all act as natural mood lifters and stabilizers). There is a direct connection between your gut and your mind, and your activity level and your mood. We can't expect to sit around and eat junk, and not feel like rubbish. If we'll clean up our diet and move more, we'll be amazed by how it impacts our mood, mind and outlook on life.

Remain + Abide: One of the first things I check when my soul's warning signals go off is where I've been turning for soul food. Have I been hustling for my worth and value, am I aching for validation and recognition? When last did I really get quiet and listen to the Father's heart? Where is the umbilical cord of my identity plugged in? If the answer is anything but God, I'm doomed. Not because Jehovah Zappa is mad at me, but because nestled in the lap of my Creator, with my heart pressed against His chest, is the only place my soul truly finds rest. When my social media consumption goes up, it's usually linked to a growing fear or insecurity I'm trying to ignore. This form of escapism is common today as many of us turn to the world to fill the void and drown out the restlessness we feel inside, instead of taking it to Jesus. That being said, it doesn't matter how much Bible study we do, how many church groups we attend, or how many great things we're *doing* for God - if we're just going through the religious motions. Our souls remain hungry for sustenance because our spirit needs to be fed from the source. Activity is a quick-fix. Intimacy and stillness take time. We were created to abide in Him, like a branch remains attached to the vine (John 15). If we're not regularly pressing into His presence and staying connected to His heart, we're denying our souls true sustenance, and will fall for any cheap scraps the world throws our way.

Outward + Otherly: One of the best ways I can tell I've fallen into a funk is by examining my focus; is it *inward* or *outward*. Am I consumed by my own woes, struggles, irritations, and inadequacies, or am I caught up in loving and serving others well? Self-absorption breeds inward focus, which incubates depression, which breeds more self-absorption. One of the fastest ways to get out of a funk and break the cycle (and please note, I am not referring to clinical depression here) is to sow into the life of someone else. There is always someone in deeper need, experiencing greater loss, or more crippling pain, and when we choose to shift our focus off of ourselves and onto others - giving away the very gift of love and hope that we're craving - our void lessens and our ache diminishes.

Do something for someone else when you're feeling blue, and it will change the trajectory of your day. I don't understand it, but it's Kingdom math. And it's from this uncomfortable, self-sacrificial posture that the #weROARproject was born. You can find out more about this sweet 'otherly' project at weroarproject.org.

If we will intentionally and regularly work to cultivate these habits and postures in our lives, especially when we're feeling the pull toward depression and anxiety, we'll notice a distinct lessening and shortening of our dips and valleys.

GATEKEEPING

Ever notice how nourishing laughter is to the soul? How a good cup of tea and a funny movie can fix a multitude of woes? Good company, good food, good news, good stories…they're balm for our weary souls. We crave the good, because we were created for love and joy, and yet we seem to live off of a steady diet of negativity. Notice how soul-sucking the media can be, and yet how easily we get engulfed in it? Kris Vallotton pointed out in his book, *Heavy Rain*, that we hear more negative news in one week than someone just fifty years ago would have heard in their entire life. We get emotionally pummeled and assaulted by the constant flow of negativity that we subject ourselves to…it's no small wonder that we're as anxious, fearful and depressed as we are. We have, nestled in the palms of our hands, more technology than NASA had in 1969 when they put a man on the moon, and we're slowly allowing it to destroy our peace and squelch our joy. We unwittingly go online to check our email or Facebook messages and, within minutes, have fallen down the rabbit hole and can't get out. And just like that, what we have isn't enough, who we are isn't good enough, our lives are pathetic by comparison, and the world is going to hell in a handbasket.

The writer of Proverbs reminds us that "when a man is gloomy, everything seems to go wrong; when he is cheerful, everything seems right" (15:15), and that "a cheerful heart is good medicine, but a crushed spirit dries up the bones" (17:22). We get to be the gatekeepers of our souls, no one else will do it for us. If you keep watching and reading smut, it's no surprise your mind resides in the gutter. If you're watching horror films and gruesome television shows, it's no wonder fear has taken root in your heart. If you live on other people's social media feeds, it's to be expected that comparison and competition will steal your joy. What you allow in, will take root and will produce fruit...whether you like it or not.

Take a break from social media, put down your smartphone, and stop reading the news. Your soul has an appetite, feed it with goodness. Your mind is hungry, feed it wisely too. It's much like a muscle in that, if you don't use it, you will lose it. Try reading a book, journaling or doing sudoku or a crossword puzzle before bed instead of the usual mind-numbing thumb scroll. Read scripture and talk through your day with God. You'll be amazed at how your sleep is affected by what you fill your mind and heart with before bed.

I was 17, and working at Pier 1 Imports, the first time God spoke to my heart clearly through a dream. Working to pay for my college classes, I'd found the perfect outlet for my OCD: visual merchandising and (wait for it) ...the cushion and pillow wall. Multiple times a day, I would straighten, organize and fluff the different pillow styles and fabric lines. I knew all their names, their style options, and where they belonged, earning me the (not so) coveted position as The Pillow Master. During this time, completely unrelated to passionate cushion organizing, I started watching gory, slasher films. I'd hit each new one at the movie theater with friends, and fill in any gaps with VHS rentals (yes, I am *that* old). The more I watched, the more paranoid I became. Running full-tilt from my car to the house, at any hint of a leaf rustle after dark, was not beneath me. I'm sure it didn't help that I was slap in the middle of my seven years of hiding, so the enemy of my soul was already having a hay-day with my secretive heart. I could see the connection in my behavior, but was fueled by the adrenaline dump of fear, and admittedly loved being a part of the post-freak-out conversation between friends.

And then came the dream. I'll never forget waking up in the middle of the night - wide-eyed and curious - having experienced a series of fragmented story lines that both compelled and convicted me. Multiple scenes and snippets played out in the dream, each one ending with a death. In every scenario the dead body happened to be dressed in clothes made from one of the Pier 1 fabrics. I sat up, shaken by the obvious theme, and tried to piece the dream together. I knew it had significance because I rarely remembered my dreams, and this one stood out clearly. As I replayed the scenes in my head, I realized the fabric - worn by each lifeless body - was the "*abundance*" line, covered in fruit and flowers. I sensed the Lord speak clearly to my heart, "Joy, you will keep killing off the abundance in your heart as long as you keep feeding your soul fear." I committed that day to be a better gatekeeper, and haven't watched a horror film since. As I see the trend continuing, and conversations among our young ones still drawn to whatever scary film is currently out, we've started to talk to our children about soul stewardship. We want them to be aware of the power of story and fear. We want them to take their responsibility to guard their hearts seriously, not only from violent or sexual themes, but from narratives that foster fear in their fearless young hearts.

Make no mistake, our souls have an appetite, and cheap

counterfeits abound. But when you stand guard at the threshold of your heart, filtering carefully what is deserving of entrance, you will cultivate life, health and wholeness in places where it matters most.

SITTING IN THE DARK

As someone who tends to avoid negativity at all cost and is naturally drawn to happy places and people, I didn't think there'd ever be anything wrong with this natural bent. But, **as it turns out, there's a fine line between being a happy person who loves to speak life, and being an insensitive one who short-circuits a healthy struggle or grieving process**. I hit on this somewhat in the pages before, but I wanted to unpack it a little further as God has been making it quite clear to me recently how unhelpful my cheery disposition can be at times - and I fear this might be somewhat of a trend in the church.

I tend to want to blaze into people's dark nights of the soul, throw some glitter in the air, and drag them out by their ankles before they know what hit them. I want to say all the right churchy things, put my spiritual maturity and coaching prowess on full display, hand-letter them an encouraging note, play happy tunes and, in so many words, help them hurry up and get over it. We prefer to abbreviate discomfort and misery as much as humanly possible because, gosh darn it, we don't like it. It makes us uncomfortable. But sometimes we just need to shut up, sit down in the dark beside our friend, and grieve with them. Not fix the situation, not hurl our pearls of wisdom at them, not offer unsolicited advice, and not quote unhelpful scripture at them. Just be with them. Simply show up, shut up, and hold space for someone to process their pain. This is the ministry of presence. Jesus extends this very gift to the disciples on the road to Emmaus. If we follow what Jesus does in the face of pain and brokenness, we'll see that He leans in. He brings compassion and presence and wholeness, not Bible verses. In fact, He even pushed back on the disciples when their instinct was to point fingers and find fault in other's pain.

I used to believe that I avoided sitting with people in their sadness because I just wanted them to emerge faster and experience the joy I felt. But now I know better. Their grief triggered my own, and I didn't know what to do with it. It would quietly bubble up and press against my well-manicured facade. As my impostor syndrome screamed louder, I would bail. It's been a slow process, but I'm resetting my default responses. As uncomfortable as it is for me, I'm learning to linger longer in the pain and remain present, even if it means allowing their wounds to press up against those things in my own soul that need attention.

If you YouTube Brené Brown's empathy talk, you'll find a beautifully animated video created by RSA Shorts that so delightfully shows the difference between sympathy and empathy. As Brown explains, sympathy drives disconnection while empathy fuels connection. Sympathy throws quippy sentiments from afar, while empathy sits in the dark with someone and whispers, "You are not alone." Connection is always more valuable than the 'right' response.

Oh, how we've wronged people with our pious scripture quoting and pithy platitudes. It didn't ease their pain, it ground salt into their wounds. Our faith in a good God is not compromised when we sit with people in the dark. We can acknowledge that this agony isn't what we were created for. That loss and pain and tragedy was never God's plan. And that this world is indeed full of trouble. Admitting the hard stuff does *not* negate God's goodness and faithfulness, it creates sacred spaces for God's presence to touch open wounds. Hear me: It's not only okay to grieve, it is often necessary for wholeness.

*Compassion asks us to go where it hurts, to enter into
the places of pain, to share in brokenness, fear, confusion,
and anguish. Compassion challenges us to cry out with
those in misery, to mourn with those who are lonely, to weep
with those in tears. Compassion requires us to be weak
with the weak, vulnerable with the vulnerable, and
powerless with the powerless. Compassion means full
immersion in the condition of being human.*

Henri Nouwen

So, what about boundaries? Because, Lord knows, there are *those* people who'd just like us to move right into their comfortable little pits with them. If fact, they've already built an extension onto their residence in Victim Valley and are just awaiting our arrival. But there's a big difference between going and sitting in the dark with someone, and moving in. This is where healthy boundaries come in. We tend to fluctuate between two opposite ends of the spectrum. We get so enmeshed in the chaos and drama of other people's lives that we don't know where their baggage ends and our boundary lines begin. And then there's the other end of the pendulum swing where we are so fearful of getting sucked into people's drama that we stay a million miles away, distant and detached from the pain of others, high and unreachable in our fortified towers of Independence. Once we've been burned out and trampled enough times (often from a lack of boundaries), it's easy to head the other way purely for recovery. Health and sustainability can only be found in the balance, in the tension, of the two. Boundaries more closely resemble fences than walls. Henry Cloud and John Townsend have written multiple excellent books about the art of boundary setting in parenting, marriage and business if this is an area you know you need to work in. And if we're really honest, who doesn't need to work on this?

~

We love the idea of growth, but man is it uncomfortable. Healing, restoration work and growth are messy, there's just no way around it. No one enjoys hard seasons or dark nights of the soul. We don't want to have to wait or suffer or endure, we'd much rather thrive, flourish and bloom, or at least remain somewhat insulated, comfortable and safe. While we can't avoid pain and discomfort, and some amount of trouble or trauma is to be expected, we can choose to shift our perspective and look for fresh revelations of God's kindness in the midst of the chaos.

Jesus says in his sermon on the mount (in Matthew 5:4) that "blessed are those who mourn for they shall be comforted". If we don't give ourselves space to mourn, we won't create space for comfort. Or the comforter. And the Holy Spirit is quite literally called our advocate and comforter. We've been so aware of the tenderness and sweetness of His presence as we've walked through particularly hard seasons in our lives. When I look back, once the pain and suffering has subsided, I'm always struck by the beauty of God's goodness and supernatural provision for us through those seasons of struggle. So, don't get discouraged or derailed when you know you need to grieve. Not only is mourning acceptable, it's healthy. Scripture says Jesus was acquainted with grief (Isaiah 53:3), but here's the catch: He didn't take up residence there. He was deeply in touch with his emotions, and His emotions served Him – He wasn't a slave to them.

Another surprising gift our struggles give us is a deeper look into what makes us tick. I wrote extensively in Penduka about passion and purpose, and how the root word of passion, "passio" in Greek, means suffering. As in 'the passion of the Christ'. What grieves us or angers us can point us toward our purpose. Some of the greatest causes in the world have been started by people who refused to allow something wrong to stay that way, or who have taken their traumatic experiences and turned them into vehicles of redemption for others. Their anger over injustice, or broken-heartedness over tragedy, compelled them to help restore brokenness in the world.

REINTEGRATION

When last did you take your pulse? More specifically, your soul's pulse? How do you first know when signs of life start to fade? Where do you go and what do you do when your soul is starving for what it needs most? What are the warning signals your life gives off before you hit a wall? I think this is one the many reasons I am so thankful for the enneagram. It has helped me identify and put words to my tendencies and coping mechanisms. I can more easily spot trends, and tell when a downward spiral is imminent. I know the song and dance I do when I start to disintegrate, and can more effectively talk myself off a cliff and reintegrate now. The enneagram has gifted me a Christ-centric compass, and I now know how to get back on course when I wander off in search of superficial significance, distraction, or a quick-fix.

※

Even today, as I drove home after dropping a van load of kids off at science camp, I could tell I was teetering. It's been building for a few days, and if I don't make changes now, it's going to make for an ugly weekend. It's here too that the connection between mind, body and spirit is painfully evident. It seems I treat my soul's capacity to hold pain like I do my bladder's ability to hold pee; I overestimate. I've been short and nit-picky with my kids for the past few days, banging heads and picking battles that don't need to be picked. This always fuels a sadness and shame in me, as I quietly grieve my seeming inability to parent graciously. I haven't worked out all week because of a change in our family schedule, and I haven't eaten well, so I'm feeling bloated, lethargic and my skin is beginning to freak out. I get overwhelmed and panicky, and even the smallest tasks feel burdensome. I just want to sleep or hide or run away. Preferably all three. We've been hustling for the past few weeks and my hubby and I both feel stretched thin. I've been slipping away to write every chance I get, while my soul is running on fumes. It's so easy, when I'm working on a book, to shift my early morning quiet time with God into writing time, so even though I'm still conversing with God throughout the day, I'm not taking time to sit in his presence and soak in His Word - and I can *feel* the deficit. All my good rhythms get tossed out, and survival mode kicks in, and one can only survive in survival mode for so long before one snaps. Thanks to being able to more easily identify my tendencies, I can virtually watch myself disintegrate, as I fight for control and shout at my kids. When my inner world feels chaotic, I counteract it with more control on the outside. I can also sense the lack of creativity and authenticity that typically accompanies my growth and integration. I notice my visceral response to be around others I can serve, encourage or charm - partly as a distraction, but mostly as a subtly manipulative way of getting my own need for love and validation met. I notice my feverish searching for something wise or funny to say online so fans and followers can like and follow and applaud, dulling the ache and helping me feel less lost and worthless. I scramble for educational or spiritual noise; a new book, podcast or sermon I can listen to in order to temporarily fill the void and feed my mind. But intellectual food has yet to satisfy the hunger in my heart.

We're pretty good at this maneuver as Christians, but just because our counterfeits are subtler in church circles, doesn't mean they're any less artificial. Or destructive. We like to increase our Bible study attendance, up our pious behavior and religious social media posts, and add more devotional readings to our day, but rarely will spiritual activity meet a need for stillness and intimacy. We can't work for or earn spiritual maturity any more than we can purchase depth of friendship. We fish for minnows while standing on the back of a whale, as we try desperately to fill a void no human can fill, and no amount of good deeds can fill. This has been one of my most well-rehearsed strategies while trying to fix what feels broken in me. I can almost stand outside myself now and watch the saga unfold. The beauty of knowing the struggles and weaknesses of my soul is that I also know what I truly need. I can see the early signs of unhealth. And I know how to get back to healthy. I can see through the pretense and grappling to what's really going on inside, so I can actually address the *real* problem. I can put on the breaks, backtrack off of the quick-fix hamster wheel, and get back on the road to wholeness. Of course, *recognizing* this trend doesn't always translate to *doing* something about it, but I'm catching myself more quickly these days, and bouncing back faster.

Every time we choose a cheap counterfeit over proper nourishment for our minds and emotions, our souls get a little more fragile. **Resilience, freedom and a deeply satisfied soul are essential for a well-lived life.** How we process our emotions, develop our minds, and what we allow to dominate our thought-life will always have a profound effect on our everyday life.

John Eldredge (one of my favorite authors), in his book *Waking The Dead: The Glory of a Heart Fully Alive*, writes about the heart and how it seems we've overlooked the fact that it "*can also be broken, has been broken, and now lies in* pieces down under the surface. When it comes to habits we cannot quit or patterns we cannot stop, anger that flies out of nowhere, fears we cannot overcome, or weaknesses we hate to admit - much of what troubles us comes out of the broken places in our hearts crying out for relief. Jesus speaks as if we are all broken hearted. We would do well to trust His perspective on this."

Despite our constant battle with them - and the church's tendency to downplay them - our emotions are a gift. What we need to understand in order to manage our emotions, and not be managed by them, is this: our emotions are excellent indicators, but they make pretty lousy dictators. When something hurts inside, it is an indicator that some work needs to be done. Instead of tending to it, taking it to a wise friend and enabling the experience to teach us something - or taking it to the Lord and allowing Him to expose something that needs to be uprooted – we give it center stage for an unforgettable performance. Or we shut it up. We stuff it with food, drown it with alcohol, or silence it with shopping sprees or porn, or otherwise shut it down with a myriad of other behaviors that aren't healthy for our souls. It's no wonder it's so hard to recognize the root of our issues. **And the truth remains: God cannot heal what we're unwilling to reveal**. In order to maintain a healthy inner life, we've got to remember that our emotions are like weather. We cannot make the mistake of thinking we are the weather. In good weather, bad weather, gorgeous weather, stormy weather...we are the mountain, God's dwelling place. Part of the problem with the way we handle our emotions is that we're trying to manage or fix on the outside what's stirring and brewing on the inside.

Several years ago, during an Indian summer, when our kids were both still young enough to require car seats, we found ourselves battling a plague. I loaded them into the car one morning to head to school and discovered four or five large house flies buzzing around in the car. After delivering kids, I returned home to swat the buggers. When there was fresh buzzing the next day, we were mystified. We destroyed them and made sure to close the windows when we got home so no flies from the garbage can in the garage could get in. Surely this would do the trick. But low and behold, the very next morning, we were met by several more. This went on for a couple of days until I could handle it no mo'. I turned the car inside out in search of the fly nursery. It wasn't until I pulled the extra booster seat out from the back row of the van that I discovered the source; a little piece of food, still wrapped in a Wendy's wrapper, shoved into the cup holder which was then slid back into the base of the seat. Out of sight, out of mind. I whipped that bad boy out and fought back hysteria as I shook dozens of fly pupae out from the booster frame. All the while we were swatting and cursing at them, we'd been *feeding* and *hatching* them in our car. Disgusting, but true. Until we go to the source and deal with an issue, we'll find ourselves mindlessly swatting at things that bug us. Restoring peace and emotional homeostasis requires inner work. Like happiness and joy, it's an inside job. Assuming there aren't medical or chemical factors at play, we are in charge of our emotions. We get to choose how to deal with them, or we can keep outsourcing our power, and skirting our emotional responsibility, by handing the remote control of our feelings over to others. If we're paying attention to what's going on inside us, we'll be able to spot trends and identify patterns. The beauty of being self-aware is that it empowers us to make changes.

As God continues to mold us more into His likeness, there are things in us that will need to come out. Habits, attitudes, faulty belief systems, and toxic thinking are all deeply embedded barbs that God wants to extract from our lives. We needn't be surprised or discouraged when turbulence hits. Whether we're a princess or a paraplegic, our condition is the *human condition*, and pain is pain. If we'll trust Him with our hearts, we can press pause on a torrent of emotion and dialog with Him about their presence in our lives. I'm learning to live by the mantra; 'He only stirs up what He intends to heal.' And that's good news for our ragged souls. Combine the careful stewardship of our emotions with a trust in God's goodness, and we'll be well on our way to nurturing wholeness on the inside of us. At the end of the day, we can be confident that He who has begun this good work in us will not grow weary, but will bring it to a glorious completion[9].

What we hunger for perhaps more than anything else is to be known in our full humanness, and yet that is often just what we also fear more than anything else. It is important to tell at least from time to time the secret of who we truly and fully are . . . because otherwise we run the risk of losing track of who we truly and fully are and little by little come to accept instead the highly edited version which we put forth in hope that the world will find it more acceptable than the real thing. It is important to tell our secrets too because it makes it easier . . . for other people to tell us a secret or two of their own.

Frederick Buechner

CHAPTER SIX

SOMA | BODY

To eat is a necessity. To eat intelligently is an art.

François de La Rochefoucauld

A former Sergeant, having served his time with the Marine Corps, took a new job as a local middle school teacher. Just before the school year started, he badly injured his back in an accident. Initially irked by his doctor's insistence that he wear a plaster cast around the upper part of his body until fully recovered, he was thrilled to discover his cast fit nicely under his shirt. His temporary handicap would not even be noticeable.

On the first day of class, he found himself assigned to the

most mischievous, unruly students in the school. These little punks, having already heard rumors that their new teacher was a marine, were a little leery of him, so decided to see just how tough he was before trying any of their usual antics. Walking confidently into the rowdy classroom on the first day of school, the new teacher opened the window wide and sat down at his desk, quietly scanning the sea of squinty eyes. When the strong breeze swept in and made his tie flap, he picked up a stapler and promptly stapled it in place to his chest, twice. Dead silence. His new charges were, of course, unaware of the cast underneath his shirt. As it turns out, he had no trouble with discipline that year.

Like an incognito upper body cast, true health isn't always obvious or visible. Sometimes it hides out beneath a somewhat more billowy exterior (hold the staple). While unhealth can subversively lurk beneath a rock-hard posterior. I know plenty of skinny people who are not healthy, and plenty of deliciously curvy people who are. In other words, physical health doesn't come in a one-size-fits-all package. But I wonder; how many of us pursue true health, and how many of us chase the magazine-cover image we've learned to associate with health? Because they're worlds apart, and the latter requires excellent lighting, a spray tan, and hours of Photoshop.

THE SKIN WE'RE IN

I've been concerned about my body, to some degree, since the ripe old age of ten. That's when I first recall the fear creeping in. And what started as a sneaking suspicion that, like my sweet momma, I was destined to struggle with my weight, blossomed into a full-blown obsession with getting skinny in my teens. As a tween I clipped health tips from magazines, ate carrots feverishly, and jump-roped as much as humanly possible. It didn't help that my older sister was built like a stick insect, much like our father, and that the density of my frame mirrored my mother's.

Around my wickedly awkward tween years, when one's body starts to do all sorts of things it wasn't given permission to do, a dear soul took me under her wing. Christine would pick me up and take me to the local fitness center where we would proceed to play on equipment, take fitness classes, and giggle in the sauna together. This new world didn't fuel my fear, rather, it lit my fire. As a middle child, stuck between an older sister spreading her rather rebellious wings, two little sisters freshly dominating the scene, and parents who both worked and were involved in ministry, I felt lost in the shuffle. I don't know if she was compelled to pursue me, suspicious that I might have felt a little forgotten and unseen, or if it was just a divine set-up. Either way, her attention ministered to my soul, and her love of fitness and nutrition nurtured my own. I discovered a passion for all things healthy, and while during my teenage years the gym became more of an opportunity to meet hot boys than to build my core, it's remained a tremendous outlet for sweat and free therapy. Later in my teens I fell in love with anatomy and physiology while studying clinical massage, and ended up training to teach group fitness classes. I eventually helped start a small women's gym when I was 22, and was a personal trainer until my 39th week of my first pregnancy at 26.

To say the pursuit of health has been a prominent theme throughout my life would be accurate. But to allow you to think it's always been a healthy, balanced relationship...would not be. More than health, I wanted skinny. I worked out for all the wrong reasons and allowed self-loathing and an incredibly broken self-image to drive my activity. As a teen, and into my early twenties, I tried diets that made my guts hurt, creams that made my thighs stick together, shakes that masterfully triggered my gag-reflex, pills that made my heart race, and coffee enemas that...well, you get the point. While I never endured the agony of an eating disorder, I was certainly fighting an image disorder. And as it turns out, binge eating, without the purging, is equally as ineffective (although gentler on the teeth). I was on a mission to get thin, whatever the cost. It took breaking my face in a car accident (public service announcement: don't drive with drunk people) and getting my jaw wired shut for six weeks for me to finally drop 30 pounds and discover an actual, discernible waistline on my body. And it wasn't until the relationship that started that fateful night (I could issue another PSA here about not dating the kinds of people who would also drive in said vehicles) failed miserably almost 3 years later, that I hit the gym with such ferocity that I dropped the weight again.

The diets I've tried in an attempt to not cry at the sight of my naked body have yo-yo'd my already small breasts into oblivion (additional thanks to pregnancy and nursing) and seriously jacked up my hypothalamus (I get so bitterly cold in Winter that I struggle to warm back up). Why? Because I loved the idea of dropping pounds fast! I lived for the day that no part of my body would spill over my clothes. I was absolutely certain that all of the other messed up parts of my life would somehow shift into place if I could just wear something below a size 8. Which, in my post-pubescent life, has never actually happened.

I love a quick fix, people. In honesty, my perspective has been so backwards that I've actually waited until I've dropped enough weight to look good in workout gear...so I can go back to the gym again. I can't make this level of crazy up, folks.

I'd love to tell you that all my body image issues are a thing of the past, neatly sealed up in some box of embarrassing memories in the basement, only I don't have a basement. And I'm practicing brave truth-telling, remember? I still have a way to go here, friend, but I am on my way. I still wince a little when I catch a glimpse of myself in the mirror in an unflattering outfit. I still have a touch-and-go relationship with my soft, squishy belly; where my belly-button permanently looks like a sad camel snout, and where the lightning bolts that streak across my mid-section remind me that at one point in time my skin was only stretchy enough to contain one human. I may have cried more about those silly streaks than I did over my southern parts getting torn and stitched up. Oh, bless me and my naive little heart.

Friend, I'm learning to love my body - all of it - and to allow that to be the impetus for physical health.

...to move and sweat and stretch it, not because I'm punishing my body for eating the fries, but because it's strong and beautiful and capable.

...to run those miles, not because something is chasing me, or because I enjoy it for a second, but because it is hard for me – and because I was made to do hard things.

...to fuel my body with whole foods, not because it's the only way I'll get thin, but because the vibrant colors, tastes and textures make me feel as happy as they make my body feel alive.

...to down that spinach, turmeric and ginger smoothie, not because I hate myself, but because I'm learning to nourish this one extraordinary body I've been given in the best way possible.

...to listen to my body, to trust it, and to respond to the cues it's giving me - not because I worship this skin-covered tent, but because I believe it's my job to worship Him in the way I steward this temple He fashioned uniquely for me.

༄

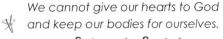

*We cannot give our hearts to God
and keep our bodies for ourselves.*

Elisabeth Elliot

LET'S GET PHYSICAL

In this chapter we're focusing on the body; the tangible, palpable part of our being. While, as with each of the dimensions of our being, there are *more* overlaps and interactions than there aren't, we're going to focus primarily on the essentials of physical health and wellness. This can be a tricky undertaking seeing, for example, anxiety manifests in a very real, physical way, but has its roots in our souls and minds...which could be classified as the 'brain', which is physical. Totally confused? Need a nap? Me too. In short, we'll continue navigating these unique 'chunks' as well as we possibly can, in light of them being but a portion of the whole. So, let's do this!

You might be relieved to know that while we're going to unpack the building blocks of physical health and wellness, we're going to take a balanced (read: non-fanatical) look at nutrition and fitness. It's a pretty daunting topic these days, with more dietary opinions and precautions than ever before, and contradictory 'scientific studies' and evidence emerging constantly. If we thought the butter vs. margarine conversation was an exhausting one, batten down the hatches, ladies. It is a war zone out there. And don't even get me started on coconut oil.

When average people (that's you and I - not to be confused with supermodels, elite athletes, or highly-allergic-this-book-is-giving-me-hives people) talk about diet and exercise, we seem to fluctuate between obsessive and dismissive. Neither end of the spectrum is healthy. Keep in mind as we work through this content that our bodies are all so incredibly different. What works for one, may not work for another. Your chemical makeup, hormone levels and genetic profile is unique to you, so figure out what makes your body thrive, and do that. And I get it. It can be hard to sift out the fundamental from the fanatical, the factual from the faddish, but there are some basic principles we can implement to start getting healthier together.

We'll figure out what our body's essential needs are, what the cheap counterfeits are that we're so tempted to settle for (and possibly need to detox from), and then we'll figure out how to satisfy the valid appetites of our bodies so we can wisely steward these amazing temples of ours.

The first thing you need to know is: **health is not a vain pursuit**. If you've ever made a resolution, set a goal, or just sensed the need to lose weight, eat better, or live healthier, you are not alone. Obviously. Humans spend billions of dollars in pursuit of smaller waistlines and bigger muscles every single year. This is no surprise. While the methods might be unorthodox, or in some cases illegal and downright dangerous, what you need to understand is that your desire to be healthy is not a bad one. In fact, I believe God Himself put that desire in us. This may surprise some conservative church-goers, as it seems the church - in their attempt to avoid culture's obsession and glorification of the body - has erred on the side of denigration or avoidance.

I've already spelled out the importance of viewing our bodies as a sacred place - as the actual temples God deemed worthy enough to carry His very spirit in - so let's look at this concept in a more practical way. Let's say, for instance, that you had saved up for years to finally purchase a sexy, sunflower yellow Shelby GT350. You did your research and you pinched your pennies, and the day came that you drove that baby off the lot. You would, without a doubt, be mindful of who you gave the keys to and where you parked her at the grocery store. You'd take great delight in keeping her in tip top shape, keeping up with oil changes, and listening to the engine for any peculiar signs or sounds. You worked hard for this beauty and you're going to do whatever it takes to maintain her so you can milk every exquisite mile out of her that you possibly can. You would not, under any circumstance - and I can bet my very life on this assumption - fill her tank with Mountain Dew and bonbons. And you would not even consider dropping some magic pill into her tank that wasn't crafted by someone who knew her inner-workings intimately. You know where I'm going here, don't you?

Why is it, sweet friend, that we cannot even fathom treating our bodies with the same respect and awe as we would some man-made vehicle? I mean, sure it's a Shelby, but please. You're a hand-crafted, one-of-a-kind, fearfully and wonderfully fashioned, made-in-the-image-of-the-Creator thing of glory! I mean, seriously. How is our sense of value this screwed up that we'd never consider feeding our pets what we cram in our own faces?

Might we treat our bodies any better if we truly understood how precious they are? How stunningly - intentionally - unique they are? How valuable they are to their Maker, and how much delight they give Him?

May it be so.

God created it. Jesus died for it.
The Spirit lives in it. I'd better take care of it.

Rick Warren

On my wedding day, that adorable man-child I had just

said "I do" to, and then smooched every chance I got (it had been 6 weeks, so you know...priorities), surprised me with a speech. It was the kind of speech that melted you like butter while simultaneously making you want to holler, "You're the best male specimen on the planet!!". If I wasn't the one marrying him that day I would have been quite tempted to deck the bride and steal him for myself. I'm only half kidding. After telling me how beautiful and true and pure I was (astonishing in and of itself, if you know my story), he went on to say that he believed God had given him a gift in me, and that it was his responsibility to care for me and nurture me and celebrate growth and wholeness in me so that one day he could release me back to God in better shape than he'd found me. See what I mean? It is a miracle he didn't get groom-napped that sunny October day.

As hefty of a responsibility as that might be, and as burdensome a task as it might feel at times, it is a commission he takes seriously. It's one he's worked hard to uphold and one he returns to, time and time again, through the seasons and struggles and rough patches. In much the same way, God gave us the gift of these tridimensional bodies, and it is our responsibility to steward them well so we can offer them back to Him in service in the best possible condition. And don't choke on the word 'service' here. I'm not talking about some stuffy, religious duty, or a distant-lands mission trip experience. I'm talking about everyday, ordinary life...lived to the fullest measure. Paul tells us in Romans 12:1 that offering our bodies to God as living sacrifices is actually an act of worship. I love this because it speaks to the heart of our God. He doesn't just want our words, or our offerings, or our good deeds. He wants - and treasures - all of us. The problem with a living sacrifice is that it constantly crawls off the altar and we have to keep offering it back up. Sacrifice of anything personal, let alone our whole being, isn't something that comes easily to humans. Offering our bodies to God as a sacrifice, or in service to Him, doesn't mean we have to craft perfect bodies – and it certainly doesn't mean that we punish ourselves. What it does mean is that we need to take care of them so we're able to show up and be available.

Have you ever noticed that there are things that we cannot naturally or permanently change about our bodies? Sure, we can stick a pair of contact lenses in, color our hair blue, rock out a pair of Spanx or two, and sport an exceptionally well padded bra, but those contacts will come out, the hair color will fade, our bodies will escape from their elastic tubes, and we'll discover the true meaning of the word "wonderbra" when we take it off, and wonder where our breasts went. But there are aspects of our appearance we cannot alter; our height, our skin color, our face shape, our bone structure, the size of our hands or feet, the way our personality shows up in our expressions, just to name a few. In spite of all the 'un-editables', God has given us the freedom and ability to have an impact on the shape and health of our bodies. I must confess, I haven't always wanted this "gift" or "privilege" - but it's a hopeful one, because it means we're not stuck. We are not helpless inside these unmalleable shells. We have a choice to make the most of these bodies we've been given, and what we do with that choice is up to us. And a healthy outside starts with a healthy inside.

ᷓ

I have loved anatomy and physiology for as long as I can remember. In fact, my hubby and I used to pore over my old college books, trying to guess which muscle, ligament or bone he had injured that week. We were total geeks. It should also be noted that we broke out in song multiple times a day in the early years, and are working on bringing that magic back. Thanks to children, and The Greatest Showman, it's slowly becoming a reality again. We remain enamored with the human body. My husband used to come home and tell me about the autopsies he'd witnessed at work, detailing the tissues and interesting internal discoveries. Yeah, we're not weird at all. A few years ago, I added neuroscience to my list of obscure things I love to learn about. I am utterly gobsmacked by the way God wove us together. It is extraordinarily the way our bones and ligaments, tissues and organs, nervous systems and neural pathways work together to make up who we are. I don't understand how someone can study the human body and not be blown away by its divine design. I remember reading[10] about how our hands are perfectly proportion. It floored me that God would pay such great attention to the way He made our *fingers*. Did you know that each section of our index fingers, from nail to wrist, is larger than the preceding section by 1.618%, what mathematicians consider to be the 'golden ratio'? And that while our hand's twenty-seven bones, combined with joints, nerves and tendons, are strong enough to wield tools and coordinated enough to type books on keyboard, they're sensitive enough to estimate a child's fever and tender enough to wipe away tears. It's mind-blowing! We love to watch documentaries with our kids, discovering the secret life of algae, the extraordinary migratory patterns of hummingbirds, and the insane way lungfish have learned to adapt to their environment. I am consistently blown away that this Creator, who puts so much thought into mollusks and cephalopods, chose *us* to be His masterpiece, the pinnacle of all creation, and His beloved.

God spared no expense knitting our bodies together in our mother's wombs, and He has the capacity to stick with us through our gazillion failed attempts at caring for these wild and wonderful vessels He's given us. He is there, cheering us on from within, as we make baby steps toward physical breakthrough, not for one minute sighing or rolling his eyes when we choose the chocolate-chip ice-cream over the kale. Again. He is ridiculously patient, even when we are not. Because, believe it or not, He wants vibrant health and wholeness for you even more than you want it. And that's very good news.

> Dear friend, I pray that you may enjoy good health
> and that all may go well with you, even as
> your soul is getting along well.
>
> 3 John 1:2

FOOD IN THE WORD

Just for the fun of it, let's look at where and how food shows up in the Bible. You might be surprised to discover how much it's woven into the narrative, from the infamous fruit eating in Genesis to the marriage banquet in Revelation. Food is a thing. It shows up so frequently as a teaching tool or a symbol for a greater spiritual lesson, that we're only going to look at some key verses.

If you don't geek out on this type of thing, just skip ahead a couple of pages to the next section (food, glorious food).

We'll start at the very beginning (because I hear it's a very good place to start): in the Garden of Eden. Not to be confused with the Garden of Eatin', a company that happens to make the best darn blue corn tortilla chips on the planet. I mean, speaking of food.

In Genesis 2:9 we've got God springing trees up out of the ground, foliage that was beautiful to look at, and delicious to eat. It could be noted that until the Fall, when Adam and Eve were booted from the garden, they were vegetarian. When God sacrificed an animal to clothe them, covering the nakedness they felt after eating the fruit from the Tree of the Knowledge of Good and Evil, this is the first we see of slaughter or bloodshed. So it's probably safe to assume that this is how life will be when God restores everything to its original glory. Considering there will be no death, you might want to come to terms with the fact that there probably won't be sirloins and T-bone steaks. Because, as rare as you might like to eat it, that filet mignon still requires death. This might not be good news to my meat lovin', hunting buddies, but I'm quite certain the redeemed world will be so wildly satisfying in every way that you'll have plenty of new hobbies to take on and new foods to fall in love with.

Speaking of eating meat vs. the vegetarian lifestyle, and all the arguments that swirl around these two very different ways to view food, here's an interesting little nugget for you to stick in your back pocket for later consideration. And don't fret; convincing you not to eat meat is not the purpose of this chapter. I love meat. I eat everything from lamb to fish, and enjoy every bite, and my husband is a hunter. So, there's no hidden agenda here. I can almost hear Kris Vallotton's voice here..."If God didn't want us to eat them, why did He make them taste so good?!". I hear you, Kris. I hear you. However, I think it's important that we be wise and humble enough to dialog about stuff like this, rather than merely sticking our fingers in our ears because we don't like to be challenged about the way we eat. So, let's put on our big girl panties and create space to think about these things, okay?

Think about your teeth for a moment, or any other person's mouth for that matter (teenage vampires not included). Assuming you have all of yours, you have 32 permanent teeth made up of incisors, canines, premolars, and molars. If you were to Google pictures of human teeth alongside those of herbivores, omnivores and carnivores, you'd notice some interesting things. For instance, how much *more* like the herbivore our tooth structure is, and how very unlike the carnivores we look (thank you, sweet Jesus). Sure, we've got "canines", but they're broader and blunter than even those of most omnivores' out there. While I don't think this boldly declares, "Y'all should not be eating meat," I do think it gives us a pretty clear idea of what proportion our intake should be of the not-meat variety. With most of our teeth designed to mash and grind vegetables, fruits, nuts and seeds, it does sort of make sense that this might be what we should consume the most of, doesn't it? If this subject interests you, you'll find more fascinating information about how our saliva, digestive enzymes and gut more closely resembles that of a herbivore than a carnivore, so research away, my celery-munching friend!

Back to the Bible we go for more food-centric moments. Toward the end of Genesis, we have Joseph helping Egypt navigate a seven year famine after seven years of plenty. He was prepared for this extraordinary opportunity to serve and lead by interpreting Pharaoh's odd food-inspired dreams. His wise stewardship – of food and his prophetic gifting – saved a nation.

Moving on to Exodus, we find what becomes known as the Passover festival taking place as the Israelites prepare for their escape from Pharaoh and all of Egypt. It's an incredible foreshadowing of what happens hundreds of years later, when Jesus becomes the sacrificial lamb, and His blood becomes what protects us (you can read about this first Passover meal in Exodus 12, where they paint the blood of the lamb on the doorposts of their homes, so that death will 'pass over' them). God continues to use food to teach his people about his character through the arrival of manna and quail (Exodus 16) in the dessert, providing miraculously and faithfully for them despite their less than pleasant dispositions.

These people are headed for the Promised Land, a land "flowing with milk and honey". While there could well have been an abundance of actual milk and actual honey there - which would have made this black tea drinking gal really happy - I think there's more to it than that. God loves to weave spiritual lessons into physical realities, speaking in metaphor and symbolism. While He absolutely intended to meet their dietary needs in this new land, the milk may also have represented His ample provision and the honey might have spoken of His sweet presence.

In 1 Kings 17 we have Elijah on the run from King Ahab and his wicked wife, Jezebel. Food shows up prominently and miraculously here twice, with God providing for Elijah by having ravens feed him by the Kerith ravine, and then meets his needs - along with those of a widow and her son in Zarephath - with the never-ending flour and oil extravaganza.

The Old Testament is full of food; we see plenty of rules and restrictions regarding food in the Pentateuch (first 5 books, also referred to as the 'books of the law'), Psalms and Proverbs are filled gratitude for provision and wisdom around moderation, and then we see a sumptuous involvement of food in Song of Solomon. Who knew pomegranates could be so sexy?

In the New Testament, with the arrival of Jesus, we find food being woven into miracles and used regularly as a teaching tool around the table. Jesus' first miracle in Cana (John 2:1-11) was turning water into wine (and yes, I'm classifying wine as food here), and we know the disciples 'break bread together' regularly, a word picture of them sharing meals - and life - together. There's the feeding of the crowds with the fish and the loaves (this actually happens on two separate occasions, with a crowd of 5,000 and then of 4,000). God uses bread and water throughout scripture to remind us that while we consume them, we'll inevitably end up hungry and thirsty again, and that Jesus - the living water and bread of life - came to satisfy and replenish us completely (Matthew 4:4, John 4:14, John 6:35, John 6:27,

John 6:51).

A foodie favorite that reminds us not to worry is Matthew 6:25-27, "Therefore I tell you, do not worry about your life, what you will eat or drink; or about your body, what you will wear. Is not life more than food, and the body more than clothes? Look at the birds of the air; they do not sow or reap or store away in barns, and yet your heavenly Father feeds them. Are you not much more valuable than they? Can any one of you by worrying add a single hour to your life?"

In Matthew 26:17-30, we have Jesus breaking bread with his friends. However this isn't your typical Passover meal; it's the last supper. And with this somber breaking of the bread and passing of the cup, our sacred act of communion is born. An opportunity to remember the body that was broken, and blood that was spilled, so that we might have life.

And the grand story that started with a piece of fruit in Genesis 3 is drawn to an epic close with the marriage supper of the Lamb in Revelation 19. Food is woven in and out of the Bible with great significance, and – like every other good gift – needs to be kept in its right place. The whole subject of food tends to expose what's going on inside us, revealing a deep rebellion, insecurity and fear that's common to humanity.

> So whether you eat or drink or whatever you do,
> do it all for the glory of God.
> *1 Corinthians 10:31*

With the Bible brimming with food references, how does the church approach nutrition and physical health today? Well, while the world has tended to lean toward obsession, the church has tended to err of the side of apathy. "Well, my flesh is just going to fade away…what does this shell matter anyway. Besides, it's potluck Sunday!" But if you were paying attention during the first few chapters, you'll know that our bodies - and how we steward our physical health - is incredibly important to God, and hugely involved in how well we're able to love and serve the world.

You better believe that if you eat crappy food, when your neighbor shows up at your door because her marriage is in crisis and she needs somewhere safe to fall apart, you won't have the mental or physical energy to be present with her. Poor food choices have ruined many a date night (who really feels up for a little mambo-jambo in the bedroom while feeling stuffed to the gills with pizza?), and have sabotaged multiple opportunities to be fully awake and sensitive to a friend who is struggling. I can't even tell you how many times a carb-coma has wrecked a potentially sweet moment with my kids.

How we fuel our bodies matters, and it matters more than we often realize. In the same way an expensive car isn't designed to run on soda pop and ding dongs, our bodies aren't designed to run on highly-process, nutrient-deficient, fried food-like-substances.

FOOD, GLORIOUS FOOD

The nutritional landscape can be a completely overwhelming one to navigate indeed. What apparently is nature's best kept secret one week, is going to kill me the next. One group tells us to drink milk like it's going out of fashion, another is quite convincing in its argument against consuming bovine udder fluid. We've been told for years to fill our diets with whole grains, but now we're being urged to eat off the wheaten path. To eat meat, or not to eat meat...this is still a nagging question. In a world where you can eat or avoid anything and not be looked at askew, what's a middle-of-the-road, just-want-to-live-well gal supposed to do, for the love of all that is holy?

While obscure diets and food fads used to rule the shelf - as in 'South Beach Diet compatible' or 'Atkins diet friendly', it now seems that dietary restrictions, allergies and sensitivities direct the market. Just scan food packaging to see the acronyms that cater to the avoidance, and are often used as persona descriptors on social media. As in 'Jane | creative + foodie | PNW | THM, GF, DF, & ENTJ', (insert flower, leaf and praise hands emojis here). You wouldn't want to eat an ENTJ (the 'Extraverted, iNtuitive, Thinking, Judging' personality in the Myers-Briggs typology), and if you're like me, you might have had to Google PNW (Pacific Northwest). THM is the 'Trim Healthy Mama' plan and you're most likely familiar with 'gluten-free' (GF) and 'dairy-free' (DF) by now. What started as a need, due to allergies and sensitivities, has become a pretty trendy way to eat - and for many, it's an incredibly restorative and healthy way.

Extreme diets still very much exist, and still occasionally catch my quick-fix-loving eye, but there does seem to be a slow shift taking place. A diversion from short-spurt diets that are unsustainable to food philosophies that are crafted around lifestyle changes. The emphasis on healthy, whole and real over canned, processed and packaged is really exciting. Not to mention the shift from waist-size minimizing to gut and brain health maximizing.

Healthy eating may have been confusing and overwhelming in the past, but it doesn't have to be moving forward. There are basic guidelines and building blocks that, in most cases, will work beautifully to decrease excess weight (and the ailments that accompany it) and increase vibrant health. And, as always, if you're battling something that just won't go away or continues to be a stumbling block on your journey to healthy living, seek professional help from someone whose core values align with your own.

BASICS + BUILDING BLOCKS

Our bodies have needs, some obvious and others more subtle. It doesn't take much convincing to say our bodies need sunlight, water, nutritious fuel and oxygen. They also need rest and physical connection. As we established in the first section, each dimension of our being has an appetite; a valid craving for things it was created to experience and be nourished by. I think it's safe to assume that if God has given us an appetite for something, He's also provided us with a way to satisfy the hunger that is both enriching and beneficial. Our job is to discern, in each of these dimensions, what the good stuff is, and what the counterfeit is. Because, believe me, if the body has a craving for something, the world is going to find a way to mass-produce a cheap imitation that, while more convenient, is actually depleting and destructive in the long run. This applies as much to our sexual health as it does to our nutritional needs.

Everything is permissible, not everything is beneficial.
1 Corinthians 10:23

One of the first things I used to encourage my clients to do was simply to pause before putting anything in their mouths, and ask themselves two questions:

- Am I actually hungry right now?
- Will this help or hurt my body? In other words, will this *nourish* me?

Listen to your body, and then choose wisely. So many of us

don't pause to think before we eat because we graze mindlessly throughout the day, and because we've lost our ability to read the signals our body sends us. Most of us don't actually know what it feels like to be truly hungry. Or satiated, for that matter. We go from "ravenous" to uncomfortably stuffed, and back again. My husband and I both struggle with this. When something tastes good, we inhale it so fast and furiously that by the time our brain is letting us know that our appetite is officially satisfied, we've had a second helping and are down for the count. We've dulled our senses from repeated overeating, and don't listen to our bodies while we nourish them. We don't eat until we're no longer hungry (which, for most of us, requires an intermediate pause and consideration), we eat until we're bursting at the seams. Ann Wigmore, a holistic health practitioner and raw food advocate, cautioned that the food we eat "can be either the safest and most powerful form of medicine or the slowest form of poison." I share this quote every time I teach on this topic because it's a poignant reminder of how God's provision for our appetites fosters life, and how the cheap counterfeits we so easily turn to peddle death, even if doused in frosting and sprinkles.

When we pause, as a rule of thumb, to just connect with our bodies before we put anything in them - stopping long enough to check our hunger level and question whether what we're about to eat is going to hurt or heal us - we're honoring them and their God-given appetite.

I realize "hurt" might sound a bit of a dramatic when talking about food, but I fear we don't realize what the "food-like substances" we mindlessly inhale actually do to our systems. Think doughnuts in a gas tank. We were created to run on good fuel, but the fuel many of us tend to run on can hardly be considered food. It's highly-processed, chemically enhanced, and includes ingredients even the smartest among us cannot pronounce. When did this become accepted as "real food"?

Okay, breathe. I'm not going to get all crunchy on you, friend. I too have watched the shockumentaries that strike fear, stir up shame, and pretty much tell you everything in your house is going to give you cancer. That's not my game plan. I tend to turn those off, reminding myself that fear is a lousy motivator or sustainer of change, and that God's given us tremendous wisdom and discernment...we just have to use them.

The nutshell version is: if it was made *by* a plant, it's probably good for you, and if it was made *in* a plant, it's probably not. General rule of thumb: say 'yes' to plant-based and 'no' to boxed factory foods. Sure, some people have sensitivities to natural home-grown foods, but as my granola friends remind me; what we harvest now is a far cry from the nutritious, perfect food God created for us. Not everyone is going to thrive on everything, and you need to listen to your body to figure out what that is. And it's easier to figure out what our bodies respond to when we're eating food in its purest, healthiest form with the least amount of additives or manipulation. If I really pay attention to what I put in my mouth, I can tell pretty quickly how my body responds to it. I know what energizes me and what makes me lethargic and groggy. I adore bread and pastas, but gosh, I feel drugged after I eat them. If I've been cutting back on refined carbs and then eat a sandwich, I can barely keep my eyes open. I wouldn't have noticed this had I not started paying attention, cutting back, and being more intentional with my food choices. Sugar and gluten also show up pretty quickly in my skin. A lot of sugar still makes me break out, and breads make my facial skin flushed and red. I had heard about the inflammation attributed to gluten a while back, but in my refusal to give up bread, I hadn't paid much attention to it. Until I did cut it out. When I caved and ate a burger bun (rather than wrapping my meat in lettuce), my cheeks got hot and prickly and my face felt flushed. And - I'm sad to admit this in writing - my belly hurt.

Ever notice how we don't know how regularly we feel like garbage, until we don't? It takes eating well for a while to realize how badly our old food habits made us feel. But if it's all we know, we simply don't know any better. While my hubby and I have cut out most of our bread consumption, giving up dairy is a no-go. I've been drinking black tea with milk since my parents gave it to us in baby bottles as toddlers. Tea time is my favorite time. It's my thing, and until nut-milk makes my tea taste the way it did back then, cow's milk will remain in my fridge.

GO WITH YOUR GUT

You've probably heard that the stomach is the way to a man's heart, but you may not have heard that your gut and your brain are besties. Believe it or not, some scientists refer to the gut as our "second brain". In fact, the enteric nervous system (ENS) - consisting of the 100 million nerve cells that line our gastrointestinal tracts, and the central nervous system (CNS) - the brain and spinal cord, are formed from the same tissue in fetal development. And their relationship doesn't end after birth. The brain and gut connect in ways few of us can wrap our heads around. Our digestive system sometimes responds to fear or anxiety before our brains even have a chance to comprehend what's going on. It gives a whole new meaning to the phrase, "go with your gut", doesn't it? Another fascinating thing about the importance of gut health is that 90% of serotonin - known as the "happy chemical" - is made in the gut[11]. If that doesn't motivate us to keep our digestive tract happy, I don't know what would.

Eating well doesn't have to be as complicated and

exhausting as we've made it out to be. We need to listen to our bodies better, respect what our gut is trying to communicate, and follow a few simple guidelines. If I'm honest, this part of the book has been a huge reason why I've dragged my feet in writing it. Not because I'm uncertain of what I believe on the subject, but because I anticipate push-back. I don't like to argue, and I find endless debate over opinions exhausting. I'm sure I'll get some emails about studies that contradict what I'm going to share - along with a couple of MLM sales invitations - so I've been hesitant to step onto this mine field. But I'm less concerned with the opinions of others these days, so you're absolutely free to disagree with me and eat whatever the heck makes your heart and body happy.

Take what I share, not much of which will be new or revolutionary, and find what works for your body. Do what it takes to care for yourself and grow in strength and health. If this doesn't jive, or you just know your system needs something a little more unique, speak to a nutritionist or someone who specializes in functional medicine. But please, do *something*.

This body is the only vehicle we have to go through this earthly life in, and we've got to prioritize its care. Yes, this also means calling your lady-parts doctor and getting back up on the table. Yes, it means keeping your teeth healthy, your skin healthy, and your insides healthy. As the saying goes, being healthy comes at a cost, but we get to choose whether we pay now, investing in fitness and nutritious food choices, or pay later, in sickness and doctors' fees. Sometimes we have to be sick and tired enough of being sick and tired to change the course we're on. I look back, as a 37-year-old, and mourn the wasted health, strength and beauty of my younger body. I was so obsessed with fitting into the mold, that I bemoaned and diminished what I had. I don't want to look back, as a 70-year-old, with the same regret. I don't want to miss what is, because I'm so focused on what isn't. Let's celebrate and honor and cultivate more of the health we have been given. We live inside bodies that God molded just for us, ones He called good, let us treat them as such. May we give Him the same delight we get when watching our children enjoy and care for a precious gift we've given them.

NUTRITION 101

We're not going to look at the food groups as they've historically been laid out, for two main reasons. First, because much of it is rendered useless for those who are gluten or dairy free, or have opted to not eat meat, and second, because I am admittedly skeptical about the motivations behind some governmental guidelines. Rather let's look at the basic building blocks needed for the average body to grow and function well. Some of this might be elementary information, but sometimes a quick refresher is just what we need. It also might feel obscure, as this book is not intended to be a predominantly educational resource, and a little nerdy. But seeing I totally geek out on anatomy and physiology, just humor me here, okay?

In order to grow and thrive, every human body needs protein, carbohydrates, fat, fiber and a blend of essential vitamins and minerals. And lest we forget; water. How you choose to satisfy these requirements is entirely up to you. As a rule of thumb, the fresher, cleaner, less processed it is, the better it will be for you. Unfortunately, friend, sugar is *not* on that list. If you need a moment, you can put this down and come back after a good cry.

Below is a quick explanation of each nutrient, along with a list of food sources. If you're a visual person and want a beautiful, educational book on food, pick up a copy of '*The*

Food Doctor: Healing Foods for Mind and Body' by Ian Marber and Vicki Edgson. I spotted it at my father-in-law's home several years ago, and fell in love. It's informative, easy to navigate, and the cross-section food photography is gorgeous. My kids even use it as a quick reference when they want to know what nutrients are in whatever food they're eating in the moment. "Look mom, ginger is high in calcium, magnesium and potassium, and is antibacterial, anti...something else, and a natural decongestant. It's called nature's antibiotic!". This little gem resides on a little IKEA cart in my kitchen, next to my red onions and squash, and is pulled out regularly.

There is so much good information out there that I'm just going to give you the 30,000-foot view. Feel free to zoom in on your own. Now, let's get a little geeky together!

MACRONUTRIENTS:

Protein: a complex organic compound formed from nitrogen and made up of chains of amino acids, and after water, is the most abundant substance in the body. It is in all of your cells and is essential to all living things. It's required for growth, maintenance and repair. I remember associating protein with body builders growing up. And chicken livers, because that's what my mother fed us in an effort to provide iron and protein on a dime. Women didn't used to think too much about their need for protein-rich foods, and yet everything from our skin to our blood requires it to function. When you read a food label (which, if you don't do already, I'd strongly suggest you do), look for protein. If something you're about to purchase or unwrap doesn't contain protein, don't get it. Try and get some protein in every single time you eat, which is as simple as throwing a handful of almonds in with that apple.

Good sources: while the standard list is lean meat, fish, eggs and dairy - and this remains true - we underestimate the protein content of beans, quinoa, lentils, chia seeds, nuts, chickpeas, oatmeal, and a host of green veggies, namely green peas, edamame, spinach, broccoli, asparagus and green beans.

Whenever possible, choose grass-fed meat and cage-free eggs. Our freezer is currently filled with locally grown lamb, pork and venison, along with lake trout and salmon we caught. There's something to be said about knowing where your food comes from, and how ethically it was sourced (happy animals = healthier meat).

Carbohydrates: carbs are said to be the body's main source of fuel and the macronutrient our bodies need in the largest quantity, but with the rise of low-carb lifestyles, there's been a lot of debate surrounding this theory. All carbohydrates are made up of sugars and starches, which are key for optimal brain function, but complex carbohydrates carry the additional benefit of insoluble fiber, which is essential for digestion. Complex carbs (cc) and simple carbs (sc), while both eventually break down into sugar (bar the fiber in cc's), are *not* created equal. Cc's are processed slowly, satisfying your hunger for longer and delivering a steady source of energy throughout the day (thanks, in part, to the fiber), while sc's break down into sugar quickly, rapidly turning into glucose, and delivering an almost instant shot of energy. While a combination of the two makes for a great balance of energy, the short-lived spikes in blood sugar from a diet high in sc's come with an inevitable crashes. While most of the simple carbohydrates people consume come from highly-processed foods, fresh fruits and veggies are great sources of sc's when we're on the hunt for a quick burst of energy.

You'll find that most cc's come in a more whole food form. While the term 'whole' food has become a buzzword in recent years, I think its simplicity is sometimes lost on people.

Simply put; whole food is food that's consumed in its natural, whole, unprocessed state. The best way I've found to pinpoint the difference between complex and simple carbs is by contrasting whole foods to processed foods. Whole foods, rich in complex carbohydrates, force the body to work hard in order to break down the complex chains of sugar, where the fiber has not been stripped, which makes for a slower, more sustainable source of energy. While processed foods, loaded with simple carbs, have already been broken down. I like to tell people it's like eating already chewed food, baby-bird style, which always gets a satisfying "Eeeew!" from the crowd. Another distinguishing factor is that whole foods provide calories that are nutrient dense, while processed foods are often referred to as 'empty calories'. These foods tend to be high in calories (along with sodium, saturated fat and preservatives), and are practically devoid of any actual nutrition as what little nutrients or antioxidants existed in the raw material have been destroyed in processing. Think whole grain over enriched flour, which has been stripped, processed and bleached, and includes 'white' breads, rices, and pastas. So don't eliminate carbs - they're essential for your body to function, rather choose your carbs wisely. Read food labels; if there's no fiber in it, and there's a high carbohydrate content, it's not worth putting in your body. Most fresh, whole foods don't require labels, and that's what we should be filling our plates with anyway.

As a side note: my husband and I have been eating a more ketogenic diet over the past few months and have drastically cut back on our carb intake. While I've always been leery of low-carb diets, there's no denying that we feel great on less. We still eat plenty of healthy colorful veggies (drizzled in healthy fats), we limit our fruit intake, and avoid most starchy vegetables, pastas, rice and wheats. In other words, we're gluten-free and then some. While we don't see ourselves maintaining this level of strictness forever, we certainly plan to adhere to a lower-carb diet moving forward.

Good sources of Carbohydrates: vegetables, fresh fruit, dairy, legumes and lentils, brown rice, barley, oats and wholegrain foods. You can sweeten your foods with healthy, natural simple carbohydrates like honey, maple syrup, coconut sugar and brown rice syrup.

Fats: a macronutrient that tends to be vilified, but is essential for healthy function, essential fatty acids are substances that the body cannot manufacture by itself, and must be derived from one's diet. They are essential for brain function, cell membrane formation, provides cushion for both internal organs and the external body as a whole, and helps transport and dissolve fat-soluble nutrients. Like carbs, not all fats and oils (collectively called lipids) are created equal, and rather than being eliminated from the diet, they should be carefully selected. In short, saturated and trans fats (also known as 'partially hydrogenated oil') are not your friend, and should be avoided, while polyunsaturated and monounsaturated fats are good friends to a healthy body.

When I started teaching nutrition classes over a decade ago, or would help my gym clients with meal plans, I had a handy list of good oils to consume and bad oils to avoid. Funnily enough, coconut oil was high on the bad list. Imagine my shock when, just a few years ago, one of the crunchiest, most health-conscious women I knew had a massive jar of coconut oil on the counter. It was the beginning of our wild love affair with the coconut. While coconut oil is high in saturated fat, it is naturally saturated and contains medium-chain triglycerides which are easy for your body to digest, are not readily stored by the body as fat, has anti-inflammatory properties, and because they're small in size, they infuse cells with energy almost immediately. We use it for everything from popping popcorn (amazing with a sprinkle of brewers yeast) and to make homemade peanut butter, to rubbing it on dry skin in winter.

When the low-fat and fat-free craze swept the nation, it caused more damage than good. In part because low and no-fat products required more sodium and sugar to taste good (and sugar is the real issue we're facing today), but also because there are certain vitamins (namely A, D, E and K) that require fats to dissolve and assimilate into the body. In other words, drinking skim milk is pointless...you need fat to utilize the vitamin D in milk.

If you're following a paleo or ketogenic lifestyle, you'll want 65-75 percent of your calories to come from healthy fats. Before you freak out and envision three quarters of your plate filled with egg yolks and coconut oil, may I draw your attention to the calorie breakdown: while protein and carbohydrates each offer 4 calories per gram, fat carries a whopping 9 calories per gram. In other words, fats have over twice the number calories of protein or carbs.

Good sources of healthy fats: avocados, avocado oil, coconut oil, nuts and seeds, extra virgin olive oil (evoo), egg yolks, fatty fish (rich in omega-3s), dairy, dark chocolate, grass-fed meats.

MICRONUTRIENTS:
Essential nutrients, needed in minute amounts, that the body cannot manufacture by itself and must glean from one's diet for optimal health. Vitamins include Vitamin A, Vitamin B, Vitamin C, Vitamin D, Vitamin E, Vitamin K and Carotenoids. Minerals include Boron, Calcium, Chloride, Chromium, Cobalt, Copper, Fluoride, Iodine, Iron, Magnesium, Manganese, Molybdenum, Phosphorus, Potassium, Selenium, Sodium and Zinc.

While it is better to fuel your body with nutrient-rich, fresh foods than relying on a pill to meet your daily requirements, a quality multivitamin is a great option for filling in the gaps. Because a deficiency in one of these micronutrients can wreak havoc on your system, checking in with a doctor, having some tests run if need be, and getting a specific supplement might make the world of difference in your health.

～❧～

As with each dimension of our beings, our bodies have appetites. The above info hopefully gives you a good overview of how our God-given appetites were intended to be satisfied. That is healthy fuel, and healthy fuel makes our bodies run in the way they were intended to. Real bodies require real food. But we like quick fixes, and businesses like to make money, so today we're faced with more food-like substances to stuff our faces with than ever before. But this fake, highly-processed 'food' is making us sicker and fatter than ever before.

SWEET POISON

Brace yourself for a quick word on sugar. It is the devil, dressed like an angel. Okay, that might be extreme, but my nurse father-in-law aptly refers to it as 'white death'. There are some hard truths that we need to understand about sugar, what it does to our bodies, and why we keep coming back for more. I mentioned in the fats/oils section that when the low-fat and fat-free craze swept the nation, companies pumped more sugar and salt into their foods in an attempt to make them more palatable. More sugar snuck in to everything from crackers to condiments. Even some nutrition-packed smoothies in the healthy, refrigerated section of the grocery store are chock-a-block full of sugar. Take a peek at labels and you'll find it. In 2014, Dr. Mark Hyman wrote an article[12] for the New York Daily News, with the headline:

'Sweet Poison: How sugar, not cocaine, is one of the most addictive and dangerous substances'. Based on his book, The 10-Day Detox Diet, he uncovers the massive amount of sugar Americans consume in everyday foods, and what it does to the brain and body. In a review[13] written for the British Journal of Sports Medicine, the medical authors write: "In animal studies, sugar has been found to produce more symptoms than is required to be considered an addictive substance. Animal data has shown significant overlap between the consumption of added sugars and drug-like effects, including bingeing, craving, tolerance, withdrawal, cross-sensitization, cross-tolerance, cross-dependence, reward and opioid effects. Sugar addiction seems to be dependence to the natural endogenous opioids that get released upon sugar intake. In both animals and humans, the evidence in the literature shows substantial parallels and overlap between drugs of abuse and sugar, from the standpoint of brain neurochemistry as well as behaviour." Citing rodent studies which show that sweetness was preferred, even over cocaine, and that the mice experienced sugar withdrawal, they go on to say that "Consuming sugar produces effects similar to that of cocaine, altering mood, possibly through its ability to induce reward and pleasure, leading to the seeking out of sugar". Well, there you have it. If you've wondered why once you open that box of cookies, you'll probably empty it single-handedly, it's because sugar is legitimately addictive. When you stimulate the pleasure center in the brain, which is exactly what sugar does, your dopamine levels spike and you immediately crave more. According to The American Heart Association, the recommended daily sugar consumption for women is 100 calories a day (6 teaspoons) and 150 calories a day (9 teaspoons) for men. Keep in mind that this is intended to be a cap, or maximum, not a friendly reminder to get your daily sugar in. A study[14] done in 2009 revealed that the average American adult consumes 22 teaspoons per day, while teenagers inhale a whopping 34 teaspoons. And seeing our consumption has only increased over the years, it's most likely higher today.

Sugar is not only addictive, it's also destructive. Not just for our waistlines and heart health, but for our brains. There is mounting evidence that high levels of sugar consumption can negatively impact our cognitive function and psychological well-being, impairing learning and memory[15] and even contributing to an increased risk of anxiety[16] and depression[17]. Those Little Debbie's look a little less darling now, don't they? For a visual representation of your brain on sugar, go watch neuroscientist Nicole Avena's TED-Ed presentation[18], 'How Sugar Affects The Brain'.

If you're craving something sweet, enjoy the real thing - in moderation. Or get creative with healthy, natural sweeteners, like dates (and date sugar), coconut sugar, raw honey, pure maple syrup, sprouted barley malt syrup, brown rice syrup or monk fruit. As you start to lower your sugar intake, you'll find your palate adjusts and is satisfied with naturally sweet foods, while artificial and refined sweeteners become too sweet. You'll also be more aware of what sugar does to your body. The average sugar consumption is so high, whether we realize it or not, that it's as if we live on a constant drip of the stuff. Once our bodies have detoxed, we're able to more quickly identify the negative effects of sugar on our systems once we reintroduce it. I can tell almost immediately when I've had too much sugar by the pressure I feel in my eustachian tubes, the little channels that link the middle ear to the upper respiratory tract. I've heard that this pressure is due to an overgrowth of candida, a form of yeast that feeds off of sugar and as it grows, can result in inflammation and yeast infections. As woo-woo and crunchy as it might sounds, I can feel the effects of sugar in my ears hours after a binge. I just didn't know how bad it was until I cut it out for 6 months. Sugar has actually been proven[19] to dampen our immune systems and cause inflammation, which can wreak havoc on our bodies.

So remember that every time you put something in your mouth, you're either feeding disease (sugar-laden and highly-processed foods) or fighting it (nutritionally-dense and whole foods).

TO THE MAMAS

Now listen to me, mamas of the world, the struggle is real. There are days I've fed my children Cheerios for dinner, and my kids have eaten their fair share of mac n' cheese and ramen noodles. Read: I am not here to make you feel guilty. But I do want to speak brave, hard truth to you. If we don't start falling in love with real food, and filling our plates with it, we're going to raise children who will choose the cheap counterfeit over the real thing, and their health will suffer in the long run. We have to, as families, retrain our palates to enjoy the tastes and textures of fresh, healthy food. Our kids are watching us. They will eat the food we stock the fridge and cupboards with.

While we're talking about kids and food, there are two parenting habits we've got to rethink. We have got to stop rewarding and comforting our kids with junk food. There are far better, healthier ways to celebrate wins, reward great behavior or provide emotional support than taking a trip to the ice-cream store. Rather than ingesting a thousand calories, give them the gift of your uninterrupted time and attention and get stuck into Lego, books or a good movie. Cook them a special meal. Go for a nature walk, or climb a tree. Paint their nails. As long as we connect fatty foods and sugar with reward and comfort, we're laying the groundwork for habits that will be hard to shake once they're grown. Think lonely tears and a tub of Ben & Jerry's. Also, if you grew up in a home like mine where food was not necessarily plentiful and waste was completely unacceptable (neither thing being inherently negative), you know how to clean a plate. A dear friend cautioned me, as I sat at the table with my toddler, insisting she remain until her plate was licked clean, to be more aware of personal appetites and levels of satiation. She very wisely observed that if we continued to insist that our kids finish their food at every meal, no matter the portion size - as responsible and logical of a parenting move as it might seem - they would eventually dull their senses and not know to stop eating when they're satisfied. Which would explain why my husband and I are both experts at eating until we're bursting at the seams. We're good eaters, and we know how to clean a plate!

If you know you need to make a change in your family's diet, stop dragging your feet and putting it off. Your little people will only complain for so long before they realize that if they're hungry, they're going to have to eat what's available. So carefully filter what's available. Get healthy foods prepped and available, so grabbing celery sticks is as easy as grabbing a handful of pretzels. If we don't do our part to set them up for success, we can't expect them to make good choices. Get your family excited about real food. If they're old enough, watch a documentary with them. There's nothing like education and powerful visuals to shake us out of our unhealthy ruts. When your family members become your teammates, instead of what holds you back, it can make a profound difference in the long run. The key is to make it fun and involve them. Our kids have grown up helping us juice; they scrub carrots, press the apples and carrots down the tube, wait for the burst of scent when the lemon or ginger hit the blades, or the burst of color when the beets get smashed, and then they drink it up with us.

They get to choose new and unusual veggies (the artichoke was our most recent 'project'), and research how best to prepare and eat it. It's not only a fun connection point for us, but it expands their palette, teaching them to experiment and enjoy a broad range of foods. They now love Middle Eastern, Indian and Thai food as much as we do.

As they've been a part of our adventure in growing our own sprouts, making yogurt, and grinding our own peanut butter over the past several years, it's just become a part of what we do. It's normal family stuff. We had chickens for few years, and they fell in love with farm fresh eggs in any form. They help us plant and harvest whatever veggies and herbs we're growing, and have grown to appreciate raw, healthy food in the process. We make our own hummus, occasionally trying our hand at black bean hummus and beet hummus. They've loved the process of us creating healthy dessert options, from chia seed pudding (coconut milk, chia seeds and honey) to raw fudge (dates, cashews, cocoa powder, peanut butter, coconut oil and whatever nuts or seeds we feel like throwing on top). They get a say in how the chickpeas get seasoned before we roast them...cinnamon and cloves, lime and chili, or nutmeg and coriander? And can we just talk about salads for a minute? If you give a kid a handful of iceberg lettuce with an onion ring and 3 cherry tomatoes, they're going to decide that they hate salad. Who wouldn't when that's someone's idea of a salad? Geez Louise. Get creative! We love to make salads with fresh greens, piling it high with quinoa, northern beans soaked in balsamic vinegar, roasted butternut squash, red onions, fresh beets, craisins, feta cheese and pepitas. We drizzle it with a great dressing and our kids gobble it up. It also makes for a complete meal because the beans provide a large dose of protein. Salad options are as endless as the ingredients you decide to throw in them, but you've got to get creative or no one in your house - including you - will ever want to eat them.

My hubby and I are pretty adamant about not buying anything with artificial food coloring, and when the kids were younger, we simply made that choice for them. Now that they're getting older, we don't want to constantly be declaring, "No, we're not buying that!" Or "You shouldn't eat that!", we want them to make educated and wise decisions for themselves. And occasionally, they do. Halloween, Valentine's Day and parades used to strike fear into my young, crunchy heart. I didn't want to fight with them, visions of Willy Wonka's neurotic dentist father flashing through my mind. I didn't want to be *that* parent, but I didn't want to do nothing either. So we started offering up a trade; they get 10c for every piece of candy they throw away, a quarter if it was big and colorful (read: loaded with food coloring). These kids are smart, and they quickly learned they could make a few bucks by saving the chocolate, and a few favorites, and purging the rest. This left the locus of control squarely in their hands. We initially bagged it up and donated it, but then realized we were sending a mixed message: 'the chemicals, dyes and sugars in this are bad for you, but we're okay putting it in some other kids body'. So we just started tossing it out. Sure, you might resent my kid taking candy at a parade if it's going to end up in the garbage, saying it's a waste of money, but I'm okay with that (see how much I've grown?). I'd rather it go in the garbage over treating their growing little bodies like garbage. They now check labels and exclaim excitedly, "Yay, this is colored with turmeric and beets!!", or "This has aspartame in it, yuck!". It's more about empowering than it is about enforcing. This way they choose wisely for themselves, rather than resenting us and quietly sneaking things when we're not looking. And yes, they occasionally walk over to the campground store and buy a gross popsicle or slushy and I die a little bit inside. But we've decided that while we're willing to fight for their health, we're not willing to fight with them about every little thing they put in their mouths. They're smart kids and they're learning to make their own choices with the tools we're slowly equipping them with.

With all of that being said, please hear me: occasionally my children eat Happy Meals and Hot Pockets. Culvers is a special date place with dad, and there's just nothing quite like a Whopper. Once a week during the colder months the kids and I have a hot chocolate and basket-of-fries date at our local diner after school. We've done it for years and we don't even need to order, the servers just know us. It's what we do.   And as the weather gets warmer, that weekly tradition gets replaced with weekly trips to the Whippy Dip. Every Friday is family movie and pizza night, and we love us some pizza. Ya'll, we know how to indulge.   But we've chosen to focus more on incorporating the good than avoiding the bad. Rather than obsessing over what we're cutting out, we're stocking up on what we need to incorporate the most. The more good stuff we get into our bodies, the more satisfied and healthier they are, and the less we crave the crap. I remember when the 'sneaky chef' craze swept through when my kids were still tiny. Healthy moms with picky kids were sneakily slipping pureed veggies into all their kid's favorite foods...so they'd actually ingest a vegetable.   Only they didn't know it, so there was no gagging, tears or trauma. I made the chicken nuggets battered with squash, and they were great. I'm all for incorporating more veggies into our meals in creative ways, but here's the issue: it shouldn't be smuggled in the back door like a forbidden friend. It should be welcomed and celebrated in the kitchen. We should be teaching our kids to enjoy real food from such a young age that they don't know any differently - not sneaking it in without them knowing it.

My husband and I are not stick-figures. We both have the astonishing ability to pack on the pounds without trying, so we *have* to be wise. But we don't want to pass on an unhealthy view of our bodies or an obsessive relationship with food to our children. It's up to us to break the cycle and model what a healthy diet and lifestyle looks like.

TIPS + TRICKS

Remember: the food we put in our bodies, and the bodies of our little people, can help and heal, or hurt and hinder us. We get to choose - so choose *wisely*. Select fresh, colorful, whole foods as much as possible.

Shop around the exterior of the store - that's where all the fresh stuff is. Be aware of how much you fill your cart with processed foods versus the real thing. When you do head in to the aisles of prepackaged foods, read labels and only buy what you know will nourish your body. Stock up on beans and frozen veggies so you'll never have an excuse to not include some colorful veggies and lean protein in your meals.

If **meal planning** helps you lessen the number of drive-thru's or boxes of mac n' cheese you go through, get on it. There are a multitude of great free resources out there (Pinterest for the win).

Avoid having packaged, processed snacks on hand or that's exactly what you're going to eat. I adore white cheddar Cheez-its, so I just don't buy them. If they're in my pantry, I will choose them over raw broccoli and carrots sticks 10 out of 10 times.

Stop letting the healthy stuff go bad in the fridge. If it's not prepped and readily available, you're not going to grab it when you're hangry. You're going to choose crackers. Once a week, or for a few minutes after you grocery shop, wash and chop veggies. If I have fresh fruit on hand, and chopped veggies on the ready - along with a steady stream of boiled and peeled eggs - we all snack better and as an added bonus, my kids pack healthier school lunches.

Eat the rainbow (Skittles not included). Not only is a dinner plate more visually appealing when filled with fresh, colorful foods, but the nutrition is more expansive and complete. If you're living on meat and potatoes, friend, you've got to get out of that rut).

Rather than counting calories, look for nutritionally dense food. Pay attention to your macros. If you're going to put calories in your body, make sure they're calories that come with protein, fiber, healthy fats and some vitamins or minerals. Don't waste your limited belly space with empty calories that do nothing but spike your blood sugar and make you feel like rubbish.

Drink more water. I'm not going to tell you to stop drinking pop (because you already know it's dreadful for you), but I will urge you to drink half your body weight in ounces of water. Drink a full glass when you first wake up, before you eat a meal, and at the end of the day (assuming your bladder can contain it through the night). If you don't like water, figure out a way to like it - by adding fresh fruit, essential oils, herbs, etc. High water intake isn't optional when it comes to your health, so do what it takes to up your intake.

Break the mold and try a meatless meal once a week (we like 'Meatless Monday'), and explore other plant-based ways of getting your daily dose of vitamins and nutrients.

143

Start small. One pound equals 3,500 calories (remember that each gram of protein and carbohydrate has 4 calories, while a gram of fat has 9). So to lose one pound, you must burn 3,500 calories than you consume. While it's not about counting calories, it is all about simple math. Twenty pounds is equal to 70,000 calories - spread over the course of a year, that's only 191 calories a day. Easy to gain, and easy to lose. If you're consuming just 191 calories more than you need each day, in a year, you'll be 20 pounds heavier. If you consume just 191 calories less than you burn each day, you'll lose 20 pounds in a year. Baby steps add up, so take them in the right direction.

Protect dinner time with your family. Eat at home, around a table - without technology, as often as humanly possible. Not only is it cheaper and healthier to eat at home, but the conversations and connection that happens around the table are essential to cultivating a sense of safety and belonging in your family.

Listen to your body. Eat when you're hungry (not bored or emotional) and stop when you're satisfied (not stuffed or uncomfortable). Eat slowly, enjoying the different flavors, scents and textures. Food was designed by God to be enjoyed - or else He could have fueled us through an umbilical cord beyond the womb. God gave us multiple senses with which to engage our meal experience - enjoy each one for what it is: a gift. If you find yourself rummaging through the cupboards or hurriedly reaching for the ice-cream in the freezer, pause. What is it your body really needs? What is it your heart really needs? If it's comfort, or encouragement, or distraction, there are better ways to nourish your soul, that won't deplete your body.

As Lysa Terkuerst so aptly put it, we were "made to crave". The question is not *whether* we have cravings, but rather what we will choose to satisfy our hunger with? If we can retrain our brains to see food as a gift, a divine opportunity to connect with our bodies and with each other, and to carefully nourish these incredible bodies of ours, we can start rewiring our relationship with food.

Play, explore, get creative. Find something that works for you and your family, and establish a rhythm. Make sure it's simple and sustainable, or you just won't do it. As Michael Pollan puts it, "Eat food. Not too much. Mostly plants." I have found that if I'm willing to put in the time to chop and roast a butternut squash, slice peppers and red onions, boil and peel eggs, cook quinoa, chop broccoli and cauliflower, and purchase ready-washed mixed greens once a week, I can make a beautiful salad for lunch in 5 minutes flat. Suddenly eating a crazy nutritious lunch isn't hard. The alternative is, well, laziness…and toast. I love bread, people. Or not eating at all, which makes me crabby, and more likely to overeat later. When I fuel my body well, giving it the sustenance it deserves, I'm a better mom and wife. My belly is happy, my skin clears up, I sleep better, and I have more energy. When I don't eat well, the opposite is true. I am not getting any younger, and nor are my kids, and I don't want to look back and wish I'd spent more time playing tag and riding bikes with them, instead of wanting to lay on the couch. The saying that 'nothing tastes as good as healthy feels' is absolutely true. And I've tasted White Cheddar Cheez-its. And molten chocolate lava cake. And the Banzai burger from Red Robin. *I get it*. But no 5-10 minute craving fix will ever trump how good it feels to get healthy and zip up my jeans without having to get horizontal. I can't tell you how many times I've been discouraged by fads and headlines. It can feel like we just can't win at this healthy eating game, and so we just throw in the towel and go out for nachos. So here's what's working for me: I'm listening to my body more than any expert, crunchy friend, or headline. I'm filling my bowls with all the goodness God made and trusting that if there's anything in there I shouldn't be eating, He'll let me know. End of story. Amen.

The bottom line is: when we eat crap, we feel like crap. When we feel like crap, we eat more crap - either because we see no point in eating well after already failing, or because the endorphins released while inhaling the fried sugar temporarily numbs the ache inside - and then we feel even more craptastic. We quickly acquire an appetite for the counterfeit fuel and literally have to retrain our taste buds to crave and enjoy real food again. But if we're not willing to wean ourselves off of the junk - and detox our brains and bellies - we're going to remain stuck in the cycle, and our bodies are going to pay a high price. I've heard it said that many people spend their health pursuing wealth, and then find themselves having to use their wealth to regain their health. Let's not lose it in the first place.

When you start eating food without labels,
you no longer need to count calories.

Amanda Kraft

While depression and anxiety are very real things (these topics are touched on in the soul section), much of the slumps and frumps we deal with - emotionally, mentally and physically - can be traced back to what we put in our bodies. How we fuel our temple matters, and we have got to take greater responsibility for how our food choices are impacting our lives. The ripple effect is far broader than we realize. What I put in my body influences the energy level with which I parent, the frequency with which I'm willing to get naked with my husband, and the depth of engagement I'm able to offer my friends in conversation.

We also have an incredible spiritual responsibility to steward our bodies well and to nourish them wisely. The fulfillment of your calling on this earth will either be assisted, or crippled, by what you put in your mouth. It sounds a little dramatic, but sister, it's the truth. My waking hours will always be more focused and fruitful when the vessel in which I live has been properly fueled. Thomas Edison wisely observed, "The doctor of the future will no longer treat the human frame with drugs, but rather will cure and prevent disease with nutrition."

Along with our nutritional hunger, there are other physical appetites that we need to acknowledge, manage and wisely nourish.

Sexual appetite | Much like real food, real intimacy takes work, preparation and forethought. There are healthy outlets, which cost more of us, and cheap counterfeits, which cost little up front, but a whole lot eventually. Much like the processed cookies and crackers we like to satisfy our food cravings with - because they're quick and easy, and because they light up all the right reward centers in our brain - there are unhealthy sexual experiences that, rather than being nutritious and deeply satisfying, are shallow and addictive in nature. One takes work and discipline up front, but has a massive pay-off in our marriages long-term, while the other fosters a more drive-thru, instant-gratification mentality and causes a ripple effect of long-term damage.

In the same way we can pause when tempted to stuff our bored, emotional faces with food, we should pause and ask ourselves some questions when we're drawn to turn to porn, masturbation, or illicit sexual encounters. Soul-digging questions like, "What is it I'm really looking for right now?"(i.e. distraction, numbing, attention, adventure), and "What am I feeling right now that has me turning to sexual things in an attempt to meet emotional needs?" (i.e. lonely, unwanted, abandoned, powerless, restless). I dedicated an entire chapter to this topic in my first book, XES, entitled: '50 Shades of Counterfeit', if this stirs something up for you and needs a little more exploring, consider picking up a copy.

Skin hunger | Multiple studies reveal that we have what scientists refer to as 'skin hunger', and it would seem in this technology-obsessed age, we're hungrier than ever for physical connection. We literally *need* to be touched, some more than others, and were created for affectionate connection with each other. This, while meeting a tangible sensory need, also touches our souls and spirits, and can foster a sense of belonging and safety in us. If you've ever needed a good hug, you know this well. I touched on this in the section on soul health.

Tender touch increases the level of oxytocin in our systems, the 'bonding' hormone that acts as a neurotransmitter in our brains that is kicked into high-drive during breastfeeding or sexual intimacy. As oxytocin levels go up, stress and anxiety go down.

In controversial experiments done in the 50s and 60s, American psychologist Harry Harlow discovered that infant rhesus monkeys, separated from their birth mothers, would overwhelmingly cling to a cloth surrogate, even though the alternative - a wire and wood surrogate - held a bottle of milk. It's as if their instinct to be *physically* nurtured was so strong that it overrode their instinct to be *nutritionally* nurtured. Numerous other studies have been done on this attachment theory, confirming that animals and humans alike need physical touch to thrive. From a 2017 article[20] in Psychology Today, "In 1994, the neurobiologist Mary Carlson, one of Harlow's former students, travelled to Romania with the psychiatrist Felton Earls to study the effects of severe deprivation on the decretei children who had been abandoned to understaffed orphanages. Typical findings included muteness, blank facial expressions, social withdrawal, and bizarre stereotypic movements, behaviours very similar to those of socially deprived macaques and chimpanzees. Recent studies have reinforced the developmental importance of childhood physical contact, which has been associated with, among others, better performance on cognitive and physical tests, a stronger immune system, and reduced aggression. All else being equal, premature infants that receive a course of massage therapy gain considerably more weight and spend less time in hospital."

While researching skin hunger I stumbled upon an article[21] in Time magazine about 'no touch' policies in school. Because of the focus on negative touch education, in an attempt to minimize violence and sexual touch, this article was highlighting the downside of no touching. The authors wrote, "When we ban touch altogether, there are no opportunities for healthy contact. That is a huge loss. The health benefits of touch are well-known, from stress relief to lowered blood pressure. But in school, the main benefit of touch is to build friendships and human connections, whether it is brushing one another's hair or roughhousing playfully. Like adults, children touch to say hello and goodbye, to express affection, to test their strength, and to give and receive comfort."

I see this in the kids in the juvenile detention facility where

I've preached for the past couple of years. I shake hands with the boys before they leave the gymnasium, while the girls stay to put away the chairs and take their jumpers off for gym class. I always linger to make contact, and the ones who are there for an extended period of time, or repeatedly, make a b-line for me. I squeeze them, stroke their hair, and cup their faces. I tell them how beautiful their eyes or freckles or smiles are, and they drink in every ounce of closeness, before reluctantly returning to the officer waiting for them. They are so hungry for connection, for affection and for non-sexual touch. We have seen the studies fleshed out in this age group repeatedly; when young girls don't receive the tender love and affection they were created for, they will meet these legitimate needs in illegitimate ways. Girls from fatherless or distant-father homes, where there has been little to no healthy male touch, are more likely to be promiscuous and are more vulnerable to the advances of predators[22] who see their emotional needs and can profit from them through commercial sexual exploitation. In fact a study[23] published in the New York Times found that girls whose fathers disappeared before the age of 6 were 5 times more likely to end up pregnant as a teenager.

If you needed any more convincing that our need for physical touch is vital to our overall well-being, consider the experience of convicted murderer, Peter Collins. Before dying of cancer after 32 years in a Canadian prison, he became an advocate for the health and human rights of prisoners, making a short film[24] called 'Fly in the Ointment' about his time spent in solitary confinement. As a single fly moves around inside a jar, Collins narrates: "I felt her soft finger tracing a line along my back as she whispered loving words to me...I dreamed of being held, touched and loved. Somehow, I felt her fingers on my leg. Shocked and excited, I opened my eyes only to realize it was a fly walking on me. I was greedy for human touch so I closed my eyes and

150

pretended it was her fingers. I tried to stay perfectly still because I didn't want to frighten the fly off and be left alone." So desperate for what had become his only source of living touch, Collins would bite his cheek and apply a mixture of his own blood and saliva to his skin to attract the flies.

This need for human connection transcends basic sexual contact, in fact most marriages are as starved for tender non-sexual touch as they are for genuine sexual intimacy. The satisfaction of this appetite, as voracious and vulnerable as it is, touches our spirits and is directly connected to our soul health.

As we nourish and tend to our bodies with more thought and care, flexing and strengthening each part, we get a beautiful picture of what it looks like to care for and appreciate the broader body. As Paul explains in 1 Corinthians 12, we are all part of the body of Christ, no portion being more or less important or valuable than the next. There are parts of our bodies we're not too fond of, areas we forget exist because they function so quietly behind the scenes, but each is an essential part of the whole - necessary and significant in their contribution. We are, after all, a motley crew, and clearly God's favorite sort to work with.

I don't know about you, but I'm running hard for the finish line. I'm giving it everything I've got. No sloppy living for me! I'm staying alert and in top condition. I'm not going to get caught napping, telling everyone else all about it and then missing out myself.

1 Corinthians 9:26-27 (MSG)

MOVE IT, MOVE IT

With the basic elements of nutrition out of the way (the 'input'), let's take a look at movement and the foundational pieces of physical fitness (or 'output').

Not too much is said in scripture about physical fitness, outside of metaphors for training and running the race, but this shouldn't be an excuse to neglect it. Netflix and air-conditioning also don't show up in scripture. So, there's *that*. The theme of wise stewardship and developing what we've been given is woven throughout God's word, and what other resource or gift is as essential to our earthly purpose than our bodies? Once your body is done, friend, it's game over. It's really hard to have an effective and energetic influence on your corner of the world when your body decides it's done.

When God was speaking to Moses in Deuteronomy 30 about life and death and good and evil, He said that his mission was not out there somewhere. "It's not on a high mountain—you don't have to get mountaineers to climb the peak and bring it down to your level and explain it before you can live it. And it's not across the ocean—you don't have to send sailors out to get it, bring it back, and then explain it before you can live it. No. The word is right here and now—as near as the tongue in your mouth, as near as the heart in your chest. Just do it!" (Deuteronomy 30:12-14). God was reminding Moses that his body was a very real center for spiritual discernment and engagement. The Kingdom of God is present and visceral, and if our bodies and spirits will remain attuned to each other, we will more naturally walk out our purpose here on earth. The overlaps in our physical, emotional and spiritual health are stunning and undeniable, aren't they?

I've heard church folk quote scriptures about long life, declaring their firm standing on the promises of God, while chasing their daily fast-food fix with a supersized diet Pepsi.

But here's the deal; no amount of scripture quoting or Bible study is going to negate our responsibility to care for our bodies. Yes, God has a good plan for our lives, but how many of us miss out on the fullness of our calling because we've not taken care of our health? Our ability to fulfill our purpose is directly linked to how healthy our bodies are. As Gary Thomas explains in his book, 'Every Body Matters', the temptation we face to eat more, sleep more and lie around more are great thieves of life's purpose, and this ingrained physical laziness inevitably leaks over into a spiritual laziness. He explains that "**protecting your health is the same thing as protecting the vehicle through which God wants to change the world**". We just can't pass the buck on this anymore.

I would hazard a guess that the reason we don't find mention of fitness or physical activity in scripture is due to the fact that you didn't have to tell ancient civilizations to move. Their very lives depended on it. Everything they did - from gathering food and water to connecting with their family and community - required some level of activity. There's no need for a "Thou shalt exercise" when your daily rhythm - and survival - involves movement. I love that the quintessential woman we love to hate in scripture (also known as the Proverbs 31 woman) is described not only as wise and savvy, but strong and capable. But we modern folk are creatures of habit, and comfort is our thing. We like life easy, comfortable and convenient.

So, with all the grace and love I can muster, let me emphatically say these 8 words to you: *get off your blessed assurance and do something*.

Much like our battle with food, it's less about knowing *what* to do and more about *doing* something with what we already know. We all know we shouldn't run on pizza and camp out on the couch. We all know the insane health benefits of regularly working out - from improved mood and better sleep to weight management and disease prevention

- and yet it's *still* the first thing to go when we get busy. That and self-care in general. Why is that? Have we believed the lie that taking time to exercise is self-indulgent or vain? Or that creating margin in our schedule for a workout is a luxury? Because let's just smash that right up front, okay? It's no longer about whether you can afford to make fitness a priority, we can no longer afford *not* to. There are few things exercise *doesn't* improve in our lives (and I'm not actually sure what those few things are).

Isaac Newton was a pretty smart guy. He observed that objects at rest tend to stay at rest, and objects in motion tend to stay in motion. In other words, couch potatoes on couches tend to stay couch potatoes. As someone whose work schedule is flexible, I see this play out every single day of my life. If I don't get up and get moving, I'm more likely to be as sedentary as humanly possible for the rest of the day. But when I get up, slip on my tennis shoes, and get moving first thing, I'm considerably more active throughout the day. I'm more aware of my body, and intentionally move it every chance I get. So, what does this look like for the average person who doesn't have an hour each day to dedicate to fitness? Three key things: keep it *simple*, make it *fun*, and be *consistent*.

Carve out 15 minutes a day to move. Heck, start with 5. Just do *something*. Anything that gets your body moving and your heart pumping. Find something that delights your soul and lifts your spirit - be it belly dancing, hiking, swimming laps, playing tag with your kids, walking with a neighbor, or doing a YouTube workout on your living room floor. The options are endless! For my birthday last year, I got a pair of rollerblades, and every chance we get, we slip out to the local park and do several laps. There's something magical about gliding along, feeling the wind in my hair, and pushing 40 without face-planting in skates. Two birthdays ago I acquired a long yoga silk that hangs from a sturdy hook in our family room ceiling. It makes for a fun and unique workout (also doubles as a giant cocoon for the kids). We also own a 6-pound hula-hoop that I acquired over a decade ago. While initially it beats your torso up a little (I've had the hip-bone bruises to prove it), the weight actually makes it easier to keep the hoop going. It's a great core toner, and it's really fun to stand on the back porch and hoop while the kids play. Most recently, I started doing cardio drumming with a group of women in our little community. It's a blast, and we're dripping with sweat by the end of our 45-minute jam. It adds a little bit of spice to my weekly workout routine.

Whatever it is, find your thing and do it. More moving, less sitting. I've spoken to women who say they don't have time to exercise, but then excitedly tell me about all the TV shows they're loving right now. Busted, girls. Maybe squats and push-ups need to be a prerequisite for another episode? There are ways to work fitness into even the busiest schedule, and your soul and sanity will thank you. Even if you set a timer each day and dedicate 10 minutes to movement, it'll be 10 more minutes than you would have participated in had you sat on the couch. Ask your friends to hold you accountable. Make it a family thing. In April I participated in a workout challenge with my 10-year-old daughter, and while I still hit the gym 3 times a week in the mornings, each night her and I would do our allotted sit-ups, crunches, push-ups and squats, and I loved it so much. It didn't take long to get our reps in and it was such a sweet time of bonding, complete with the occasional squat-induced giggle fart. I'm sure it helped that I promised her $10 if she stuck with it for the entire month. I was amazed by her strength and dedication, and giving each other a high-five after each workout was the cherry on top. My hubby plays basketball with "the guys" 3 times a week, and tries to get some weight training in on the other days. This, like eating well, is something we are modeling for our children. We're always modeling behavior, whether we like it or not - it's simply the *type* of behavior that we get to choose. If they don't see us prioritizing health and fitness, what makes us think they're going to prioritize their physical health? Go for a walk after dinner, ride bikes together, play basketball, run around the yard. You officially have no excuses.

But I'm too tired, you say. Guess what; exercising actually builds stamina and endurance. But I don't look good in spandex, you say. Nor do I. But guess what; you can work out in whatever you feel good in. I even see people pop in to the gym in jeans to walk on the treadmill in winter. Hey, whatever works. But I'm too old, you say. Guess what; exercise keeps you young and if you've still got breath in your lungs, you're the right age to start. Take Mavis Lindgren[25], for example. Or 'Amazing Mavis' as she's known in some circles. She ran the 50-yard dash at a church picnic when she was 10 years old, and then took a bit of a break from running. 60 years to be exact. The extent of her exercise as an adult, she confesses, was knitting. In her 50s she was diagnosed with pneumonia multiple times in just a few years, which slowed her down further. At age 62, after hearing a doctor speak on the benefits of walking and jogging, she committed to walking every day, gradually increasing her pace to a mild jog and an eventual slow run. Donning a homemade running dress and canvas shoes, cars would roll to a stop beside her, concerned that this frail old soul was running from home. But as it turns out, she was running from old age. Now on a roll, Mavis became unstoppable. By age 84 she had completed 64 marathons. Retiring from running at 90, Mavis logged her 75th - and final - 26.2 mile trek in 1997. Phil Knight, founder of Nike, had a custom pair of "Air Mavis" running shoes made especially for her final marathon, and she rocked them out in style at the Portland, Oregon event. Thanks to Amazing Mavis, we'll never again be able to legitimately say "I'm too old" to get moving, or get started on the road to health.

Whenever I'm tempted to sit rather than move, or stop

running before I reach my goal, I think of Amy - a friend who's lost both legs to diabetes, who would probably give anything to walk again. Or of Ruthie, my baby sister who fell down a mountainside in Botswana and broke her leg. After several surgeries to fix metal plates and screws that kept dislodging after the original 'fix' (acquiring quite the exquisite scar up the side of her lower leg), the girl never gave up. She never stopped pushing herself, despite the pain and frustration of multiple setbacks, and eventually rocked out a half-marathon on the Great Wall of China in 2016. When I don't feel like exercising, I think of the people who no longer have that choice. And do it because it would be wrong to squander the ability, strength and energy I do possess, just because I don't *feel* like it.

FITNESS 101

As you find a rhythm and activity you enjoy, try to implement 3 core fitness elements into your routine; cardiovascular training (get your heart pumping and building endurance), strength training (get your muscles contracting), and flexibility (stretching your muscles back out). Because there is so much good information out there on each of these categories, along with plenty of differing opinions on what is best or enough, I'm going to give you a brief snapshot of how you can implement each into your life in a simple and sustainable way - which is the only way we'll actually do something, and keep doing it.

Cardiovascular exercise (building cardiorespiratory endurance) is all about moving fast enough, or getting your large muscle groups working hard enough, that your heart rate is elevated and your heart and lungs are working hard to supply your muscles with nutrients and oxygen. You'll notice that if you're pretty sedentary, just getting up a flight or two of stairs leaves you a little out of breath, while your heart thumps out of your chest. This is good, albeit uncomfortable. The problem is, most of us don't like this feeling, so we return to the couch, and we never build our cardiovascular endurance. Cardio refers to the heart (the walls of your heart are made of cardiac muscle), and vascular speaks to the circulatory system of blood vessels. Needless to say, this muscle - and form of exercise - is not one you want to neglect, as it's central to your overall health and your ability to stay alive. Aerobic (meaning 'living, active and requiring the presence of oxygen') exercise builds your cardiovascular endurance, and includes activities like biking, jogging, swimming, and dancing. Really any activity that forces your heart and lungs to work hard, for an extended period of time, is classified as aerobic or 'cardio' exercise. With as busy and demanding as our lives can be, it is essential that you find exercise that you enjoy and can do regularly. Get creative, find something that feeds your soul as much as it feeds your body, and protect time in your schedule for it - or it just.won't.happen.

As I mentioned, there are plenty of differing opinions regarding how much cardio is necessary to make an impact on your health, and here's what I've discovered over the years; if the 'prescription' of exercise feels too daunting, or minimizes the effort I am able to put in now, I'm more likely to throw in the towel altogether. So, do what you can do. Start small and build. Set a timer and move for 15 minutes. Turn up some good music and have a dance party in the kitchen with your kids. Tune into a good podcast and go for a brisk walk. Grab some girlfriends and train for a local 5K. By getting fresh air and sunshine, or laughing and connecting with your people, you kill two or three birds with one stone. Getting your heart thumping and your blood pumping isn't just good for building endurance, building a higher energy level, and dramatically lowering your risk of death from cardiovascular disease, it also burns calories, which helps keep your weight in check. Plus, breaking a sweat is excellent for purging the system and skin of toxins (just be sure to stay hydrated).

Strength Training, also known as resistance or weight training, is another important component of physical health. As I've spoken to women over the years, I'm amazed by how many of them write strength training off as a 'man's thing'. "Oh, I don't want to get big manly muscles," I've heard more than once. To which I laugh out loud every time. I've been trying to work on muscle growth and definition for the past twenty years, I tell them, to no avail. This is thanks, in part, to the lack of testosterone in our bodies. Also, I like muscle definition a little less than I like sleep, so there's that. And consistency is key. I have actually developed some pretty great muscles over the years...I just have them tucked away beneath some pretty stubborn protective padding.

When I talk about strength training to women over the age of 40, I typically get a befuddled, glazed over look. It's as if they're imagining big sweaty gym rats in their minds; if they don't care for big bulging muscles, why would they want to flex their own? What most middle-aged women don't understand about resistance training is what an important role it plays in fighting osteoporosis. Yes, weight-bearing exercise (like walking) is vital, along with taking a quality calcium supplement, but lifting weights can also help protect bones and prevent osteoporosis-related fractures. Building core strength and maintaining strong muscles also helps with balance and coordination, key factors in preventing falls. There's no question that we feel weaker and more tired as we age. This makes us move less, and lift less, which in turn, makes us weaker and more tired. It is absolutely true that if we don't *use* our muscles, we will *lose* our muscles. We can fight the downward spiral of strength and agility by increasing our movement and adding some simple weight-training to our routines. For older women, that might simply be doing bicep curls with those large cans of beans. For busy moms who have littles around their ankles, it might mean keeping a resistance band in a kitchen drawer and doing some reps while you wait for the potatoes to boil. Or while squatting to smooch little cheeks. Whatever it looks like for you, find a way to incorporate some strength training into your week. There's plenty of information available online on muscle groups and the best way to develop them, so I won't get into the nitty gritty here, but if you have access to a gym, most facilities will have a resident trainer who can walk you through some basics and get you going on a routine. Just remember this: fatigue is good. If you don't exhaust a muscle, you won't strengthen it. You want to choose a weight that you can lift 10-12 times before 'failure' (you can't possibly do another rep), and then take a break and do another set or two. If you work one muscle group (for example your quadriceps - the muscle group on the front of the upper thigh that extends your leg at the knee), you should also work the opposing muscle group on the same day (in this example, it would be your hamstrings - the muscle group on the backside of your thigh, below your booty, that flexes or bends your leg at the knee). This keeps 'opposing' muscle groups equally strong and healthy, and reduces the chance of injury due to over - or under-development of one or the other (think tight abdominals and a weak lower back).

Flexibility (also referred to as stretching) is another essential element of exercise that seems to get overlooked and yet becomes even more important as we age. Think of bringing your heel back and up to your bottom; that's a *contraction* of the hamstrings. These muscles are connected at the base of the pelvis and again just below the knee, to the tops of bones in the lower leg. This act of contraction literally shortens the muscle fibers, which in turn moves a part of your body. It's brilliant, really. Divine design for sure. When you exercise, during cardio or weight training, your muscles do what they do best: they flex or contract, repeatedly. With repeated contraction, the muscle fibers can remain in a semi-shortened state, and need to be stretched out to return to their natural, elongated state. This helps lessen day-after pain and stiffness, and keeps yours muscles long and lean. Which is why you'll want to do the bulk of your stretching *after* you exercise, and be sure to stretch the specific muscle groups you've just worked. Holding, and gradually increasing, a stretch for 10-20 seconds is ideal, just be sure to never 'bounce' a stretch. Stretching before you exercise is fine too, just make sure you've warmed up your muscles and got your blood pumping a little first, as muscles are a little like sponges - you'd never wring out a dry sponge for fear of ruining it.

As we get older, we'll want to incorporate some balance work in there too, as the less steady on our feet we become (and the more fragile our bones become), the more valuable our balance becomes. Incorporating core training, like yoga or pilates, is an excellent way to get both flexibility and balance work into your day. Even just 5 minutes is better than nothing.

I'm quite certain I don't need to convince you of the benefits of exercise. Remember, **it's not about knowing more, it's about doing something with what you already know**. Which is to say: you probably need to move your body more.

As you start to incorporate more movement into your day, chances are, you'll be more inclined to make healthier food choices. This is where we can use the ripple effect of influence to our benefit. In the same way we're more inclined to skip the gym when we've just gorged on pizza (or maybe you're one of the crazy ones who just works harder to burn it off), you're more apt to move more when you eat well. This is the power of momentum at work, and it's a beautiful thing. As you fuel your body better, you have more energy to connect with friends and family. As you feel better in your skin (which, admittedly, is even more about how you see yourself that what physical shape you're in), you're more apt to want to be seen naked, which is great for your marriage. You're more apt to play with your kids and get connected in your community, which help fulfills your mission to engage and love on the people God has place in your life.

⚬⚬⚬

Friend, if ever you've doubted whether your body matters to God, remember that you are a tangible expression of a unique part of the body of Christ, and without a healthy physical vessel to carry His presence in, our impact and influence are diminished, or worse yet, cut short. You matter. Your *body* matters. Your *health* matters. A lack of training and equipping in faith circles has church leaders crashing and burning because they don't know how to steward their soul health, manage their sexual appetites, and fuel their bodies wisely. The Church, as a whole, has got to get a handle on this, and Christians should be leading the charge to live vibrant, healthy lives because of the treasure we carry inside us.

Please know that there is a distinct difference between condemnation and consequences. If you're a Jesus follower, there is *no* condemnation. Nope, nada, nothing. So, if this section has left you feeling a little heavy-hearted and ashamed, make sure you're listening to the right voice. The Holy Spirit is called 'the comforter' for a reason. Not 'the condemner'. Conviction is a gift, as it moves us and compels us to change, and is always laced with hope and grace.

Condemnation and shame, on the other hand, leave us feeling hopeless, unworthy and stuck. That's the voice of the liar, and you can tell him where to stick it.

But, with that being said, we often get to walk through the consequences of our actions. And occasionally, *inactions*. We cannot super-spiritualize our foolish choices. If we eat badly and never exercise, no amount of Bible study is going to change what is going to happen to our bodies. **Prayer was never supposed to cancel out our responsibility to practice self-discipline and self-control, and our bodies will reap what we sow into them**. You may have some negative consequences to navigate due to years of inactivity and foolish food choices. Be it high cholesterol, 40 pounds of extra weight, or a complete lack of cardiovascular strength. *But take heart*. God is a good Father, and while good parents don't remove the weight of consequences from our lives, they walk with us through them, reminding us that there's a better way and that it'll be worth it in the end.

SMALL STEPS

If you're anything like me, you've started and bailed from half a million different attempts to 'get healthy'. Exercise routines, diets, you name it...we've failed at it. And each time we start and stop, our faith in our ability to actually make lasting change decreases. But don't quit just yet. Remember, it's not how many times you've fallen that matters, it's how many times you've gotten back up again that makes all the difference. Get back up again, and start small. Take some simple, strategic steps toward health - small ones you'll be able to sustain - and keep going. When you get sidetracked, refocus and keep moving.

We have a bad habit of diminishing small change. We like big, flashy, night-and-day transformations, but that's the stuff of Hollywood studios, not real life. Slow and steady wins the race. Think of the humble little penny. It's so small and insignificant that I can almost guarantee you that you've walked over them on the sidewalk, or tossed them away while cleaning. They seem to have little value. But in this upside-down Kingdom in which we live, **small is valuable, insignificant is precious, and impossible is the stuff of miracles**. If I were to give you a single penny today, and then double it every day for the next 31 days, would it amount to much? You start with a single penny, then I double it and give you 2 pennies tomorrow, followed by 4 pennies the next day, and 8 pennies after that, constantly doubling the amount. How many pennies do you think you'd have at the end of 31 days if we just kept doubling the amount? A few bucks in pocket change? No siree! You'd be sitting with a whopping $21,474,836 dollars...and 48 cents. Incredible, isn't it? All by starting with a single penny and doubling it each day.

What small, simple change could you make this next week that would add up over time? What single negative habit could you nix this week, starting today - or tomorrow - if you've already scratched that itch? What single good habit could you implement this week, starting today? Remember to focus on the good first, and *most*. This applies to our spiritual lives as much as it does to our nutrition and exercise habits, to our minds and our thought life as much as it does to our sexuality. It is true for each and every appetite we have. When we're consumed by eliminating the negative stuff first, it becomes a losing battle because we've given what's unhealthy prime real estate in our heads and hearts. Where our attention goes, our energy flows. We get to choose which area this is. When we focus on filling up on the good stuff, the more satisfied we become with the real thing, and the less room there is for the garbage. As our appetites are well satiated, we crave the counterfeit less and less. We feel better, and we make healthier decisions.

People try repeatedly to change their habits, and continue to fail, because they give all their attention to eradicating negative trends before implementing the positive ones. They give up the goose, before they even have the chance to put good habits in place because they run out of steam fighting the bad. There is an incredible power in momentum, and we can certainly use it to our advantage here. Detoxing is good. Removing harmful habits is important, absolutely. But while there are things that need to get extracted from our diets and routines quickly, the power and longevity is in keeping our *focus* on life-giving things. We will thrive with healthy habits in place, but a life dictated to by rules and restrictions is no life at all. A rhythm of grace is what we were created for, after all.

Small investments in our health have a tremendous ripple effect as we age. But know this; we rarely reap in the same season that we sow. So, have a vision for the future. Keep showing up. Keep doing the work. Keep putting one brave foot in front of the other. Start small, focus on incorporating more goodness into your day, weed out the bad as you go, and just keep plugging away. Keep saying yes to nourishment and no to depletion. Be consistent, celebrate the small wins and bounce back quickly from the fails. Again and again. And again. When you feel like quitting, revisit your vision and remember why you started. Your temple is worth it.

The part can never be well unless the whole is well.

Plato

CHAPTER SEVEN

PNEUMA | SPIRIT

We need never shout across the spaces to an absent God. He is nearer than our own soul, closer than our most secret thoughts.

A. W. Tozer

It was a sunny Saturday morning in New York City when the pope landed. Waiting at the airport for him and his small team of noble guards, was a chauffeur from one of the finest limousine rental companies in New York. Once the pope's luggage is loaded into the limo, the chauffeur notices that the pope is still standing on the curb, staring starry-eyed at the beautiful vehicle. "Excuse me, your eminence," says the

167

chauffeur, "would you please take your seat so we can leave?"

"Well, to tell you the truth, young man," says the pope, "they never let me drive at the Vatican, and I would really like to drive today."

"I'm so sorry," protests the driver, "but I cannot let you do that! I would lose my job, and what if something should happen to you?" Smiling mischievously, the pope replies, "No fear, son, God is with us. And there might be something extra in it for you." Reluctantly, the chauffeur gets in the back with the guards as the pope climbs in behind the wheel.

The chauffeur quickly regrets his decision when, upon exiting the airport, the supreme pontiff floors it, accelerating to 105 mph in a matter of seconds. "Please slow down, your holiness!" pleads the distressed chauffeur, but the delighted Pope keeps the pedal to the metal. Until they hear sirens.

The pope pulls over and rolls down the window as the officer approaches, but the officer takes one look at him, returns to his patrol car, and gets on the radio. "I need to talk to the chief," he says to the front desk. The chief gets on the radio and the officer tells him that he's stopped a limousine going a hundred and five.

"So bust him," says the chief.

"I don't think we want to do that...he's really important," replies the officer.

"Who ya got there, Anderson, the mayor?" asks the chief.

"Bigger," he responds.

"The governor?"

"Bigger."

"The president?"

"Bigger."

"Well," sighs the chief finally, "who is it?".

"I think it's God!", comes the sheepish response.

"What on earth makes you think it's God?" growls the chief.

"Well, sir, he's got the pope for a limo driver!"

I laughed out loud the first time I heard this joke. And then it struck me; while it's easy to dismiss the chauffeur as a less important job, we forget that who - or what - is in the driver's seat of our lives is the single-most influential force in guiding - or in some cases dictating - the direction in which we move.

I trust that as you've found yourself in these pages, that you've gained a new respect for the brilliant mind you house in that head of yours, a greater awareness of that tender soul of yours that is unlike any other, and a fresh appreciation for the beautiful vessel that is your body. But we need to remember that all of these components within our tri-dimensional being function at their best when they're being inspired and led by the spiritual part.

SPIRITUAL HUNGER

In much the same way our bodies require food, sunlight and oxygen, and our souls crave significance, affection and belonging, our spirits literally need communion with God. This isn't optional. They *need* worship. They *need* prayer and intimacy. They *need* time in scripture.

God intentionally created us with an appetite for spiritual things. This hunger, and the many attempts to fill the void, are undeniable when you look at the myriad of supernatural and other-worldly media movements growing rapidly in culture today. The church can stand by and be judgmental, fearful or offended of this emergence, or we can recognize it for what it is; a world that is searching and starving for spiritual food to satisfy the ache.

Because our kind Creator always provides sustenance for an appetite He gives us, we are offered a stunning buffet of tastes and textures in order to satisfy this hunger. They show up in the form of spiritual rhythms and practices that draw us into His presence and closer to His heart.

As with the other two parts we've already looked at, there are plenty of pseudo satisfactions eager to meet our needs. Because they don't tend to show up sporting a red cape and a pitchfork, counterfeits in the spiritual realm can be a little trickier to identify. While there certainly are frauds that are *blatantly* corrupt, these easy-to-identify substitutes are far less of a problem for the average person just trying to grow in their faith. One of the most subtle and subversive ways we embrace a fake is when the enemy waltzes right in through the church doors, in the form of organized religion. The counterfeits we find ourselves drawn to most often are those that carry kernels of truth in them, ones that have become so broadly accepted - and even expected - within our religious subculture that it feels almost scandalous to question them. It can be scary to ask questions in an us-versus-them environment that favors certainty and uniformity. But what if those things we've been fed as gospel, are opinion? Like the little boy who pointed out from the sidewalk that the emperor was butt naked, I'm learning to lean toward uncomfortable honesty as I sense God allowing, and even encouraging, me to ask questions.

When it comes to spiritual counterfeits, rather than remaining hyper-vigilant to avoid dangerous imposters, I wonder if many of us who grew up in the church might need to funnel our energy toward disentangling our limping faith from the matrix of motions we've grown accustomed to going through. If your experience was anything like mine, then when you said yes to Jesus, you also somehow acquired an entire shipment of other requirements - lenses, beliefs systems, political views, rules and expectations - that seemed to come with Him, like an unexpected package deal. Buy Jesus, get all this other baggage free of charge. You don't question the package, you don't push too hard against it, and you certainly don't start unpacking it. It's easy to be a holy rule follower at first, because a glimpse of eternity has a way of turning your world upside down. Running on your love for Jesus and your desire to be a good Christian, you simply build your life around it, like one might attempt to accommodate an elephant in the middle of their living room. You read, you listen, you learn, you pray. You *behave*, because the world is watching and you're representing. But **the moment protecting our Christian *culture* becomes more important than Christ Himself, we've danced our way dangerously close to idolatry**.

We were created to belong, and because the prospect of being 'outed' is terrifying, we keep showing up, keep punching the clock, and keep going through the motions - even if we don't know who's actually driving the limo. Until we finally run out of gas. The gig is up, we're tired of pretending, and we don't even know what we believe anymore. We quietly lament that there has got to be more to life than this, and it's at this point that people feel they have only two choices; jump ship, or try harder. The try-harder crowd has gotten good at fixing spiritual crises by upping their involvement and engagement. If Jesus doesn't feel real anymore and my life isn't any better, it's because I'm not trying hard enough. We read more books, sign up for another discipleship program, jump a little higher during worship, volunteer at church more, and map out a fool-proof strategy to finally kick that bad habit to the curb. But we can only *try harder* for so long before we burn out completely and start to resent the gig all together. That's when option two begins to look more appealing; *bail*. Whether bailing takes the shape of apathy and indifference, or an active - and often angry - departure from the faith, these weary souls find themselves standing alongside the very people they'd previously judged for jumping ship. Those people who decided the entire kit-and-caboodle is a farce and if they can't have God apart from that ridiculous bonus package, they'll just pass. Thank

171

you very much.

But there is a third way. A way for those of us who are sick and tired of the religious charade, but who love Jesus too much to bail altogether. Those who have experienced the beauty and power of God's presence, but can no longer accept the implied non-negotiables of the bonus package. Those who long to engage the world through a Kingdom lens, but refuse to do so by aligning with a prescribed political party. Those who don't want what the world offers, but can no longer embrace the us-versus-them undercurrent of westernized Christian subculture. Those who cling to the ineffable goodness of God, but find Christian clichés and catchy verse applications lousy band-aids for the battle wounds of a life lived in this sin-stained world.

They know community is essential, so the lone-wolf approach is not an option. They know others wrestle with the same holy discontentment, but the new terrain still feels risky and lonely at times. They somehow know that this was supposed to be about friendship with God, about enjoying Him and learning to love what He loves, rather than guarding a set of doctrines. They have more questions than answers, but have decided to take Jesus up on his offer to learn the unforced rhythms of grace.

"Are you tired? Worn out? Burned out on religion? Come to me. Get away with me and you'll recover your life. I'll show you how to take a real rest. Walk with me and work with me — watch how I do it. Learn the unforced rhythms of grace. I won't lay anything heavy or ill-fitting on you. Keep company with me and you'll learn to live freely and lightly." (Matthew 11:28-30 MSG).

And like Truman Burbank - crashing his little fishing boat into the wall of the elaborate film set in a desperate search for truth and freedom - we set out on a journey to escape the show and find what's true. *Performance-free authentic spirituality; Jesus plus nothing.*

This is the road I'm on, and it is a pilgrimage I wholeheartedly believe Jesus is tenderly and patiently navigating with me.

DIVINE ROMANCE

This may come as a surprise to you, but Jesus wasn't a Christian. He didn't actually come to start a new religion; He came to set people free from the law of religion – law that they could never uphold – and invite them into relationship with Himself. A divine romance. True story. You see, Jesus wasn't - and isn't - obsessed with behavior modification and sin-management. That was the Pharisees, and sadly, many religious organizations today. Jesus didn't come to initiate a new set of beliefs and motivate good behavior, He literally put on skin and stepped down into our depravity to rescue the world He so loved. He is and always will be *liberating*, not suffocating. God knew we couldn't fall in love with words and belief systems - we needed flesh. So He "became flesh and blood, and moved into the neighborhood", as Eugene Peterson so beautifully put it in the Message (John 1:14). The intimacy of this imagery is stunning. It's all a part of their master plan; Jesus, Father God and Holy Spirit are fully engaged in the renewal and restoration of all things. Jesus brought with Him the *initiation* of this grand restoration, and until its *consummation* upon His return, we will live within the tension of the 'now' and the 'not yet'. What amazes me is that we get to play a role in the redemption. God invites us into His rescue mission. He hands us *His* power and authority, and while He slowly molds and mends us, we get to link arms with others and invite them into the renewal.

We get to remind people of their inherent goodness, not point out their dirt. We get to point them to the lover of their souls, not assume the position of official kingdom gatekeeper. We are called to be agents of change and brokers of hope; to glorify Him and enjoy Him forever. We get to take down our fences and build bigger tables, reminding people that there is room at the table for even the doubters and the questioners. When we really, truly stop seeing people as projects, we're free to love them right where they're at. And I'm realizing that this won't happen until we've learned to love ourselves right where we are.

> *Preach the Gospel at all times and*
> *when necessary use words.*
> *Francis of Assisi*

When did the Christian life get reduced to a 'repeat after me' prayer and a list of rules and to-do's to live by? On what planet is the dilution of this epic love story actually *good news* (the meaning of "gospel")? If we've become bored, predictable or too comfortable in our faith, might we be missing something? We've taken what only God can accomplish - draw and restore the hearts of mankind - and have manufactured it into a slick evangelism program, complete with fish bumper sticker and #blessed t-shirt. What a travesty.

When Jesus called His disciples, not even once did He say, "Okay boys, drop your nets and repeat after me." He didn't instruct them to believe in Him, He invited them to *follow Him*. He called them beyond intellectual or verbal response into *action*. **Following Jesus was never supposed to be about attending church once a week, dropping money in the dish, and not cussing**. The Christian life isn't just about coming to Christ, it's about becoming Christ-like. We can't afford to get stuck at *salvation*; it's about *transformation*. The gospel was never supposed to be about fire insurance. Say this prayer and you'll secure your free ticket to heaven, then just sit tight until your time comes and then you can escape your miserable existence to don wings and a harp. By relegating life and death, and heaven and hell, to the next life, we've anesthetized ourselves to the reality of embracing eternity in the now. Ecclesiastes 3:11 says God has put eternity in our hearts, and I believe it's so we can partner with God in bringing heaven to earth in our lifetime.

Becoming a Christian is not a one-time jig followed by a lifetime of mostly moral behavior. Simply *believing* in Jesus is one thing, it requires head knowledge and, well, little else. Walking with Jesus involves movement and action. It shifts from information and education to transformation. As long as we prioritize our heads over our hearts, we'll keep plucking fruit from the tree of good and evil, instead of feasting from the tree of life. The Christian life is meant to be an adventure; alive, effervescent and evolving as we grow with Him.

When I think about how clever the devil is and how destructive religion can be, the connection seems obvious. The enemy of our souls has used the church to lull people into complacency – *warm a pew, sing a song, donate to the church and you'll be okay.* **While offering some sort of cosmic security, religion always comes with performance-based rules and stipulations, and what promised to protect us ends up being the very thing that imprisons us.**

In *Waking The Dead*, John Eldredge explains, "Religion and its defenders have always been the most insidious enemy of the true faith precisely because they are not glaring opponents; they are impostors. A raving pagan is easier to dismiss than an elder in your church. Before Jesus came along, the Pharisees ran the show. Everybody took what they said as gospel — even though it didn't sound like good news at all. But we wrestle not against flesh and blood. The Pharisees and their brethren down through the ages have merely acted — unknowingly, for the most part — as puppets,

175

the mouthpiece of the Enemy."

Mahatma Gandhi is recorded as having said, "I like your Christ, I do not like your Christians. Your Christians are so unlike your Christ." Ouch. The sad truth is that this statement could be echoed by many today. In fact, when I survey the Western Evangelical church in general, I can't say I disagree with his observation. We have done a less than fabulous job of being his hands and feet to the world. We've not learned what it looks like to be *in* and not *of*. We've separated ourselves into our safe little Christian bubbles, created our own sources of media, apparel and entertainment to protect and insulate our families, and have pretty much removed any need to cross paths with scary outsiders at all. We know what we believe, whether we know *why* we believe it or not, and anything outside of the established parameters is off limits. We've taken what Jesus offered and fashioned it into something that's more *exclusive* than *inclusive*. We learn all the right verbiage, follow the rules and dress up on Sundays, keeping our pain and struggles under wraps for fear that they'll damage our witness or undermine our theology. But humans can only keep up appearances for so long, and the holy pedestals we've unwittingly placed ourselves on make for an awfully ungraceful fall. The crazy thing is, Jesus never called us to all of this. He rebuked the Pharisees for these exact same performances, and yet here we are again, setting ourselves up for disaster. It makes us wonder, whatever happened to *love*? Richard Rohr, a Franciscan priest whose teaching I stumbled upon through enneagram research, reminds us that, "If love is the soul of Christian existence, it must be at the heart of every other Christian virtue. Thus, for example, justice without love is legalism; faith without love is ideology; hope without love is self-centeredness; forgiveness without love is self-abasement; fortitude without love is recklessness; generosity without love is extravagance; care without love is mere duty; fidelity without love is servitude. Every virtue is an expression of love. No virtue is really a virtue unless it is permeated, or informed, by love."

Jesus said his disciples would be known for their love, but today it seems Christians are better known for hypocrisy, being judgmental, our myopic political stances, and the myriad of things we're against or disapprove of. It's no wonder the world doesn't want in. It should be of no surprise to us that this next generation is largely unchurched. People don't want what the church is peddling, and oddly enough, I don't think Jesus would have either. He came to set the captives free and bind up the broken-hearted, but that isn't what his followers are known for. The word "Christian" writes Eugene Peterson, "means different things to different people. To one person it means a stiff, upright, inflexible way of life, colorless and unbending. To another it means a risky, surprised-filled adventure, lived tiptoe at the edge of expectation... If we get our information from the biblical material, there is no doubt that the Christian life is a dancing, leaping, daring life."

At the end of the day, religion - defined by Miriam-Webster as an institutionalized system of attitudes, beliefs, and practices - will inevitably suck the life out of us, while an intimate relationship with our Creator will foster life. May we always choose life.

Stay clear of silly stories that get dressed up as religion.
Exercise daily in God — no spiritual flabbiness, please!
Workouts in the gymnasium are useful, but a disciplined life
in God is far more so, making you fit both today and forever.
You can count on this. Take it to heart. This is why
we've thrown ourselves into this venture so totally.
We're banking on the living God, Savior of all
men and women, especially believers.

1 Timothy 4:7-9

TRAILBLAZING

A born rule-follower, I took it seriously when well-meaning youth leaders and pastors cautioned us naive teens to be super careful what we believed or who we listened to. Don't watch Ninja Turtles, it's eastern mysticism. Don't go to dance parties, disco stands for 'dancing in satan's co.'. Harry Potter; black magic. Yoga; new age. Sex; dirty. Anything not overtly Christian; too risky. Oh, the infamous "satanic panic" of the 80's. We were pretty gifted at determining, with just a glance, whether people were "in" or "out". We needed to be hyper-vigilant and ever on guard or else we would risk being corrupted by the world, or misled by false doctrine. We embraced fear and called it wisdom. There was an overwhelming concern drummed into me that I might not make it out alive. I was convinced that my fickle little heart and wayward mind could not be trusted. I relied heavily on those in authority to define the boundary lines for me. Theologians were gospel, and anything that didn't fit into the little glass box of acceptable beliefs was dangerous. Without question. **I had unwittingly outsourced the leading of the Spirit to the powers that be.** Rather than being taught how to manage our freedom and spiritual authority, we simply handed them over to those who were older and wiser than us. Please don't hear what I'm *not* saying. I am not advocating for a lack of discernment or common sense in how we conduct our spiritual growth, nor am I minimizing the importance of having wise counsel in our lives, especially as young believers. However, I don't believe that slapping a religious ribbon on fear makes it any less destructive.

I've spent my whole life being tentative and on guard, in the name of protecting my faith, and it has cost me greatly. It grieves me to admit how much of the freedom and boldness Christ purchased for me has been sacrificed on the altar of fear. We deny our spirits the liberation they were created for in favor of safety and suffocation. We have forfeited intimacy in our need for understanding. But I suppose it was our obsession with knowledge that got us into this pickle in the first place. As has always been the case; sin management makes good converts, while the good news creates passionate disciples.

Mistaking this active life of faith for an institutionally backed and culturally bound belief system is similar to reducing the Mona Lisa to paint-by-numbers.

Dan Taylor

I'm sure these tendencies and teachings emerged as a form of damage control, and as a way to reign in reckless behavior and loose-cannon theology within the church. That being said, we should know by now that confining the Spirit of God to a box we can wrap our arms and heads around has never served us well. **The moment we've reduced God to something we can put in a box, we've taken from Him the very thing that makes Him God**. I've come to realize that many a Christian has been guilty of the sin of certainty. We prefer to call it conviction and confidence, but this posture is both myopic and dangerous. We so fear getting it wrong that we draw boundary lines in the sand that Jesus never drew. We don't explore, we've lost our wonder, and we no longer allow faith and risk and mystery to be a part of our spiritual experience. Facts don't change lives. People can read and believe the Bible, and not be changed. Desire and experience change us. This is the difference between believing and *beloving*. It's not that knowledge is *not* important, it's that it must remain subservient to trust, faith and love.

179

Never lose a holy curiosity.

Albert Einstein

As someone who grew up terrified of the demonic realm, I'll never forget the first time I heard Robbie Dawkins speak. Robbie, a Vineyard pastor who's known for his love of the prophetic and healing ministry, joined forces with the passionate Todd White and set up a table at an occultic festival in Salem, Massachusetts. Immersed in a sea of fortune tellers and crystal sellers, their sign simply read: "*Spiritual Readings*". They marched right into what most Christians would have deemed no-man's-land, and set up shop. Confident in the authority and call they had from God, they loved on people, shared God's heart for the wizards and witches that stopped by, and brought a bright light into a very dark place. They asked if they could pray for people, and several of them were physically healed. Many just quietly basked in the tangible presence of a Creator who loved them. I find Robbie's faith and courage so inspiring. It flies in the face of the fear-driven separation I was so familiar with growing up. Graham Cooke is another delightful Jesus-follower who makes a beeline for people caught up in the occult, when most of us would hide. His confidence in God's goodness gets me every time.

Then you have XXX Church, led by founding pastor Craig Gross, a movement of people who feel called to not only educate the church on the destructive effects of pornography, but love on those men and women actively working in the sex industry. Even if it means setting up a booth at the Sexpos in Las Vegas. Robbie, Graham and Craig all run in, when the church tends to run out. They move *toward* the pain, in pursuit of the hurting, the rejected, and the lost. Isn't this what Jesus repeatedly modeled for us?

Rather than cultivating a fear of being misled, maybe we should teach people to hear the voice of the Father, to seek wise counsel and scriptural alignment, and then to bravely step out in faith. Do we trust God will carry us, catch us, and correct us if need be - or don't we? What is the actual depth of a relationship with God, after all, if it requires an intermediary to exist or grow? Jesus was so eager for us to know Him intimately, face to face, that even if it killed Him, He'd make a way. We no longer need a go-between, Jesus tore that curtain in two when He took His last breath on the cross. Rather than hope someone will enter the Holy of Holies once a year on our behalf, we can have peace and strength knowing we house His very presence. We are, after all, a royal priesthood (1 Peter 2:9).

One is sometimes glad not to be a great theologian; one might easily mistake it for being a good Christian.

C. S. Lewis

I took a break from writing this morning and went for a walk on the trail through the campground woods behind our house. This is a trail I've walked or run many times over the past few years, especially when the shift in seasons highlights the extravagance of the trees. As I walked the trail on this muggy September morning, wrestling with the connections I see between religion, duty and control, I realized I'd made it halfway through the woods and hadn't looked up once. I was so preoccupied with dodging the puddles and avoiding the muddy tracks caused by the heavy rain over the past week that I hadn't taken in any of the beauty I'd set out in search for. I slowed down and scanned the horizon. It was extraordinary this morning. It took me recognizing my bent toward caution to even notice that the birds were singing, or the way the sun flickered through the yellowing leaves. It was lush and stunning. I sensed the Lord whisper, "That's what you've spent most of your life doing. That's where fear has been your guide, rather than faith. You've been so scared to veer off the marked course that your spiritual eyes have been locked on safety and security, instead of looking for me and what I might be doing off of the beaten path. You have been so scared to mess it up...but do you trust me? Walking with me will feel risky and messy at times, but I will lead you." Yes. *This*!

When did we stop believing that the very God who created us, loves us, and lives within us, could lead us and protect our hearts and minds on the journey? At what point did we think man could do a better job? That our fellow, imperfect humans - no matter how educated or well-behaved - were better suited for the job of outlining and mapping the appropriate spiritual course for us? If we believe God leads us, will we let Him lead? Is it possible that we'll hear incorrectly at times, and that we might take rocky detours on occasion? Heck yes! But do we trust that our kind Father, and the wise friends and mentors He's suggested we surround ourselves with, can get us back on track? Gosh, I hope so.

Friend, this is such good news! This whole Christianity thing is less about what we can do *for* Him, and more about what He's *already* done for us, and will continue to do *in* us and *through* us. 1 Corinthians 8:3 says that "The one who loves God is known by God." How did we miss this? It's revolutionary truth! It's not about us, after all. The pressure is off, beloved. The burden removed. We don't have to know more and more, and burn ourselves out in the endless pursuit of knowledge...we can be still and allow ourselves to be known by the one who loves us endlessly. In the words of Eugene Peterson, "There are no experts in the company of Jesus. We are all beginners, necessarily followers, because we don't know where we are going."

As it turns out, God will go to great lengths to expose our broken theology. As I've hesitantly sojourned off my map over the past several months, I've realized this: I would rather explore the messy, beautiful, uncharted terrain with Jesus, than tiptoe the boundary lines marked out by those who prefer predictability over presence. Jesus, after all, consistently messed with the religious people's paradigms. He made all of their red flags fly. He upset their rituals and challenged their rules. He had little tolerance for human hierarchies; He loved the unlovely, took time for the rejected and neglected, and pursued the outcast. He was a champion of the underdog, a pioneer in the women's equality movement, and a true civil rights activist. Through the eyes of the Pharisees, Jesus was a mystic and heretic. He was full of paradox. Even his death, which by all earthly standards appeared to be an epic ministry fail, meant life. The very symbol of our faith - a naked man, pierced and bleeding on a Roman cross - would seem absurd to any reasonable person.

This Jesus deemed everyone worthy of love and rescue. While the Pharisees elevated themselves and heroically talked the talk, Jesus beautifully fleshed out the contrast of Bill Bennot's convicting declaration that "how we walk with the broken speaks louder than how we sit with the great". It really doesn't matter how many times we've been through the Bible, if our lives confess that God's word never actually got through us?

Eugene Peterson explains in *The Way of Jesus* that, "To follow Jesus implies that we enter into a way of life that is given character and shape and direction by the one who calls us. To follow Jesus means picking up rhythms and ways of doing things that are often unsaid but always derivative from Jesus, formed by the influence of Jesus. To follow Jesus means that we can't separate what Jesus is saying from what

Jesus is doing and the way that He is doing it. To follow Jesus is as much, or maybe even more, about feet as it is about ears and eyes." Selah.

Friend, God is always at work, but if we expect Him to limit Himself to our methodology, formulas, and comfort zones, we will remain on the outside looking in. God gave us imaginations, why don't we engage them in our relationship with Him? G.K. Chesterton so eloquently observed that, "The function of imagination is not to make strange things settled, so much as to make settled things strange; not so much to make wonders facts as to make facts wonders." May we never lose our sense of wonder. As we say in the Vineyard Church, faith is spelled 'R-I-S-K'. If we aren't willing to open ourselves to mystery and risk, then we're going to miss his kingdom on earth altogether.

Risk, as we have seen, is indispensable to any significant life, nowhere more clearly than in the life of the spirit. The goal of faith is not to create a set of immutable, rationalized, precisely defined and defendable beliefs to preserve forever. It is to recover a relationship with God.

Dan Taylor

RELENTLESS PURSUIT

It is true; God is always up to something. And it is always good, always restorative and always fueled by love. Even when He's convicting us of sin, or putting his finger on an aspect of our lives or character that needs to change, there is extraordinary grace and endless hope in the process. In fact, that's one of the first ways my mom taught me to distinguish God's voice from the rest when I was a young teen. She handed me what has turned out to be an incredibly useful tool to sort through the noise and sift conviction from condemnation. She would ask, "How did the voice/message/impression make you feel?" If the overall feeling was life-giving and hope-laced, and very specific in its correction, then the Lord was tenderly pointing something out that He wanted to work with me on. Emphasis on *with*. But if the overall sense was a vague heaviness, hopelessness or shame, the message came from enemy lines and could be dismissed. Trampled, if need be. Because here's the thing; when God calls us on the carpet for something - because he's a good father - He actually is calling us into growth and greater levels of maturity and freedom. Specific correction enables us to make changes. It points out where we've gone off track or where our attitude or selfishness has gotten us in trouble, so we can make things right. That is what loving correction from a good parent looks like; it reminds us *who* we are and calls us upward. Condemnation and shame keep us stuck. It doesn't offer correction, it extends a death sentence to our souls. Not 'You *did* something wrong', but 'You *are* something wrong'. It doesn't seek to clarify and restore, it aims to confuse and destroy.

So, with that being said, what is God doing right now in your neck of the woods? In your heart and soul, and in your body? Where is He calling you out of your comfort zone and into growth? What is He putting his finger on in your routines and habits and attitudes? What is He up to in your family, and neighborhood, and community? Because He's always up to something, and if we'll look for His fingerprints and listen for His voice, we'll find Him. And then we get to join Him in the restoration effort.

If someone asks us to share a testimony of what God is doing in our lives, and all we've got is the same story from 18 years ago, then beloved, it's time for a fresh encounter with Jesus. It's time to go off script, and most likely off the beaten path, and figure out what He's up to. Sometimes we just have to get quiet enough to hear His voice. God rarely invades space that hasn't been made for Him, and like most other humans alive today, we're too busy for our own good. When last did you switch off all technology, escape from the chaos, and sit quietly in His presence? The incredible thing is, we don't have to go to church to find Him (He doesn't live there, I promise), nor do we have to do anything unusual to conjure Him up or convince Him to pop out. He's right here; before us, behind us, around us, within us. Deuteronomy 31:8 says that 'Do not be afraid or discouraged, for the Lord will personally go ahead of you. He will be with you; He will neither fail you nor abandon you." Here's a God who, as Cory Asbury writes in *Reckless Love*, will chase us down, fight until we're found, kick down walls, tear down lies and climb up mountains in pursuit of our hearts. It melts me every time I hear or sing it. Who wouldn't want to sit at the feet of such a kind King?

We rarely think of the air we breathe, yet it is in us and around
us all the time. In similar fashion, the presence of God
penetrates us, is all around us, is always embracing us.

Thomas Keating

David exclaims much the same sentiment in the Psalms, "I can never escape from your Spirit! I can never get away from your presence! If I go up to heaven, you are there; if I go down to the grave, you are there. If I ride the wings of the morning, if I dwell by the farthest oceans, even there your hand will guide me, and your strength will support me. I could ask the darkness to hide me and the light around me to become night - but even in darkness I cannot hide from you. To you the night shines as bright as day. Darkness and light are the same to you." (Psalm 139:7-12 NLT). What a beautiful picture of a lover who will follow us to the ends of the earth and refuses to let us go. For the first time in a long time, the gospel sounds like really good news!

SEASONS + ROOTS

Much like your fitness routine needs to evolve, because stagnancy isn't good for your interest level or your health, your spiritual life needs to grow and evolve. Change is inevitable in life, but growth and progress are optional. How are we doing with that? Are you growing? Do you know Jesus better than you did last year? Or five years ago? Are you more mature, more deeply rooted, more secure in your identity in Christ? Are you more free and whole than you were a year ago? If we're not actively growing, then we're missing out, because God is always at work behind the scenes in our lives, bringing greater levels of freedom, wholeness and revelation. Sure, it isn't always noticeable in the moment, and it certainly isn't always glamorous or exciting, but continued growth can be expected if we're walking in step with God. What worked for you when you first met Jesus may no longer draw your heart toward Him. What everyone recommends as the absolute best devotional, study guide or prayer method, may not move you. While we'll get more into unique practices that best suit your personality and season, know this; if you don't press in, experiment, and embrace change, you will feel stuck and be left wondering why your spiritual life feels lukewarm.

Seasons are to be as expected in our spiritual lives, as they are in our emotional and physical experience. We all have mountain top moments and dark valley days. We go through seasons where we feel really close to the Lord and can practically taste His sweetness. Typically for me, these seasons are conceived in the crucible of crises or tragedy, which have a way of driving me into the "cling" position. We hear His voice more clearly and feel His presence more tangibly, often because our very lives depend on it. Life has a way of bringing us to our knees, which - as it turns out - is a brilliant way to reconnect with our truest life Source.

We go through dry seasons, where spiritually we feel empty and numb. Oddly enough, these seasons often emerge on the heels of very successful times, when we've felt less of a need to cling to God. We're cruising along, running on the temporary high of happy times, and before we know it, we hit a bump in the road. Suddenly the applause is gone, our people are nowhere to be found, our money is thin, or our health fizzles. It's here that the gnawing void in our spirits becomes obvious. We feel guilty and ashamed, and increase our spiritual activity, as if earning back a position on God's nice list. Other times we just feel indifferent, disinterested and unmotivated. We question our faith and everything we've always been sure of. This can be a very scary and lonely place. But the good news is: God can handle our questions, our anger, and our doubt. None of this fazes Him. As Graham Cooke so eloquently says, God can't be disillusioned with us...because He has no illusions of us. Let me say it again, sweet friend; doubt is okay. It is unexpressed and unexplored doubt that can become toxic.

Parker Palmer, the founder of the Center for Courage and Renewal, described the divine tension we live in, in this way, "The deeper our faith, the more doubt we must endure; the deeper our hope, the more prone we are to despair; the deeper our love, the more pain its loss will bring: these are a few of the paradoxes we must hold as human beings. If we refuse to hold them in the hopes of living without doubt, despair, and pain, we also find ourselves living without faith, hope, and love."

You can tell a man is clever by his answers.
You can tell a man is wise by his questions.

Naguib Mahfouz

I heard about a conversation that went down at Home Depot a while back between a customer and a garden center assistant. The man had come in complaining that his tree roots kept messing up his grass. He had purchased the sapling from them a few years prior and was doing what they recommended. He gave it a good soak relatively consistently and was doing his best to keep the growing tree happy, but didn't understand why it wasn't taking root the way it was supposed to. "Stop watering it," the employee responded. This sounded absurd to the man until the Home Depot garden-guru explained that as long as he kept providing surface water, the roots were going to remain shallow. By not watering it, he would be forcing the tree to dive deeper for its nourishment, enabling it to sink its roots down where they needed to be for the tree to grow strong and healthy. Sounds a lot like life. We too need to train ourselves to go deep in search of the source.

I was processing through a season recently where my faith felt shallow and weak. I realized that while I was doing #allthethings - hustlin' and bustlin' doing great things for Jesus – I felt empty. This is not the first time I've been confronted by this glaring disparity. It is not at all uncommon that during these episodes, I have not been going to the Source for my sustenance. Rather than drinking from the well, my busyness – or laziness – has me drinking bottled spirituality. It's prepackaged and convenient. I don't have to sit around and wait on Him to fill me, I can take a gulp of Jesus juice and get on my way. Now listen; I am not saying that books and devotionals, audio sermons and podcasts are bad – because they're most definitely not, and they all offer value I'm so thankful for. What I am saying is that they need to be a supplement, not the main meal. No amount of information or activity can replace time in His presence. I have reached input overload many a time - listening to multiple sermons a day and devouring book after book - only to realize there's so much noise that I can't hear His voice above the clamor. Even Jesus took time away from ministry and miracles to rest and commune with His father. It was pure life to Him. As John paints the picture for us of the vine in John 15, we've been called to abide in Him, for strength, sustenance, and survival. If Jesus, being fully God and fully man, still needed connection, what makes us think we can go it alone? **Stillness, silence and solitude will always feel like death to those whose identity is tied to what they produce, but without pockets of time to spend here, we will not grow, nor will we last.** What's so stunning about exploring the original Greek roots of words we commonly use, but don't fully understand - like 'abide' - is that we see a fuller picture of God's heart. 'Abide' in Greek is 'meno', which not only means to 'remain', but also means to 'be held'. And there are those seasons that while I don't feel I have the energy to cling, I take peace in knowing that I can still be held.

What's interesting about the transition from being superficially rooted to going down deep and spreading wide, is that there has to be enough thirst created first. God will often use what feels like a hard, dry season to drive us deeper into His presence. While we tend to view these seasons with shame or disdain, He is not put off by our humanity. In fact, our weakness creates a vacuum that He is eager to fill. Our frailty is the perfect opportunity for Him to show off His strength and goodness. What seems like a tomb to us, is usually a womb for His presence.

We live in such an appearance-centric culture that it's easy to become obsessed with the external realm. We love to accomplish big things, bear fruit, and look good doing it.

We all want to produce good things on the limbs of our lives, whether motivated by pride or passion, but God is more concerned with the unseen, hidden places of our hearts. It's here, in the uncelebrated, unsexy pockets of our days that we develop our spiritual root systems and anchor ourselves in Him. **Might the Christian life be less about being in the world for God, and more about being in God, for the sake of the world?**

While I'm always more drawn to what's above ground, I know that healthy fruit is a byproduct of healthy roots. The first cannot exist without the latter. I have to pursue the eternal over the external. I have to unplug from surface busyness and dig into whatever connects my spirit best with Him in that particular season. Meister Eckhart, a German philosopher, theologian and mystic who lived in the thirteenth/fourteenth century, pointed out that deepening our spiritual life is more about *subtraction* than *addition*. Rarely do we need to add more to our lives to cultivate authentic spirituality. Rather it is the elimination of clutter, the paring back of busyness and noise that aids us. God isn't, after all, looking for us to do more things for Him - He's waiting for us to do the right things with Him. I used to read and study and devour any spiritual development material I could get my hands on, hoping that if I understood all of it, I could be a better Christian. But I've realized that by letting go and confessing my lack of understanding, it frees me to live in the mystery of a God bigger than my comprehension and kinder than my capacity to grasp. Paul prays this gorgeous prayer in Ephesians 3 about being rooted and established in the fullness of Christ's love, and asks in verse 16 that God would strengthen the Ephesians in their hidden, inner beings; making the distinction that this strength was not something they could acquire or comprehend, but one they would discover and *surrender* to.

We need to remember too that in the midst of winter, the

stark naked apple tree is still an apple tree. There are seasons in life that we won't bear fruit, times that we're just not "feeling it". Days that we are fighting just to survive the day. The season that surrounds the tree does not change the fact that what surges within that living thing, is the life of a tree. Apple tree DNA, regardless of external fruit. That outer appearance – that temporary lack of fruit – does not change what we are and whose we are. We have royalty in our veins, and us not acknowledging or seeing it doesn't make it any less true. There are seasons for rest, for dormancy, for growth, for pruning, and for fruit bearing…and He is in it all.

So we're not giving up. How could we! Even though on the outside it often looks like things are falling apart on us, on the inside, where God is making new life, not a day goes by without his unfolding grace. These hard times are small potatoes compared to the coming good times, the lavish celebration prepared for us. There's far more here than meets the eye. The things we see now are here today, gone tomorrow. But the things we can't see now will last forever.

2 Corinthians 4:16-18 (MSG)

Whatever season you're in, look for his fingerprints. Keep sowing seeds and nurturing what's already been planted. We rarely, if ever, reap a harvest in the same season we sow. You may not see His hand right now, but you can trust His heart. He is ever with you. And He's rooting for you, whether you're doing all the right things or not. Seasons in our spiritual journeys are not only normal, they're part of a healthy human experience. They're also temporary. So, if you're walking through hell, keep on walking. God wastes nothing - He will use every little thing for our good and His glory. Besides, what good gardener ever condemns the compost for being full of rubbish?

It is so important to understand that having a vibrant faith is not about being perfect, pretentious or performance-oriented. This is a lie that breeds cookie-cutter Christians with high walls and shallow faith. As long as we believe that our humanness makes us a liability to God, we're going to destroy ourselves trying to live up to some standard He never set for us. Because here's the bottom line: we don't have to strive for our place or hustle for our worth. *It's a done deal.* Let's all breathe deeply, shall we; the pressure is off. If we're bravely living our faith in action and taking risks, failure is inevitable. We are going to fall flat on our faces on occasion - in fact, if you don't fall flat on your face here and there, you're playing it too safe. The only way to guarantee a lack of failure is to avoid risk, bunker down, and do absolutely nothing with your time, talent and treasure. And the last time I checked, that wasn't the grand adventure we were invited into. Which, if we're honest, is a failure to fulfill our God-ordained purpose here on earth. It's not about how many times we stumble and fall. Our strength and resilience are displayed in how quickly we get back up again. It's about what we do with our failure. Look at Peter and Judas. They *both* denied Christ, but one committed suicide and the other became the head of the church.

God is so kind and patient with us as we learn and grow and stretch our faith legs. We couldn't fathom a father admonishing his toddler for falling when she's learning to walk. We are learning to walk by faith and run in step with the Father. He is so quick to scoop us up when we fall, and to draw us close to His side. We have to choose not to listen to the voice of shame after a stumble, but to tune our ear toward His tender encouragement. This boils down to how we view God - it influences every single aspect of our lives. If He's a grumpy dictator and harsh taskmaster, failing will cause us to run and hide. If He's a good Father and kind Savior, we'll run into His arms. This distinction is everything because it's our intimacy with God that most intimidates our enemy. It makes him crazy when we bounce back quickly from a fall. It's only when we're down that he can kick our souls and muddy our identity.

If we will more fully embrace our humanness as having been made in the image of God, and having been declared 'good', and if we'll stop elevating ourselves and pretending to have all our perfect poop in a group, the world might start paying more attention to the God we allow to shine through. People outside of the church look at our striving and pretension and are so put off by it. We're exhausted, and they can tell. **We keep making God in our image, and it's not working for anyone**. The world is craving a raw, honest encounter with a powerful, loving God – and they're watching us to know if it's possible. Let's start taking down the walls we've built to keep the illusion in place, and start building bridges of grace in their place.

MOLD BREAKER

Until recently, I hadn't dared to challenge many of our widely accepted and deeply entrenched ideas about what it means to know God, and about what it actually takes to foster true spirituality. Through this glorious unraveling I've discovered incredible freedom in allowing my spiritual feathers to get ruffled by unlikely sources (like Franciscan monks and Christian mystics), forcing me to dig more deeply into what it is that I actually believe, rather than simply regurgitating what I've mindlessly consumed over the years.

Several years ago I picked up Larry Osborn's book, *Spirituality for the Rest of Us,* and the questions posed on the back immediately grabbed me; "If you don't fit the mold, if you're tired of adjusting to other people's definitions of spirituality, if traditional spiritual disciplines just aren't working for you, if all the standard answers aren't enough, but your deepest desire is to know God more..." Wait, what? I wasn't the only person wrestling with holy discontentment, and this guy - a reputable pastor and sought-after spiritual director - was giving me permission to not be okay with the status quo? I was gobsmacked. I promptly stole the book from my parents' house and devoured it (it's still in my bookshelf in case you're wondering, Mom).

It was a breath of fresh air, and exactly what my spirit needed in that season. Larry explains in the book how much, if not most, teaching on traditional spirituality is a lot like the teaching on marriage. We may think we have a great marriage, until we start reading books and going to conferences designed to teach us how to get it right. He goes on to describe how the books and conferences enlightened him and his wife to the fact that they were doing it all wrong. They weren't eating enough meals together, the TV was on too much, their date nights were far too rare, and their prayer time as a couple was sorely lacking. The message was clear: *The fact that they had a strong marriage didn't matter; how they got there was what mattered most.* And they'd apparently gotten there the wrong way. The tools for building a great marriage had somehow become the measure of a great marriage. And on that scale, they didn't measure up. Few of us do.

When it comes to developing a great relationship with God, the same thing often happens. The tools and spiritual disciplines that can help us get there frequently become an end in themselves. Books and conferences on the inner life end up presenting a cookie-cutter approach to spirituality that focuses more on the steps we take than on the actual quality of our walk with God, he explains. The truth is, God wants a great relationship with all of us, but it can't be found in a one-size-fits-all approach. It's the end result that matters, not the path we take to get there. If something produces a great walk with God for you, it's a great path to take. If not, it's probably a waste of time, even if lots of other folks highly recommend it. In fact, what works for one can be worthless - even harmful - for another. The way we're wired really does matters. Whenever we project what works for us onto everyone else, we create frustration and legalism. When we let others project their stuff onto us, we too often end up with unfounded guilt or a nervous twitch. Neither of which is very helpful when it comes to producing a great relationship with God.

For example, my father has four daughters. Let me rephrase that. He has four incredibly unique, undeniably different daughters. In his (and my mom's) desire to celebrate and cultivate our unique talents, gifts, and "flavor", if you will, they relate to us in different ways. Growing up, a long conversation about ancient civilizations would thrill and fill his intellectually vibrant relationship with my older sister, while talk of the soccer game on Saturday would more tangibly fill my active baby sister's tank. My younger sister and him will talk about microbreweries and culture, while he and I tend to chat about relationship dynamics and theology. We are all so different. And yet we share the very same father. Out of his love for us, and his desire to connect with us where we're at, he relates to us in ways that are as unique as our personalities and passions. And he fully respects – and expects – to be related to in very different ways by each of his daughters. We are different, so it makes perfect sense that our relationships with him would look different. He's cool like that.

How much more then would our heavenly Father communicate uniquely with the vastness of His creation. After all, if scripture is inspired by God and He intentionally chose to speak through different voices and unique personalities, why do we think He'd stop now? He woos us, challenges us, teaches us and loves us in the exact way He created us to receive these things. Yup, you guessed it...He's cool like that.

In the same way, out of our inimitable make-up, we relate to Him differently. Why is it then that so many of us were taught, whether implied or articulated, that the way someone else has connected with God is the method in which we should relate to Him? And likewise, why do we project what has worked for us onto someone else? I'm sure it's not intended to wound or discourage, but it often does. I still catch myself gushing about a new book or spiritual practice I've discovered to friends in a way that carries the expectation that they match my enthusiasm and implement said items into their life in order to thrive. Of course, sharing our passion is great - and healthy - but we need to make sure our language doesn't imply that their results or experience mirror our own. Once we acknowledge the boxes we've put ourselves and others into – and those we have had the naivete to put God into – we can shatter them. And this is a beautiful thing!

When I first met my husband, I was delighted by how much we had in common. Now, fifteen years later, I'm equally as amazed by how very different we are. While neither of us are fighters, per se, we do partake in what we affectionately call 'intense fellowship'. Oddly enough, what we tend to bang heads about most these days is politics and theology. We share the same core values, and agree on all the big things, but our approaches to certain subjects, and the lenses through which we view life, are so different. I see a huge butt, and he sees a huge trunk, and while we're looking at the same elephant from different angles, we can't understand why the other can't see what we see. The more we can come to value and celebrate each other's strengths and differences, instead of bemoaning them, the better life will be for both of us. "The beginning of love is to let those we love be perfectly themselves, and not to twist them to fit our own image," said Thomas Merton. "Otherwise we love only the reflection of ourselves we find in them."

The gift of knowing ourselves, and realizing that God intentionally wove us together this way, frees us up to grow spiritually in the way He created us to. Our experience of God is shaped by our personality and history; His presence doesn't change, but the vessel that carries it does. Think about it; men and women experience God differently. Introverts and extroverts relate to God differently. Left-brain intellectuals' expression of God will look different than the right-brain creatives'. Home bodies will sense God's presence in different ways and places than the outdoor enthusiast. The young man with Down Syndrome will know God differently than the seminary professor. **Everything from our cultural background and personal history to our talents and temperaments will add color and variety to our spiritual experience**. This stunningly broad spectrum captures but a glimpse of God's expansiveness. It would behoove us to quit limiting our limitless God. As we say regularly in our house, "It isn't wrong, it's just different."

Osborn writes, "Finally, I wondered why I kept running across so many godly people who felt so ungodly. I now realize it had more to do with our faulty definitions of spirituality than anything else. In most cases, these people felt like spiritual failures not because they were far from God, but because they'd been unable to live up to generally accepted measures of spirituality. They had stalled out in Leviticus each time they tried to read through the Bible. They were kinetic types who found extended prayer not only unfulfilling, but nearly torturous. Or extroverts who'd bought one of those fancy leather journals, but never got around to putting anything in it. Mostly, they were regular folks who for whatever reason didn't fit the mold too well. They tried it, but sadly found it didn't work for them." How very true this is. I've met people who quoted scripture, said all the right things and followed all the rules, and who felt like death to be around. And then there are others who are completely rough around

198

the edges, are quirky and edgy and unconventional, and simply glowed with love for Jesus. It's as though we become like the god we've created in our own image, and wonder why people don't want what we have. As Oswald Chambers so wisely urges, "Let God be as original with other people as He is with you."

❧

Whatever happened to freedom in the church? Is it, like love and grace, something we fear could easily be abused and so requires rationing and management? In John 10:10 we read that while the enemy seeks to steal, kill and destroy, Jesus came to give life - and life *abundantly*. That word 'abundantly' in Greek ("perissos") doesn't just imply fruitful, it actually means life in excess, beyond measure, even superfluous. He offers us so much life that it literally overflows - intentionally, I might add. Jesus didn't die for mediocre, boring, restrained or stifled. He died for abundant, and that involves living free from the slavery He died to set us free from (Galatians 5:1). As followers of Jesus we're aware of the spiritual battle for our freedom, but we also tend to give satan too much credit. We don't realize that we *give* it away freely. We allow prominent people in our lives to rob us of joy and peace and delight in Christ, often unintentionally, and it makes us slaves to things that we're not supposed to be enslaved to. Christ set us free from this stuff. The only thing we're in bondage to is love (Colossians 3:12-14, Matthew 22:37-40, John 13:34).

I can preach a sermon on a Sunday morning and hear an entire smorgasbord of responses from people. "Oh, you got *that* out of the message," I've thought at times, as someone confides through tears how something I don't even remember saying touched a tender spot in their heart. That's not broken telephone...that's *God*! He's an expert at taking a simple message, breaking it like bread, and nourishing very specific needs in different people's lives.

God made us stunningly unique. Let's not disregard or disqualify that by trying to be something we're not. We try and conform to what the world says we should be, what our family says we should look like, what the church says we should sound like. Some people raise their hands, some people don't. Some people journal, some people don't. Some people find Jesus in a pew, some people don't. We repeatedly enforce rules that are not in the Bible. Who am I to quantify your faith because you experience God differently than me? And who am I to judge you because you sin differently than I do? Grace and freedom can be scary, I get it, but we can trust the One who has called us to Himself. He adores the messy mosaic of our affection and He is working in each one of us to make us more like His son. We have been set free. Free from all of our sin, all of our junk, all of our shame. The blood is enough. Absolutely enough. If we abuse it, we don't really know it.

⟡

While it's a considerable chunk of scripture, don't miss the brilliant nuggets in The Message version of Colossians 2:6-19. It's powerful and very apropos for today.

"My counsel for you is simple and straightforward: Just go ahead with what you've been given. You received Christ Jesus, the Master; now live him. You're deeply rooted in him. You're well constructed upon him. You know your way around the faith. Now do what you've been taught. School's out; quit studying the subject and start living it! And let your living spill over into thanksgiving.

"Watch out for people who try to dazzle you with big words and intellectual double-talk. They want to drag you off into endless arguments that never amount to anything. They spread their ideas through the empty traditions of human beings and the empty superstitions of spirit beings. But that's not the way of Christ. Everything of God gets expressed in him, so you can see and hear him clearly. You don't need a telescope, a microscope, or a horoscope to realize the fullness of Christ, and the emptiness of the universe without him. When you come to him, that fullness comes together for you, too. His power extends over everything.

"Entering into this fullness is not something you figure out or achieve. It's not a matter of being circumcised or keeping a long list of laws. No, you're already in — insiders — not through some secretive initiation rite but rather through what Christ has already gone through for you, destroying the power of sin. If it's an initiation ritual you're after, you've already been through it by submitting to baptism. Going under the water was a burial of your old life; coming up out of it was a resurrection, God raising you from the dead as He did Christ. When you were stuck in your old sin-dead life, you were incapable of responding to God. God brought you alive — right along with Christ! Think of it! All sins forgiven, the slate wiped clean, that old arrest warrant canceled and nailed to Christ's cross. He stripped all the spiritual tyrants in the universe of their sham authority at the Cross and marched them naked through the streets.

"So don't put up with anyone pressuring you in details of diet, worship services, or holy days. All those things are mere shadows cast before what was to come; the substance is Christ.

"Don't tolerate people who try to run your life, ordering you to bow and scrape, insisting that you join their obsession with angels and that you seek out visions. They're a lot of hot air, that's all they are. They're completely out of touch with the source of life, Christ, who puts us together in one piece, whose very breath and blood flow through us. He is the Head and we are the body. We can grow up healthy in God only as he nourishes us."

⚬⚬⚬

So, sweet one, do you know how the Lord speaks to your heart? Religious routines are good, please hear me. But they are not enough. You could go through holy motions for years, memorize scripture until you're blue in the face, and still not know the father's heart or presence, and such, still not be captivated by His love for you. Jesus admonished the Pharisees for studying scripture diligently, odd as that may sound, because while the words they read pointed to Him, they missed his very presence in their midst (John 5:39).

Let me ask you this: what fosters your affection for Him? Because you should go and do more of that. **What stirs your spirit and lights you up is a good indicator that you're discovering your sweet spot with Jesus.** You've been so uniquely created; don't underestimate the creative way in which God will commune with you. I am moved deeply by music, dance and story. And there are few places I feel as alive as I do when I'm in, on or near water. My spirit explodes when I'm in a kayak on a river, or near the ocean. It's almost overwhelming. I'm a 'little things' person - I notice details others miss. Like dew drops on blades of grass, sunrays through morning mist, and heart shaped leaves and rocks. I can feel the Father's smile over me like warm sun on my face. It stops me in my tracks. Other people may not understand or appreciate these things, but I can't deny it. It's as if heaven touches earth in those moments and every unimportant thing fades. So, if that's where God speaks to me, and that's where I feel His Spirit closely, why on earth would I neglect these practices or discard them as trivial? If you've given up on pursuing friendship with God because someone told you that you had to pray for an hour and then journal for two - or that worship had to look and sound a

202

certain way - I am so sorry. Don't throw in the towel. You are not defective, nor are you not spiritual enough. God is communicating with us all the time, you just need to figure out which frequency to tune into. You are uniquely made, on purpose, with a purpose. Why continue trying to force a square peg into a round hole? It's time to experiment and figure out what ignites your heart, fires up your soul, even what engages your body...and then lean into it, and into Him. As triune beings, we get to commune with God in and through all of it. This isn't a job only for the spiritual portion of us. He wants it all.

This journey is fluid and moving, and it requires bravery and it takes risk. Our spiritual lives will only lack excitement if we've hit cruise control, taken up residence on a park bench, or not yet found the rhythm of grace we're best suited to move in. I've heard it said that if we're bored in our spiritual lives it's either because we've accomplished our mission or lost our vision. And our mission won't be accomplished until we're dead, so there you have it. Notice that our walk with God is called just that, a *walk*. Not a run. Not a sprint. Not a nap. It's supposed to be an adventure!

There will be bumps, unexpected turns and uphill climbs on this path, but there will also be breathtaking vistas that will remind us why we walked this way in the first place. It is a hard and holy road, but it will all be worth it. He walks with us, no matter the terrain. Keep on pressing on and pressing in.

RESET THE DEFAULT

Several weeks ago, while preparing to send some large design files to a client from my studio computer, a little window popped up and informed me that the software I use to compress files was expiring soon. I scanned the fine print and scowled for a second - I'd been zipping files this way for over a decade, with no recollection of subscription or payment - and then promptly closed the window. Two weeks later the message re-emerged to warn me again of impending expiration. Irked by this sudden interference in my work rhythm, I ignored it and moved on. Much to my surprise, said pop up window wasn't lying, and the next day I was unable to compress any files. Naturally, I did what any savvy person does in order to fix anything from a fever to a broken faucet - I Googled it. "Why do I suddenly have to pay for WinZip when I've always compressed my files for free?" And then, realizing I wasn't even familiar with this software, I Googled, "What is WinZip?" I may have added a 'goshdarnit' for emphasis. As it turns out somehow, at some point, I scored this free download I never wanted. It installed its obnoxious code on my computer, establishing itself as the default compression method on my system, and then starting counting down to the day I'd have to pay to continue using it. After further digging, I figured out that by simply uninstalling it, my desktop would return to its original setting and restore the use of my regular free compression method. After my initial gratitude for the easy fix wore off, I felt violated. How had this file so easily made itself at home on my computer? Without me even realizing it, WinZip had rewritten its role as my default software, and had almost successfully duped me into paying for it.

How often we fall for this routine in life. From lies we've come to believe in our hearts and minds as truth, to hoops we've grown accustomed to jumping through for religious brownie points. We need to examine default settings that have been operating quietly behind the scenes and make sure that what's wired into us is the Creator's original code. We will most likely have to rewrite some script and uninstall some defective software because, if we blindly continue operating with glitches in our system, it will cost us our freedom.

What spiritual counterfeits have you allowed to creep in and hold you hostage? Maybe you know exactly what it is, or maybe you need to ask God to bring it to the surface. Whatever it is, I believe God is inviting us to lay down anything that doesn't align with His heart for us, to uproot the lies and lighten the burden so we can walk freely with our Maker.

While mindless activity and rote religious rituals do little for genuine spiritual health, there is something to be said about having regular practices and rhythms in place. Key ingredients, if you will, that together - in whatever order or proportion we find works well - cultivates spiritual growth in us. The terms 'quiet time' and 'devotions' are commonly tossed around in church circles, but often infer only a sliver of what we've been invited into.

We don't control how or when God's spirit moves us (notice that I didn't say "shows up", because as we've already acknowledged, He's always with us), nor do we manage or portion-control His presence. That being said, I do believe we're responsible for 'positioning' ourselves in such a way that we capture and experience everything He has for us. These practices are a readying of ourselves; we create space for God to do what He does best.

Think of gardening or sailing. I don't make the plant grow, but I can provide all the elements it needs in order to thrive. And I can't make the wind blow, but I can get out on the water and position my sail to catch the wind. And yes, it does involve discipline and patience. It's not about manipulating an outcome. It's about creating space and preparing ourselves for progress and growth. Our job is obedience, He gets to manage the outcome. This is more about a *posture* of the heart and mind than a *routine*. While I grew up protestant, and have always prided myself in the emphasis on relationship over ritual in the non-denominational sphere, I've been discovering - and treasuring - some of the rich practices and liturgical traditions of our church fathers and mothers. To say this revelation caught me off guard would be the understatement of the year. While I haven't been overly critical of other denominations, I certainly have dismissed much of outside practices as irrelevant or even silly. As a friend recently put it, we (Christians) are the product of a divorce in the church, and it's unfortunate that because of the ugly split (between Catholics and Protestants), we've been taught to throw the baby out with the bathwater. We have been so committed to *our* way of doing things that we're just not open to where God might be moving outside of our little comfort zone. To the tune of some 40,000 different denominations in the US alone. This simply reinforces how dualistic the church has become. We all think we're right and everyone else is wrong. We have the corner on God, and ya'll are phonies and fakes.

As I'm learning how to abandon my knee-jerk 'either-or' filter in favor of a more Christlike 'both-and' embrace, I've fallen in love with some of the teachings of St. Francis of Assisi, along with some ancient practices of Trappist and Jesuit monks. I've been finding gold from the Christian mystics. Even admitting this in writing feels odd. If not risky. And before you close this book and call me a "heretic", know that just 12 months ago, I would have laughed in your face at the thought of entertaining anything remotely Catholic in origin. But God continues to surprise me through unlikely sources, and the growth in my life has been undeniable. This glorious unraveling has been a watershed moment in my life, and I cannot go back. I will no longer throw the baby out with the bathwater. As my sweet momma has taught me, we need to eat the meat (and there is plenty), and spit out the bones. We're too used to choking on bones and refusing the meat.

It's easy to get caught up in the belief systems of our faith, and then get stuck. But as Aaron Niequest says in his invitational book, *The Eternal Current*, change will only happen when we shift from a beliefs-based faith to a practice-based faith. He reminds us that Sunday is not the main event, and that the invitation is *participation*. While weekly church engagement is good, it is not enough. Quoting a friend, Niequest notes that, "A person can't drink jet fuel all week and try to light a candle on Sunday nights. That's not how a human soul works." It's not about baptizing the American dream, he continues, in an attempt to spiritualize what we're already doing. It's about getting swept up into God's divine rescue plan for humanity. This great and mighty river that flows throughout history toward the healing and restoration of all things. A practice-based faith isn't a works-based faith. We don't practice for approval and love, we practice *from* a place of approval and love. Jesus didn't say, "Here is the truth, believe it," He said, "I am the truth, follow me." We're called to be practitioners, not merely orators or educators. It is essential that we stop standing on the shore, arguing doctrine and debating best practices, and actually get *into* the water. It's easy to set up shop on the shore and run at the mouth. It takes courage and trust to get in the water and let go of the shore. If we're being completely honest, can we say we're actively following Jesus if we're standing ankle deep? Authentic, raw spirituality is about following Jesus into the water and learning to swim with Him in the beautiful depths of the eternal current.

⇜⇝

SPIRITUAL PRACTICES

While this is by no means an exhaustive list, here are several postures and spiritual practices that help align our hearts with His and fortify our faith in the process.

While some of these practices are new to me (within the past year), I'm enjoying expanding my horizons and developing new spiritual muscles. Experiment and figure out what works best for you, your unique personality, and the season of life you're in. He is in it all.

> *Learning to desire God's will is not something we can accomplish by resolve and willpower. It occurs only when we live so close to God's heart that the rhythm of our own heartbeat comes to reflect the divine pulse.*
>
> David Benner

SCRIPTURE:

Getting into scripture is critical for building the backbone of your faith. The apostle Paul writes in 2 Timothy 3:16 that "The whole Bible was given to us by inspiration from God and is useful to teach us what is true and to make us realize what is wrong in our lives; it straightens us out and helps us do what is right." (NLT) Rather than a measuring stick, it serves as a filter through which to sift truth from lie. It offers us a Kingdom lens through which to see life, provides a balm for our wounded and weary souls, and is a light to guide our steps. Scripture is rich with promises, encouragement, exhortation, and wisdom. It is history and eternity, lament and hope, woven into one.

Whether you dig into scripture daily through a study guide, chip away at chunks in order to read through it within a year, or spend time soaking in single verses you feel drawn to, the key is that you spend time in God's word. As I've wrestled with things that seem contrary or confusing in the Bible, or images of God in the Old Testament that don't seem to line up with the God I know, I've taken them to Jesus - the Word made flesh. While we're typically taught to view God through the lens of the Bible, if we don't know the greater narrative and overarching character of our God, we can walk away with a very distorted view of the Father. I believe it's important to view the Bible through what we already know of Christ, because, as Brian Zahnd says, Jesus is what God has to say. Please don't misunderstand this as me having a low view of scripture - I simply have a high view of Christ. While I don't believe that the Bible is the fourth member of the Trinity, I do wholeheartedly believe it's God's word to us and there is so much treasure to be mined in it, if we'll only take the time to find it. The beautiful thing is, we get to read alongside the Author. With the Holy Spirit as our guide and interpreter - the word will come alive to us.

If you're just starting out - or restarting - spend some time in the New Testament, in the gospel of John, in Romans, or in Ephesians and Philippians (which are called the Epistles). Read the Psalms and Proverbs in the Old Testament. There are so many different translations of scripture, some that include commentary and life application study guides - find one that speaks to you. I own an NIV, the Message version (a personal favorite), an Amplified version, and am slowly building up my collection of books from the Passion Translation. Because the Bible is a collection of books written by different authors in several languages over 1,500 years, it's important to understand the history and context behind these 66 unique books. Find a wise friend or mentor who can help you get the most out of your reading, and nudge you to get back into it when you've gotten out of your rhythm. If you're a heady person, dig into the original Greek and Hebrew text. The depth and context it offers is extraordinary and is sure to satisfy your love of history and research.

While daily scripture reading is a great habit to form, don't just go through the motions. The Pharisees did this and it did nothing for them. Ask God to open your eyes and soften your heart to what He wants to show you. Read scripture with Him. Ask questions. Ask Him why He chose to include things, what they mean for you today, and how you can apply truths to your own life. If you don't get His truths and promises written onto the tablets of your heart, how will you stand on them and cling to them when trouble arises. You have to get it *in* before you can retrieve it in times of need, anxiety or temptation. His Word is a gift that we'll only benefit from if opened.

LECTIO DIVINA:

This method of reading scripture, blended with meditation and prayer, is a traditional Benedictine practice that is intended to promote communion with God and deepen one's knowledge of God's word. Translated from Latin as "divine reading", this practice does not treat Scripture as mere texts to be studied, but as the Living Word to be immersed in. To start your time of reading, spend a few moments quieting your heart and mind, and invite the Holy Spirit to speak to you.

• **Read** (*lectio*): as you read through your selected scriptures for the first time, be aware of any words, phrases or illustrations that stand out to you. Don't force anything, just patiently wait on God's guidance. Is the Holy Spirit impressing anything on your heart?

• **Reflect** (*meditatio*): as you read the passage a second time, focus further on the points you become aware of during the first reading. Maybe re-read a few verses and reflect carefully on where God might have been nudged you. What do you believe God is saying? What do you feel? Try not to analyze the passage or slip into 'study mode'. Rather than dissecting the word, we let the word dissect us. Focus on listening to what God might be saying, and how this relates to your life today. Ask Him for guidance and clarity.

• **Respond** (*oratio*): as you read through for a third time, this is your chance to respond, either verbally through prayer, or in a journal if that fits your style. What is God's personal invitation to you through this scripture? Thank Him for his presence and word.

• **Rest** (*contemplatio*): this is an abbreviated version of contemplative prayer (see below). This isn't a time of prayer or meditation, just a sweet stillness in His presence.

PRAISE + WORSHIP:

While most of us carry stereotypical images in our minds of what praise and worship look like - or should look like - if it is done in spirit and truth (John 4:21-24), it will look different for everyone. Remember that the way in which we express gratitude and adoration to God is a byproduct of how He has uniquely created us. Some people love to sing - and are good at it - others don't. While I believe worship was intended to be a mosaic of creative expression, we tend to limit it to controlled environments and displays of love that are more appropriate for public consumption. While I'm not suggesting chaos and lack of restraint, I do think we've lost some of what it means to worship God with our whole hearts. On the other end of the spectrum, we don't need perfect performances pulled off by men in v-necks and skinny-jeans, and women with enormous Instagram followings. Strobe lights and pyrotechnics are not necessary to usher in the presence of God. We also don't need hymnals and a 100-year old organ. We need hearts that are captivated by the love of the Father and lives that express that gratitude anywhere and at any time. Just look at nature. It loudly and lavishly shouts praise to its maker, without concern for what the time is or who's watching. As Mike Bickle says, "Worship is not a 20-minute period during a church service, but a lifestyle of relating to God in a particular way."

Like prayer, our grand expressions of worship don't impress

211

God if we're just going through the motions. I can't tell you how many times I've sung the right words and moved my arms the right way, while mulling over an offense or rewriting my shopping list. Our hearts matter more than any tune or tempo. My mom has always said that God doesn't listen to our words like humans do. Lip service falls flat. He places a holy stethoscope directly on our hearts, so we'd better make sure that what's going on inside of us lines up with what's going down on the outside.

While most people use the words interchangeably, there is a difference between the musical expression of praise and worship. Someone once explained it to me as praise being *about* God's goodness and faithfulness, while worship is a more intimate expression of love directly *to* God. While this may not necessarily be a theological unpacking of the terms, it helped me to see them as two different ways to love Him well.

• As I mentioned earlier, pay attention to what moves you and stirs your affection for God. I've seen people caught up in worship, head-banging their heart out at a rock concert, and I've seen people sitting quietly, enjoying God's presence, in the woods. The apostle Paul reminds us in Romans 12:1 that offering our very bodies and lives to God is our truest act of worship. So if you love to dance, then dance for Him. If you love to paint, paint for Him. If you love to cook, feed people for Him. If you love to teach, educate for Him. Whatever you do, do it wholeheartedly as an act of worship.

• I've said before that music moves me deeply, and I'm positive I'm not the minority here. There's a tremendous difference in the atmosphere - internally and externally - when I choose to pump worship music out of my speakers instead of pop songs. Sure, I love a good John Legend or Imagine Dragons playlist, but there's no denying that my heart craves the peace and hope that accompanies spirit-filled music. Whether it's instrumental (Tony Anderson and Bethel are my go-tos here), or lyrical (Elevation Worship, Bethel Music, Stephanie Gretzinger, Amanda Cook, Rita Springer and Jonathan David Helser are some of my favorites), incorporating worship into your day can have a profound effect on your mood, attitude and outlook.

Prayer is easily ruined when we make it a project - part of a spiritual self-improvement plan. Rather than pushing yourself forward by resolve, allow God to lead you by desire. The most typical evidence of grace at work within us is not awareness of duty but awareness of desire.

David G. Benner

PRAYER:

Prayer is such a broad category, with multiple different postures and purposes, that to attempt to limit it to one bullet-point would severely minimize its myriad of expressions. Merriam-Webster defines prayer as an address or petition to God in word or thought. At its core, it is communication with our Maker. It is both talking and listening to the Creator of the universe. We can pray specific prayers (sometimes referred to as 'common prayers'), which tend to be read or memorized, and we can pray spontaneous prayers. We can pray at certain times of the day (sometimes referred to 'praying the hours') or throughout the day. We can pray in church, or while waiting in the pickup line at school. We can pray standing up, kneeling down, or sitting on the toilet. We can pray out loud, in song, or in the quiet of our hearts. We can offer up intercessory prayers, petitioning God on behalf of others, or take time to practice some listening prayer, where we intentionally wait on God for direction or encouragement through scripture or a sense of his leading through word or picture (which could also fall into the category of prophetic prayer). I've been a part of personal prophetic prayer times where, as a small team, we waited on God on behalf of someone, and He knocked our socks off with his specific insight and encouragement. I've also been on the receiving end of this powerful ministry on multiple occasions, and it has blessed me to my core, bringing confirmation and affirmation each time. Another discipline that can accompany prayer is fasting. Fasting, which is typically defined as abstinence from food or drink in order to dedicate ourselves to prayer, is a great way to refuel your faith walk and reignite your passion for prayer.

The extraordinary thing about prayer is that we get to talk to God whenever, however, and as frequently as we want to. The key is that it's a dialog, not a monologue. We speak, and then we take time to listen for His voice.

CENTERING PRAYER:

While often written off as new age or confused with eastern mysticism (because evangelical Christians struggle with the words 'meditation' and 'mindfulness'), centering prayer is a part of our spiritual heritage as Christians and offers a deep grounding that is needed now more than ever. It is also referred to as 'breath prayer' or 'contemplative prayer'. In this electronic age where we're never out of reach and are fed a constant diet of drama and negative news, it's no wonder anxiety and depression rates are higher than ever. Silence and solitude are a lost art. Boredom is a thing of the past, and the concept of Sabbath rest is lost in translation. We're chronically distracted, our attention spans are shorter, and the chatterbox in our minds never seems to run out of steam. We're weary and worn out, and even the thought of spiritual growth feels like more work. Enter centering prayer.

The beauty of this centering prayer practice is that it is just that; a practice. We're not expected to get it right. There will be many failed attempts at stillness, but we just keep showing up and trying again. We keep leaning in. It doesn't replace other forms of prayer, it adds depth to them. This practice is less about escaping the outside noise and more about quieting the inner noise. It's about practicing an awareness of the presence of God, and resting in that presence. It's a fleshing out of psalm 46:10, "Be still and know that I am God". An accepting of the invitation to deep, whole-person union with God, as Jesus prayed on the night of His betrayal (John 17:21). It is a transition from mere head knowledge of God, beyond cognitive comprehension of his existence, to a tangible, experiential knowledge of His intimate presence - and all the goodness that comes with it. When practiced regularly it becomes an anchor for the rest of our day. This sweet awareness of His presence becomes a place of calm and peace that we live from. Instead of living for eventual rest and rejuvenation, we can live from a place of rest and renewal.

Based on the monastic schedule, this method of prayer was practiced twice daily for 20 to 30 minutes. I aim for a 5-10 minutes session in the morning, and trust it will grow as I do. Sometimes I only get 2 minutes, but it's 2 minutes I desperately need.

Here's what it looks like:

• **Find a quiet spot to sit down with eyes closed**. I typically sit cross-legged on the floor in my living room, in front of the bay window, right as the sun crests the trees and kisses my face. Sit up, back straight, and lay your hands in a comfortable way, open, on your knees.

• **Choose a word or short phrase as your 'sacred intention'.**
This is not a mantra to repeat as much as it's a reminder to let
go of frantic thoughts and focus your attention on being
present and open to God. My words are the breath prayer
introduced by Brennan Manning in his stunning book, *Abba's
Child;* "Abba (inhale), I belong to you (exhale)." I have them
stamped on a little metal cuff that I wear on my left wrist as a
reminder. Sometimes I whisper, "Thank you", "Jesus", or
merely "peace". God's name, Yahweh is also a beautiful
breath prayer; "yah" on the inhale, "weh" on the exhale.

• **As you focus on the sound of your breath**, deep and slow,
become aware of how it feels to have breath in your lungs.
Quiet your mind and heart. When awareness of physical
sensations or thoughts come, neither hold on to them nor
reject them. Just allow them to drift by and return ever-so-
gently to your sacred word or phrase. This takes discipline. A
wise woman in our church, whose vibrant prayer life I so
admire, gave me a visual that has really helped me fight
distraction. Because telling your mind not to think about
something simply causes you to think about it more
(remember that "don't think about a pink elephant"
experiment), it's helpful to think of this practice as sitting on
the bank of a river and fixing your gaze on a giant tree on the
other side. As things float by in the water, don't focus on
them or try to pick them out, just allow them to float by,
always shifting your attention back to the tree. This has
greatly helped me focus on "practicing the presence", as
Brother Lawrence referred to it.

• **This is not about achieving some spiritual experience or
entering a trance**. The intention of centering prayer is to rest
in the pleasure and presence of the Father. To be renewed
by the unforced rhythms of grace. If you've set a timer (a
vibration would be recommended over a ringtone), when
your time is up, simply smile and thank God for his faithfulness
and goodness.

A friend recently introduced me to a fantastic Centering Prayer App (by Contemplative Outreach, Ltd) that has an opening prayer, beginning sound and customizable timer. While this practice is remarkably simple, it is not easy. Not because much is asked of us during each sit (the term used for the allotted time of contemplation), but because we fight the inefficiency and lack of production involved. We're good at busy, we're pretty dreadful at stillness. Stillness of body *and* mind. And seeing contemplative prayer is less about praying and more about presence, it takes time and discipline to make this a part of your day. But once you do, you'll wonder what took you so long.

"However softly we speak," said John of the Cross, "God is so close to us that He can hear us; nor do we need wings to go in search of Him, but merely to seek solitude and contemplate Him within ourselves, without being surprised to find such a good Guest there."

THE EXAMEN:

This ancient exercise, developed by Saint Ignatius of Loyola (1491–1556), founder of the Jesuits, centers around reflection and review. Rooted in the Latin word, "examine", this practice involves a replay of your day, with keen attention to thoughts, words and deeds. The underlying purpose of this practice is to detect God's presence in our days and discern His direction for us moving forward. Some key elements in this practice are:

• **Find a distraction-free spot** and begin by quieting your heart and mind, becoming more aware of God's presence with you. Thank Him for His great love for you. Pray for the eyes to see and the grace to understand where God is at work in your life.

• **Review your day** - recall specific moments and encounters, and your feelings at the time. Reflect on what you did, said, or thought in those moments. Were you drawing closer to God, or further away? As you remember moments of joy, thank Him for His goodness and blessings. As you recall moments of pain or sin, acknowledge your brokenness and need for His mercy. Ask God to reveal where He was in each moment. Can you identify His fingerprints and presence throughout?

- **Look toward tomorrow** - what lessons from today can you carry into tomorrow? How might you be more aware of God's presence and collaborate more effectively with His plan. How could you grow closer to God and others in the new day? Be specific, and conclude with thanksgiving. Traditionally one would close by praying "Our Father".

DISCIPLESHIP + MENTORING:

If we are followers of Christ, then we are his apprentices, or *disciples*. Discipleship involves learning to live as Jesus lived, and do what Jesus did, so we can more effectively be His hands and feet. In our love of compartmentalizing and categorizing, it seems that we've disconnected evangelism from discipleship, discipleship from mentoring, and mentoring from spiritual direction. We need them all, and while each has distinct characteristics, they overlap in many areas and all revolve around two main themes; growing in wisdom and maturity, and deepening our intimacy with Christ.

My husband and I like to say that everyone needs a mentor, and everyone needs to mentor. We also happen to believe everyone needs a counselor, but that's another discussion. If we have good mentors in our lives who offer godly counsel and an eternal perspective, then we're getting mentorship, discipleship and spiritual direction in one. Seek out older, wiser people whose hindsight can become your foresight. People whose feet you can sit at, on a semi-regular basis, in order to glean wisdom and direction. Someone who is able to speak honestly into your life, even when it's hard and uncomfortable, and whose love and support you can rely on. Someone who's love for Jesus is contagious. At the end of the day, we become like what we love and worship, so it's essential that our passions lead us toward the heart of God. In the words of French novelist, Antoine de Saint-Exupery, "If you want to build a ship, don't drum up people to collect wood and don't assign them tasks and work, but rather teach them to long for the endless immensity of the sea." Friends that help foster that longing in us are worth their weight in gold.

If someone hasn't already come to mind while reading this, consider asking your church if they offer a mentorship or discipleship program you can get involved with. You might even consider hiring a coach or spiritual director to walk with you for a season. Whatever you do, don't miss out on the opportunity to be mentored and discipled. And in the same way someone a few steps ahead of you can add value to your life, you can add value to someone's life who is a few steps behind you. Don't underestimate the ways in which God can use you to pour into some else's life.

We don't come to the table to fight or to defend. We don't come to prove or to conquer, to draw lines in the sand or to stir up trouble. We come to the table because our hunger brings us there. We come with a need, with fragility, with an admission of our humanity...The table is the place where the doing stops, the trying stops, the masks are removed, and we allow ourselves to be nourished, like children.

COMMUNITY + CHURCH:

Gathering together as the church - not necessarily *inside* a church - is essential to your spiritual health. There's something profoundly beautiful and meaningful about breaking bread together - in meal form as well as partaking in communion (the eucharist), engaging in corporate worship and prayer together, and studying God's word as a body of believers (Acts 2:42).

Whether you're inclined to attend a mega church or are drawn to the intimacy of a small home gathering, get connected and stay connected. We were not created to do this life alone, and it is within the context of relationship that God does some of his best refining and restoration work. Find a community of people who aren't satisfied with pat answers and Christian clichés, and who refuse to accept a faux "fine" in response to an honest "How are you?" It's important to create room for gut-level conversation, without having all the answers. Where our focus is on belonging more than behavior. Find somewhere that you can be fully yourself, where you know you belong so you don't have to hide behind your 'Sunday best'. Where you can press into the transforming presence of God alongside other beautifully messy humans and be challenged to grow. Among people who will speak truth to your soul when you need to be reminded of who God says you are. Somewhere that you'll be encouraged to use your time and talent for the kingdom, and where you know you can show up, even on your worst days. Find a church where essential spiritual rhythms are practiced, and where the lead pastor is the same person on Sunday morning as they are on Thursday night. A healthy church is, after all, more of a spiritual gymnasium than a classroom.

Some of our favorite people are those we've met through our church and small groups, and to make it even sweeter, some of our friends and neighbors who we adore now attend our church. We love these folks. They are our people. But here's the thing: community isn't built during the 7 minutes of church foyer time we get before service on Sunday (and that's assuming we're actually on time). We are engaged and invested in each other during the week. We are a part of a small group of couples that gathers every other week, and during the off weeks, we get together as guys and gals. We babysit each other's kids so date nights can happen. We sit around campfires into the wee hours, over wine or coffee, and talk. We message each other in tragedy and triumph. We are in process together, all moving toward a common goal; to become more like Jesus. Our marriages are better, our families are better, our community is better...because we do life together, and because of our commitment to being a part of the bigger body of Christ.

Make gathering with other followers of Jesus, who are also learning to step out in faith and press into the mystery of God, an essential piece of your spiritual practice.

﹖

Spiritual practices are like vitamins. They're accessible and available, but they serve no purpose if they simply remain in the cupboard in our heads. We actually have to ingest them regularly to benefit from them. They're not easy, but they are simple. In the words of Marshall Goldsmith, what got us here won't get us there. We've got to establish new rhythms that make these practices happen.

I'm sure there are other disciplines I haven't touched on here, and if you're curious about them and they nourish your spiritual life, please experiment. Trust that He is a good father, and a good guide, and that if you're walking closely with Jesus - hungry for more of the Kingdom - that He will lead your exploration and bring you back on track when you wander off. There is no fear in love. Lean in.

Our research and amazing new scientific technology are
continually adding exciting new evidence that our Great
Creator, God, has equipped us with marvelous mechanisms
by which, through faith in Him, our spiritual beliefs
and behaviors can actually help heal us.

Harold G. Koenig, M.D.

As tri-dimensional beings, made in the image of a triune God, we are to love God with our whole being. Our spirituality isn't an exclusive commitment reserved for minds, spirits or Sundays. Intellectual smarts will not sustain us. We are invited to engage our bodies, minds, hearts, souls and spirits in this divine dance. In his book, "*Anatomy of the Soul*: Surprising Connections between Neuroscience and Spiritual Practices That Can Transform Your Life and Relationships", Curt Thompson explains that our spiritual experience of God has got to be rooted in relationship. In terms of neurobiology, comprehension of that truth must move from right brain to left. The right hemisphere of our brains is engaged through story, emotion, empathy and connection, and then that information is sent across the corpus callosum to the left hemisphere, where analytical, structured and logical functions take place. In essence, the left brain makes sense of what we sense. Unfortunately, much of the evangelism and discipleship methods in the west engage primarily the left brain, appealing to people through theology, dogma and guidelines. The mystery of our faith cannot be processed by our left brain, it just doesn't compute. We simply cannot reduce our spiritual journey to a logical, linear process.

Christianity is Christ, plus nothing. Nothing more, nothing less. It is not an ideology, a cause, a set of core value or a moral code. Christianity is, as Leonard Sweet and Frank Viola write it in their book, *Jesus Manifesto*, "The 'good news' that beauty, truth and goodness are found in a Person — a real and living Person who can be known, loved, and experienced — and that true humanity and community are founded on connection to that Person."

If you've felt restless in your spirit, take heart. You have eternity stitched into you, whether you recognize it or not, so there is a divine homing device within you set on the Father's heart. No amount of head knowledge will guide you there. Your heart will always be homesick for His presence. You may try to dull the ache with people and noise and busyness, but stillness and solitude is the answer. It's not about acquisition or success, it's about *surrender*. It's not outside of you, it's within.

Sweet friend, God is totally committed to your wholeness and restoration, and to accompanying you on the hard and holy road you're on. We have a God who would rather die than have anything come between us. As we close this chapter, spend some time praying about what can you let go of - or set into motion - this week, this month, this year...to further drop what you believe about God in your head to truth you know about Him in your heart. There's a tremendous difference between *understanding* that God *knows* us, and *feeling* fully *known* by God. Once we understand that we're deeply known and outrageously loved by the author of life itself, our journey back home will never be the same. And we will be more apt to want to take others with us. May we stop building walls and start building bridges. May you hear Him whisper your name, and may you know that you are forever held.

The gospel is absurd and the life of Jesus is meaningless unless we believe that He lived, died, and rose again with but one purpose in mind: to make brand-new creation. Not to make people with better morals but to create a community of prophets and professional lovers, men and women who would surrender to the mystery of the fire of the Spirit that burns within, who would live in ever greater fidelity to the omnipresent Word of God, who would enter into the center of it all, the very heart and mystery of Christ, into the center of the flame that consumes, purifies, and sets everything aglow with peace, joy, boldness, and extravagant, furious love. This, my friend, is what it really means to be a Christian.

Brennan Manning

"MAYBE IT'S OK"
by WE ARE MESSENGERS

If I didn't know what it hurt like to be broken,
Then how would I know what it feels like to be whole.
If I didn't know what it cuts like to be rejected,
Then I wouldn't know the joy of coming home.

Maybe it's ok if I'm not ok,
'Cause the one who holds the world is holding onto me.
Maybe it's alright if I'm not alright,
'Cause the one who holds the stars is holding my whole life.

If I didn't know what it looked like to be dirty,
Then I wouldn't know what it feels like to be clean.
If all of my shame hadn't drove me to hide in the shadows,
Then I wouldn't know the beauty of being free.

Maybe it's ok if I'm not ok,
'Cause the one who holds the world is holding onto me.
Maybe it's alright if I'm not alright,
'Cause the one who holds the stars is holding my whole life.

Father let Your kingdom come,
Let Your will be done,
Here, in my heart as in heaven.

Maybe it's Ok, if I'm not Ok.

Written by Darren Mulligan, Jonathan Smith & Bryan Fowler

CHAPTER EIGHT

YOU ARE HERE
ROAD TO WHOLE | WELLNESS EVALUATION

Tell me, what is it you plan to do with
your one wild and precious life?
Mary Oliver

When the Trinity mapped out their grand redemption plan, we were at the heart of it. The why behind the renewal and restoration of all things.

If we can grasp just an iota of the goodness and glory yet unfolding, it will change everything about the way we navigate our lives. The supernatural is leaking out through our natural, the extraordinary is breaking through our ordinary, if we'll only have the eyes to see it.

Why do we settle for so much less? Imagine attending a

wedding where the groom finally says to his beautiful bride, "With this ring, I will take care of you in retirement one day." It's absurd! Laughable, at best. And yet so many have approached salvation - and life - this way. **Jesus did not save us so we can go to heaven one day. He saved us so we could bring heaven to earth right now.** I trust as you've worked through this book that you have gained a greater understanding of what it means to be *saved*. That God is actively and faithfully in the process of mending us and making us whole; soul, body and spirit. Sozo is for you and me, and it's for now.

Now, if anyone is enfolded into Christ, he has become an entirely new creation. All that is related to the old order has vanished. Behold, everything is fresh and new.

2 Corinthians 5:17

So where do we go from here?

Good intentions will get us nowhere. Being intentional will. Deliberately making time to 'take stock' is essential to our overall health. Consider this final section a 'You Are Here' marker on your map, as you take time to observe from above your road to wholeness. Can you name where you actually are? We can, after all, only move closer to our destination once we've established where we currently are.

Create some space in your schedule over the next week, and then again in six months, to grab a pen and journal. Check your pulse in each of the three dimensions; soul, body and spirit.

Progress has not followed a straight ascending line,
but a spiral with rhythms of progress and retrogression,
of evolution and dissolution.

Johann Wolfgang Von Goethe

MENTAL & EMOTIONAL WELLNESS:

- How do I feel on a scale of 1 to 10? 10 being grounded and hopeful about my future?
- What is the greatest current obstacle/struggle/distraction in my life that hinders me in this area?
- Am I aware of my intrinsic worth and value, or do I allow others to determine and diminish it?
- Am I resilient? Do I bounce back quickly or do I obsess over failure or offense?
- How intentionally do I cultivate an attitude of gratitude in my daily life?
- Am I communicating my needs and boundaries or am I expecting others to guess correctly and meet them?
- Do I use my power wisely, regularly choose unity over being right?
- What feelings tend to trigger my desire to escape, numb or hide?
- What belief systems and coping mechanisms do I have in place that no longer serve me?
- Am I aware of the tapes that play on repeat in my mind, and do they speak life or death over me?
- Am I willing to have uncomfortable conversations in an effort to deepen and strengthen my relationships?
- Am I intentionally nourishing and expanding my mind, or do I consume soul-sucking media on a regular basis?
- Am I carving out time to do things that make me come alive and fuel my soul? Is soul care a priority?

- Do I have people in my life around whom I can be fully myself? Are they a safe place to become and belong.
- Do I find myself over-committed and stretched thin because of my need to please others and gain their approval?
- How well do I know myself? Am I familiar with my strengths, temperament, personality and tendencies?
- Based on the number I selected in the first question, what is a single action I could take today that would improve my mental + emotional health?

The fatal metaphor of progress, which means leaving things behind us, has utterly obscured the real idea of growth, which means leaving things inside us.

G. K. Chesterton

PHYSICAL WELLNESS:

- How is my health on a scale of 1 to 10? 10 being energetic and vibrantly healthy?
- What is the greatest current obstacle/struggle/distraction in my life that hinders me in this area?
- Am I taking care of this brilliant body I've been given, or am I assuming it will continue to function well without maintenance or care?
- Am I moving more than I'm sitting? Am I getting my heart rate up every day?
- How am I fueling my body? Is what I'm putting in it nourishing and nurturing it, or slowly destroying it?
- Am I eating as colorfully and freshly as possible, or does my diet consist of various shades of pre-packaged browns.
- Do I know the proportion of macronutrients my diet

consists of, and might it need some reworking?

- Am I aware of how what I put in my body makes me feel? Am I listening to what my body is trying to tell me?
- Do I pay attention to when I'm satisfied, or do I frequently eat until I'm uncomfortably stuffed?
- Am I aware of when I turn to food or drink for comfort or distraction instead of dealing with an issue?
- Do I take the time to care for myself daily, doing whatever little things make me feel pretty and lovely (perfume, makeup, earrings, etc.)?
- Do I consistently get enough sleep? Do I take time to wind down, to rest and rejuvenate?
- Am I hydrating my body sufficiently with clean, unadulterated water?
- Am I being kind about my body and speaking life over its shape and form?
- Do I maintain a regular schedule of check-ups to more fully understand my health profile?
- Do I have someone in my life who is able to lovingly confront me when my physical health is sliding due to bad habits?
- Do I treat my body as the sacred temple it is, and do I steward its limited resources well?
- Based on the number I selected in the first question, what is a single action I could take today that would improve my physical health?

If you can't fly then run, if you can't run then walk,
if you can't walk then crawl, but whatever you
do you have to keep moving forward.

Martin Luther King, Jr.

SPIRITUAL WELLNESS:

o How's my relationship with God on a scale of 1 to 10? 10 being authentic, intimate and growing?

o What is the greatest current obstacle/struggle/distraction in my life that hinders me in this area?

o Who do I understand God to be - in me, for me, and through me? Do I believe He is truly good?

o Is my spiritual journey centered around the transforming presence of God, or church attendance?

o Am I able to wrestle honestly with tough questions, or do I simply regurgitate what I've heard? Do I know what I believe?

o Am I actively following Jesus, or do I simply hold a membership to His fan club?

o Where am I most aware of His presence? What fosters my affection for God? Do I make time for this often enough?

o Is my faith solid enough to both ground me and free me to embrace mystery and risk?

o What is the state of my root system? Is it shallow and unreliable, or deeply anchored and established in Christ?

o Does my life produce good fruit? Is joy, peace, patience, kindness, goodness and self-control evident in my life?

o Do I fall into the trap of going through religious motions or am I working to cultivate authentic spirituality and intimacy with God in my daily life?

o Am I prioritizing the nourishment of my spirit or do I turn to cheap counterfeits (in what I read, listen to and watch)?

o Does my prayer life consist of a monologue, or am I being still long enough to hear His heart?

o Am I looking for simple ways to daily impact other people's eternity, even if simply by loving them well?

o Do I look for God's fingerprints in hard times or do I tend to assume He's punishing or ignoring me?

- What is that one thing that keeps coming up that feels like a divine invitation into greater wholeness? Can I trust Him in it?
- Where might God be calling me out of my comfort zone and into the water with Him?
- Am I generous with my resources, out of my understanding of His sufficiency, or do I struggle with a scarcity mentality?
- Based on the number I selected in the first question, what is a single action I could take today that would improve my spiritual health?

The purpose of this evaluation is to increase awareness in all three dimensions of your life.

Consider these final questions:

- Am I aware of my appetites (body/soul/spirit)? Which counterfeits do I find myself gravitating towards that I will need to detox from? What is really beneath my desire to accept these quick-fixes over true nourishment? It's only once I name it that I can tame it!
- What can I set into motion - today, tomorrow, this week - that will have a positive impact on my nutrition, my level of activity, my emotions and mental health, and my intimacy with God? What practices or rhythms might I want to implement? What unhealthy habits or tendencies might I need to address?
- Am I living with my body, spirit and soul in alignment? Does what I believe to be true about my inherent value - that I am made in the image of God - express itself in each dimension?
- Where do I want to be six months from now, and one year from now?

- What do I want to see changed/improved/transformed first? And what baby steps can I take towards making this happen?
- Is there someone - a coach, mentor, counselor or spiritual director — that I would benefit linking arms with in this process?

May God himself, the God who makes everything holy and whole, make you holy and whole, put you together - spirit, soul, and body - and keep you fit for the coming of our Master, Jesus Christ. The One who called you is completely dependable. If he said it, he'll do it!

1 Thessalonians 5:23-24

SOZO *manifesto*

I was fearfully and wonderfully made,
Woven together on purpose, for a purpose.
I will steward my soul well, it is wise and unlike any other.
I will steward my emotions well, they are a blessing and not a curse.
I will steward my mind well, it is smart and creative.
I will steward my body well, it is strong and capable.
I will steward my spirit well, it is tender and open to His leading.
I will choose to lay down those lesser things that
I have tried to satisfy my deep hunger with,
In favor of the nourishment I was created to thrive on.
I will choose to be brave and honest with my soul.
I will choose to be kind and compassionate to my body.
I will choose to be still and led by the Spirit.
I will make time to play and create and laugh.
I will take time to mourn and grieve my pain.
I will cultivate an attitude of gratitude and generosity.
I will detox from the counterfeits that have numbed me.
I will nourish my mind with beauty and truth.
I will listen to my soul and tend to its needs.
I will establish boundaries and honor my limits.
I will allow my emotions to teach me, but not lead me.
I will fuel my temple with wisdom and care.
I will move my body with strength and dignity.
I will learn to love the skin that I'm in.
I will feed my spirit with connection and life.
I will silence the noise and unplug from busyness.
I will uproot the lies and listen to truth.
I will live with an open heart and mind.
I will create space to sit in His presence.
I will take off the mask and lean into community.
I will own my story, cling to His promises,
And choose to be patient with the process.
I will embrace the hard and holy road I am on,
Staying in step with the One who loves me fully,
Because I was created to be free and whole.

I pray that out of his glorious riches he may strengthen you with power through his Spirit in your inner being, so that Christ may dwell in your hearts through faith. And I pray that you, being rooted and established in love, may have power, together with all the Lord's holy people, to grasp how wide and long and high and deep is the love of Christ, and to know this love that surpasses knowledge—that you may be filled to the measure of all the fullness of God. Now to him who is able to do immeasurably more than all we ask or imagine, according to his power that is at work within us, to him be glory in the church and in Christ Jesus throughout all generations, for ever and ever! Amen.

Ephesians 3:16-21

JOURNEY OF JOY
THE BACKSTORY | EXCERPT FROM XES

My older sister and I were born in Cape Town, South Africa, and grew up in Windhoek, Namibia, where our parents moved a few years later to avoid the discrimination of the apartheid, among other things. That may sound unusual coming from a white South African, but my parents were passionate about us growing up in multiracial schools, and felt led to transplant our family in what was then called South West Africa. A few years later, my younger sister arrived, and 3 years after that, our baby sister.

If you're doing the math, yes, that's 4 girls. And a mum. And yes, my dad is a rockstar.

Random fun fact: with my dad also hailing from South Africa and my mom emerging in Zimbabwe, our family of six were born in 3 different countries across Southern Africa.

I have many fond memories of childhood, and a startling amount of negative ones. Not because there were more negative than positive, not by a long shot, but because I think that this tends to be the way our brains process life. And the way our enemy wages war on the battlefield of the mind.

It floors me how, looking back, how I can recall things my parents did in complete innocence that were misinterpreted and twisted in my vulnerable little heart. My older sister, with her skinny little body, did ballet. I, however, was 'muscular', so I did gymnastics, even though I ached to dance. Sarah, with her beautiful brown eyes, looked lovely in pink, so she got a pink ballerina dress. A blue dress was a natural fit for me with my piercing blue eyes. Sarah's hair was straight and long. Mine, on the other hand, was curly. Only nobody knew it. We lived in a semi-arid desert climate, much like Arizona, which is very unsupportive of follicularly swirly girls. And let me just tell you, if you're going to brush a gal's hair like it's straight - when it's not - and not give her any anti-frizz serum to make it look good, it is not going to cooperate. And it didn't. My super fine, frizzy hair went every which way, except when we made trips to the coast. Then it curled and looked lovely. Who knew!? So, my mum kept it cut short because it was the only way to manage my mop.

Blue dress. Short hair. No ballet. Large unabomber glasses. They all spelled out the same thing: "You are not feminine, Joy, in fact you're sort of like a boy." It didn't help that I naturally gravitated to the boys, because they were uncomplicated and fun, which further alienated me from the girls. When my body started to do weird things and the boys wondered what was going on, I simply lifted my shirt and said, "Yeah...check it out...isn't that crazy? I'm sprouting boobs! Wanna touch em?" I was just one of the boys, and while I loved feeling like I belonged, I ached to feel accepted within my own tribe.

One negative memory can completely obliterate the sweetness of 10 precious moments in our minds. We tend to dwell on and relive the memories that stirred up shame, insecurity, humiliation, discomfort or fear. Maya Angelou explained it like this, "People will forget what you said, people will forget what you did, but people will never forget how you made them feel."

And while my childhood was saturated with love and comfort at home, insecurity and self-loathing were my perfected skills for much of the latter portions. I have gaping holes in my memory, mostly between age 8 and 18, where I cannot remember anything. It's as if the shame and regret I wrestled with daily blotted out massive portions of my life. The self-hatred made those memories too uncomfortable to recall.

I distinctly remember a recurring daydream I started having around 7th grade. And the dream always unfolded in the exact same way: me, in all my spectacled, short-haired clumsiness, awkwardly toeing the cracks in the playground while the popular kids played elsewhere. Some sort of chaos would inevitably break out amongst my classmates and the distinct need for a hero would arise. This is when my fragile heart would practically beat out of my chest in excitement - it was my cue, my moment to shine. Even if it was painfully nonexistent.

I would step forward and, reaching around to the back of my neck, would fearlessly unzip the ugliness - shedding my unsightly exterior, effortlessly stripping away the insecurity and stupidity, peeling back the too-tall, too-thick, uber ungraceful facade to reveal the jaw-dropping beauty within. I'm sure she responded to a considerably sexier name. Like Jessica. Or Veronica. Anything but "Joy". Boasting long, gorgeous hair, a tiny waistline, and a beautifully feminine face, she turned heads and won hearts and solved schoolyard problems.

And she was everything I was not.

This was usually where the daydream would end, but it was enough. Enough to temporarily satisfy the ache in my heart. To be beautiful. To be confident. To be someone other than who I was.

I started snipping diet tips from beauty magazines and compiling health folders before I hit my double-digits. I became obsessed with my appearance, desperate to battle the bulge before it battled me. Watching my mom struggle with her weight for as long as I could recall, and seeing the resemblance in how we were built, struck a fear in me that fueled my obsession.

Despite the lies I believed about my lack of worth and value, I became that girl. The one making out with the boys at every middle school dance, not because I really loved to suck face, but because it made me feel pursued and valued, and was, admittedly, rather fun to shock the other girls. I had a new 'boyfriend' every week and lapped up the false sense of confidence it provided me.

While I started to appear happy and confident on the outside, I was empty and broken inside.

My family moved to America near the end of 1994, where I attended my second high school. Talk about culture shock. By the time I had found my feet and nestled into a good group of friends, our visas had expired and we were moving back home to Namibia. With the difference in school year (our school year mirrors the calendar year, while a school year in the States runs from September through June), I begged my parents to allow me to try correspondence schooling, rather than repeat 6 month of school, and struggle once again to fit in with the other kids who'd maintained their friendships in my absence.

The few friends who had stayed in touch with me during my 18 months overseas, sans email or social media, were eager to hear how life had treated me. And I was not one to disappoint. I conjured up all sorts of stories about beach volleyball and cheerleading, of which I knew nothing, because the pitiful time I'd spend shuffling through the halls, trying not to be noticed, was too painful to relive. Lying became second nature to me, and with no one to contradict my stories, I simply painted the picture of the life I'd wanted to live. I created the image of the girl I wanted to be, and they bought it, hook, line and sinker.

It seemed, for a time, that life was looking up for me, but the veneer was only paper thin.

After years of childishly dabbling in promiscuity, and yet never crossing the virginity line firmly established in our conservative Christian home, I started dating older boys on

240

the sly. In September of 1996, shortly after I turned 15, I met the sons of one of my dad's colleagues who were visiting from England. I quickly connected with the older one and started spending more time with him. Little did I know of the competition raging behind the scenes in this testosterone-charged household, and the night before their family flew back home, they spiked my drink and the younger one took me downstairs to his room. I don't recall much of the rest of the night, except spending the wee hours of the morning rocking in the fetal position in my older sister's bedroom repeating, "I'm not a virgin, I'm not a virgin, I'm not a virgin". And then there was the phone call I received from a very angry older brother who wanted to know what the hell I'd done with his brother (that I'd refused to do with him) the night before.

I knew little, but I knew enough.

This was a pivotal point in my journey. Life as I knew it had officially changed. The little value I felt I had left had been taken from me, and I suddenly had no reason to say, "No". I threw myself into the arms of any interested male in a hopeless attempt to find significance. I used people and pleasure to temporarily numb the pain, desperately trying to quench my thirst for meaning and value.

Following in the steps of Adam and Eve, I allowed my shame to drive me into hiding, away from exposure and away from God.

The deeper I slipped into promiscuity, the harder it was to get out. Not only was I worthless, now I was dirty.

I jumped from relationship to relationship, going home from the bar with boys I barely knew, often much older than myself. I was only 15, but looked much older, and in a country where underage drinking was the norm and no one was carded, I continued to slip beneath the radar. I had a love-hate relationship with this thing I had going on. I loved the temporary thrill of being pursued, but I hated that it only briefly drowned out the loneliness and isolation. Once over the high, I slipped further into the dark.

> *One who is full loathes honey from the comb, but to the hungry even what is bitter tastes sweet.*
>
> *Proverbs 27:7*

I remember laying dazed in some guy's bed late one night when his roommate returned home. There had been no tenderness, no affection. Only business, without any form of protection. And now, with a third person in the room, there was no introduction. No closing of doors. No respect. Only a sick awareness that I was his prey for the night and the joke was on me. He threw me my clothes and quietly drove me back to the bar where he left me. The next time I saw him was on the rugby field, where I discovered he played for our national team.

I couldn't escape the hell hole I'd dug for myself, so I learned quickly to run away mentally, while remaining present - albeit half-dead - physically. A habit it took me years to break once married.

I was drowning, and no one knew it.

Looking back I've wondered where my parents where while I traipsed around town, wasted and used. But as I get older and wiser, and after several hard conversations with them, I've realized that they were battling their own devils. Knee-deep in good works, they were busy proving their own worth and value, while raising four girls.

While my older sister had openly rebelled and fast earned herself the label of 'black sheep', I was still trying desperately to keep my iniquities hidden. I had seen the devastation my sister's exit from our faith had caused my parents, and had determined to not put them through that again. So I was a respectful, hard-working student by day and a faithful pew-warming kid on Sunday mornings…and a bar-hopping floozy by night.

During this same year, I started shoplifting. It started small, with a chapstick here or a pack of gum there, and grew to include near daily fixes of clothes, CDs and make-up. Getting things for free became such a thrill, despite the gnawing awareness that what I was doing was wrong, that when I finally committed to stop (years later), it was incredibly hard. Unless you've experience the pull of an addiction, and the cycle of adrenaline and pleasure you experience, it's hard to understand the way in which it sucks you in and then quickly spirals out of control.

I lost two little side-jobs that year as a result of stealing. I even stole several home pregnancy tests that I hurriedly took in grocery story bathrooms, vowing to God that if He would not make me pregnant, I would stop what I was doing. I knew that if that little line were to imply 'with child', that I would be thrust into a new world of scary choices and heart-breaking consequences.

When my parents discovered I had stolen their bank card and had made several withdrawals, and after they'd driven around town early one morning trying to locate me after I'd lied about where I'd spent the night, they knew correspondence schooling had afforded me freedom I had no place managing. Into my third high school I went, where I earned the nickname "the body" and started dating the older brother of a school friend. I kept the fact that he had a son a secret, as I was sure my parents couldn't handle the truth.

More secrets, more separation.

As the crowd I spent time with morphed into a different breed of people, pornography became something I was regularly exposed to. Once again fueling the dump of adrenaline that coursed through my young veins, I got

243

sucked further out to sea.

When we got the news that our visas had been renewed, and that we would be returning to the States, I was all too happy to leave a country that had grown to represent a season of so much guilt and shame.

Two weeks before we flew out, while visiting family in South Africa, I met a young man. I had just turned 16, and he'd just turned 21. We got hammered, along with 2 others, then went for a joyride out on the town. Trucking down a main street in Cape Town at a ridiculous speed, we hit the broadside of a taxi that had pulled out in front of us. The next thing I knew I was getting a morphine shot in my butt and surgery scheduled for my twice-broken jaw, You would think that the events of the evening would act as perfectly clear warning signals, but I was too blind to recognize them.

Our relationship continued, long-distance, over the next two and a half years.

I viewed moving across the world as a much-needed fresh start, and I could, once again, present the image of the person I hoped to be. Only this time...one unblemished by sexual baggage. I started my senior year at a small country school (my 4th high school, if you're keeping track), and slunk into the background. Sadly, having an accent makes you stand out by default, but with 'insecure' written all over my face, I became a prime target for those meanies looking for a target.

I had transitioned from a young girl who loved people and thrived in school to a shattered young woman who was afraid of letting people in and who hated the emotional torture of school. I was terrified of my mask slipping, convinced that if anyone knew who I really was, I would be hung to dry.

While I wasn't physically bullied or tormented, the battle that raged in my head made any encounter with unfriendly people miserable. If someone laughed in the hallway while I was walking through it, they were laughing at me. If more than one person smiled at me when I walked in the room, it was because I was the butt of their joke. When people didn't greet me in passing, I thought it was because they didn't like me. I longed to be invisible, and yet, watching others blossom in things I was too scared to try out for - like sports or theater - made my heart ache for more. I was desperately jealous of their confidence and courage, but the thought of risking failure was too much to bear.

So I stayed in my shell, dragging my dirty-girl secrets everywhere I went. When my boyfriend would come up to visit, for months at a time, I'd quietly slip back into the lifestyle I'd lived back home, and then seamlessly revert back once he left.

After I had graduated, and while working on my massage therapy certification at the local community college, this boyfriend of mine popped the question. It wasn't really a lovely surprise seeing I'd sort of pushed him into it. I was convinced he was the only one who would ever want me, so I informed him that this was the natural progression of our relationship. I bugged him to hurry up and buy me a ring... while simultaneously insisting that we stop having sex. Not really a good combination for the average male.

God had started to woo my heart and there where certain things I knew I had to weed out of my life in order to get my life back in order.

Little did I know, a new girlfriend had popped up on the other side of the globe - one who wasn't insisting on a ring or pushing for purity - and when the email arrived that 18th day of February 2000, informing me that it was no longer working out and that we should go our separate ways, the world as I knew it crumbled. I slept and wept, unable to get out of my bed, spinning that meaningless new ring on my finger.

RENEWED

But this, my friend, is where it starts to get good. The very same week my world fell apart, Jehovah Sneaky was at work behind the scenes. The women's Bible study that my mum led on a Thursday morning was taking a trip down to North Carolina for a conference, and I was just desperate enough to go along for the ride. While I don't recall too much from the weekend, teaching or ministry wise, I distinctly remember the women who carried me through some of the loneliest days of my life. They scooped me up, lifted my chin, and like a flock of mommas, enveloped me with love.

I spent the next couple of years digging into my relationship with God, avoiding boys like the plague, weaning myself off shoplifting, and trying desperately to avoid the temptation to slip into the sexual habits I had created years prior.

Painfully aware of my inability to have healthy relationships, I told God that my heart was His. Fully and completely. I knew I couldn't be trusted with my heart, as I had flung it at every passing boy over the past several years, so I surrendered that decision to Him, committing to not pursue a relationship again without knowing He was releasing my heart into their care.

I started leading youth group, teaching a Bible study, and even stumbled my way into Christian radio. I had started over, stuffed my past down deep enough that it was hardly even discernible, and was now determined to earn my way back into God's good grace. I was going to prove to Him that I was worth saving.

After three years of celibacy, while perfecting my new 'God's girl' image, a pastor I worked with at the radio station introduced me to a young man. While I didn't notice him at first, we kept running into each other at random media events, first at a Michael W. Smith concert, then at a

SonicFlood concert, and again at Festival Con Dios. We finally started to connect the dots when the general manager of the station, and our pastor friend, exchanged our emails and got the ball rolling. Because of the hour long distance between us, we got to know each other via phone and email, and after a month of lengthily conversation, we had our first date.

When I had surrendered my heart to God a couple of years prior, I had begged Him for wisdom. Having run so quickly into physical encounters with boys in the past, rarely connecting emotionally, and never sharing a spiritual bond, I had asked God to reverse that trend when the man He had for me came along. I watched Him honor this request in the following months as we connected instantly over our mutual love for Jesus first, developing a sweet friendship after that, and carefully putting boundaries in place for sexual purity. Everything seemed to be going just peachy!

An interesting thing happened on our second date, however, when the topic of sexual purity arose. Sitting in his Ford Taurus in the Farmer Jack's parking lot, I panicked. The conversation had turned to me and I had a choice to make. To tell, or not to tell. Dry heaving out the window, I turned back to him and whispered, "I was date raped when I was 15." Nothing more. I had decided to share the 'poor me' part of my story, and keep the 'bad me' portion in hiding, assuming the basic knowledge of me being 'used goods' would validate the presence of some junk to work through.

Heaven knows, if he really knew the amount of sexual baggage I came with, he'd head for the hills.

Our relationship progressed and in March of the following year, he proposed in the white sand of a Florida beach at sunset. It was beautiful and glorious, and on that day I was only slightly aware of the farce I had become. I had grown so accustomed to pretending that I had almost managed to convince myself that my ugly past was simply a figment of my imagination. I would go through the mental motions of carving out ground at the bottom of the ocean, dumping all my iniquities into the pit, and then smothering them in cement. I would repeatedly drown out the memories each and every time they threatened to rear their ugly heads and remind me who I was.

From the outside looking in, I had it all. The perfect job, a wonderful family, an amazing fiancé, and impeccable faith. The only problem was, I knew my life was a charade, and the fear of exposure - and the subsequent ruin - kept me tightly enslaved.

While everything blossomed on the outside, I was quietly withering on the inside.

Secrets will do that to you. I have learned over the course of the past decade or two that whenever I keep dirt hidden, it has power over me. These secrets fester and take on a life of their own, devouring my confidence and joy, and driving me further back into the shadows of insecurity. But when brought out into the light, they lose their power, and I gain power over them. As long as we allow the enemy a foothold in the darkest recesses of our heart, in amongst the secrets and cobwebs, he will poison our self-image, smudge our purpose, and chain us down with fear.

I love the picture we have painted for us in the story of Rapunzel. Here's this princess, who doesn't even know she's got royalty surging through her veins, held captive in a castle she could easily exit, by lies and fear of the unknown. That was my life for so many years. I was utterly terrified of what people would think, of how loved ones would react, that I shoved all my sin and shame into the nooks and crannies of my soul and allowed them to rot. I hoped that if I could stuff it all down far enough, and convince myself that none of it actually happened, who on this side of the world could argue any differently.

This thinking is not only ineffective, but it's about as

248

ludicrous as burying dead bodies in your backyard and thinking their eerie presence won't affect the way you live your life. Garbage stinks, no matter how you gift wrap it, and it's intended to be purged. But when your junk is too painful and ugly to even consider sifting through, you get awfully good at blocking your nose and stifling your gag-reflex.

I developed such a warped sense of reality that I - to this day - have chunks of memory completely blotted out. I remember several times waking up in a cold sweat from a dream that left me gasping for breath, heart pounding out of my chest. Vivid scenes of my involvement in a murder, and the messy attempt to cover it up. I spent many days searching through my fractured memories, desperate to know whether this was something I had actually been a part of, or whether the devil was simply capitalizing on my inability to separate fact from fiction.

In the months leading up to our wedding, we did everything we knew to do in preparation - we took every marriage class, read every book, and spent time with older, wiser couples who invested in our relationship. While at times I felt like a fraud in talking about past experiences, simply leaving out massive chunks of my history, I had finally managed to convince myself that as long as I could keep up the performance, no one would ever be the wiser. The alternative was no longer an option.

It was mind over matter, and I was determined to protect this beautiful new life I was living.

Two months before our wedding, in the August of 2003, I ended up driving to New York with a close friend for a media event. I assumed it would just be a fun-filled few days at Six Flags, hobnobbing with artists and brushing shoulders with the big wigs of the music industry. But God had other plans.

On the final evening of the event, I found myself sitting front and center in the stadium, media pass hanging proudly around my neck. After Michael W. Smith's set, TobyMac rocked the stage, followed by the delightful presence of Kirk Cameron. I was loving my front row seat, until she came out. Pam Stenzel, purity advocate extraordinaire. She talked about abstinence and purity and virginity and boundaries, all the things I assumed I didn't really need to hear at that point. After all, I was gettin' hitched in 2 months. She went on to share how important it is to live with full disclosure in marriage, to dialog with honesty and transparency. And I wanted to die. I hoped the earth would just open up and swallow me whole. This was not what I wanted to hear. After all, I had quietly dragged these secrets around for the past several years, and with my wedding just around the corner, it made no sense for me to go rummaging through the trash now. Let bygones be bygones. Don't stir up this hornet's nest, woman.

But the pit in my stomach deepened as she drove home the need for relationships to be built on foundations of trust. "Fine, God. Just fine. I get it," I whimpered. Paralyzed in my seat I watched as people flooded the prayer tent. I was so very aware of an urgency in my spirit, a sense that God was saying, "Joy, I'm giving you the opportunity of a lifetime...but you have got to act within the lifetime of this opportunity." I knew that window would close quickly, as making it to our wedding day without telling him the truth, would mean taking my secrets to the grave. I couldn't possibly burden him with that after he was tied to me.

It was now, or never.

The thought of allowing my fiancé into those dark, dirty places of my life seemed impossible, so I thought I'd outsmart God at His own game. "Okay, God. Let's make a deal," I started, "if I speak to Pam and she tells me I should tell him everything, I'll do it." By the growing mass of sniffling bodies in and around the prayer tent, I was certain this was my ticket out. I wandered over, sheepishly standing off at a distance, trying to plan my next move, when I turned to go. Standing directly behind me was Pam Stenzel. How He did that, I will never know, but there she was in all her purity-advocating glory, and I couldn't escape. Seven years of running came to a screeching halt and I fell apart in her arms. She cried with me, prayed with me, and confirmed what I felt God was prompting me to do; it was time to take out the trash.

I am so thankful for the precious friend who accompanied me on this trip, a dear friend of my fiancé's long before she became my own. She quietly listened as I processed through my raw emotions, ranging from terror to anger and back again, and then helped me prepare my heart for what was about to take place in my relationship. She, too, prayed with me, encouraging me and speaking hope into my heart, and was the first person to hear snippets of the life I had kept in secret.

Once home in Michigan, I went to the apartment we were renting, where my fiancé was currently staying, and waited for him to return home from work. Apart from the day I spent staring at my newborn son through cold ICU glass, being intubated and cardioverted, as medical staff fought to save his life, this was the longest day I'd ever known.

After avoiding eye-contact and dancing around the subject for as long as possible, he pried, and I cracked. I don't recall how the words emerged from my lips, but through snot and tears, he heard snippets of a life very different from the one I had painted. Certain the filth of my true identity had manifested on my face, my chin remained planted on my chest as I drudged the secrets up from hiding.

Lies upon lies. Relationship after relationship. Sin cloaked in more sin.

And then he asked me what I feared most he might ask. "How many were there?" The number slipped from my lips, and then I was gone.

Convinced this sealed the fate of our relationship, I left my engagement ring on the couch and ran for the bathroom. Curled up in the fetal position on the bathroom floor, I ached for God to just take me home. I was an undone, incoherent and utterly destroyed by my own failed masquerade. Surely death would feel better than this mess I had made.

What felt like hours later, but I'm sure was closer to 30 minutes, I heard him in the doorway. He bent down, scooped me up and, hands firmly holding my face, forced me to look at him. I will never forget the pain I saw in his eyes. A pain I had caused. But mingled with the hurt, was a compassion I didn't understand.

He took my hand, got down on his knee, and asked me - once again - to marry him.

RESTORED

Oh, friend. This moment will forever be sealed in my memory. Heaven kissed earth in the wee hours of the morning in that little apartment on Potter Street, and through this extravagant expression of grace and forgiveness, that boy changed my life. For the first time, truly, in my life, I understood - tangibly - the radical love of Jesus. The love that says, "Even though I know you completely - with all the ugliness and brokenness you carry - I still want you!"

I was utterly wrecked in the most beautiful of ways.

The next morning, puffy-eyed and surprisingly courageous, I sat on my momma's lap and told her what had happened on the night of September 15th, 1996, and how it had impacted the choices I'd made over the next few years. We wept together as she wrestled to understand how they'd missed the warning signs that I was so deeply in trouble. She asked to share it with my dad, and shortly afterwards asked that I share my story with our women's group at church.

Faster than I ever thought possible, this terrible tale that had held me captive all these years lost its power and become a powerful weapon against the very one who had tried to destroy me.

The following year, as we navigated the unchartered territory of newlywed life, we spoke at a purity conference. Sharing honestly and transparently from our personal journey, we were able to reflect on some of the struggles we were working through as a couple as a result of our poor choices, while celebrating God's extraordinary faithfulness.

And while I'd love to tell you that our life has been sunshine and roses since the truth emerged, we've had a whole heck of a lot to work through.

My husband wisely sought counsel from a Godly mentor. He reminded him how hard it must have been for me to bring this to him, and how important it was that he work through it, forgive me, and then let it go. "Never bring it up again," he added. And I am so incredibly thankful and blessed to say, he never has.

While I'm still uprooting lies I believed and associations I made during sexual encounters as a teenager, we've come a mighty long way! Despite the years of junk we've had to wade through, the many soul ties we've had to sever, and the deep insecurities I continue to wrestle with, the sweetness and freedom of our intimacy has grown exponentially over the past several years.

To add to the sexual baggage, I dragged a boatload of emotional wounding into our marriage. I had so cemented into my mind the notion that 'conflict destroys relationships' that it took me years to not shy away from it. Past experience had proven this theory time and time again, so when something was bothering me, I stuffed it. And when my hubby picked up something wasn't right, and brought it up...I hid.

Fear of disappointing him fueled my drive for perfection and gave voice to my inner critic. The lingering sense that I was never good enough, in the kitchen, bedroom or laundry room, bubbled close to the surface, rearing its insecure head in hyper-sensitivity and defensiveness.

This poor guy had NO idea what he was getting himself into.

I cannot imagine what life would be like for us today, had I tried to keep everything locked up inside. I wonder whether we would have even survived. Secrets tend to breed more secrets, which destroy the trust and safety of a marriage, and eventually unravel the very fabric of your relationship.

While those tools we'd placed in our marital tool belt came in handy when dealing with love and respect issues, or gender roles, and finances, nothing could quite prepare us for the daily walking out of married life. Especially one that required much healing and reprogramming between the sheets. Our sex life, once settled into, was lackluster at best, as I struggled to stay emotionally present, while shying away from anything creative that might resemble the experiences I'd had years earlier. Honest, open discussion, coupled with prayer, really helped us overcome much of these issues, and continues to act as our go-to when unexpected things emerge from time to time.

It's been amazing watching God use our journey and our struggles to encourage other couples wrestling with the same stuff. We've had the opportunity to mentor several couples, and lead many different marriage courses, simply because we've made our imperfect selves available to Him, and because we truly love watching our resourceful God redeem our brokenness and use it for His glory.

REDEEMED

We had the opportunity to fly home to South Africa and Namibia in 2006, in celebration of our third anniversary, and to connect my hubby with the family of mine he'd not yet met. Many of our fondest memories together were created during the 5 glorious weeks we spent gallivant across the countryside.

On our last evening in South Africa, before heading over to Namibia for our final week of vacation, I had another of those 'God opportunities'. One of those, "I'm giving you the opportunity of a lifetime...but you have to act within the lifetime of the opportunity" moments.

We had spent a week with my parent's best friends in Johannesburg and I had been sharing how I was still wrestling with some severe insecurity. In fact, my people-pleaser streak was threatening to become a fully-blown way of life. I was terrified of disappointing people and in my effort to never rock the proverbial boat, I had become relatively passive-aggressive in the way I dealt with things.

My mom's bosom buddy, who had headed up their area's Theophostic Ministry (and inner healing ministry; "theo" meaning God, "Phos" meaning light) had asked whether I'd wanted to set aside some time to really pray about these things and ask God what the root issue was. Initially I'd been eager, but as the clock ticked down and our final hours with them became fewer, I felt a mild panic. "I don't really feel like being an emotional, snotty mess," I reasoned. "Don't worry about it...I'm good." But there, in the pit of my stomach, was that bubbling sense of urgency.

Don't miss it, Joy. Don't miss what I have for you.

Just before we were scheduled to be picked up by my dad's sister, who was going to take us to their place, and then drive us to the airport in the morning, I dove in headfirst.

Wait. I want in. I want everything God has for me...bring it on!

So we called and asked her to come 2 hours later, then jumped in with both feet. As I sat cross-legged on her bed, begging God to uproot this life-sucking burden from me, we waited. Allowing God to take me back to the beginning, where lies took root and truths got twisted, the tears and snot began to pour. From the forgotten parts of my heart, God brought to mind snippets of scenes that had taken place when my older sister and I were 4 and 6. He took me, in my mind's eye, to the white garage door of our favorite worker's apartment on the grounds of the hostel we'd lived in. My dad had worked as vice-principal to this German girl's hostel for years, and it's the place we called home upon our arrival from Cape Town.

What took place in that small bedroom had been all but erased from my memory. Only fragments had remained, but slowly things shifted into place. Suddenly it all made sense.

All those years I'd wrestled with shame and guilt because something about our childhood had felt mysteriously dirty, but without remembering what had actually happened, I simply stuffed the feeling, owned the shame, and believed that something must just be wrong with me. I was broken. And dirty. And disturbed.

All those years my sister and I dabbled in things we had no place dabbling in. And now it made sense.

This was the missing piece of the puzzle I'd been desperately trying to assemble, and God - in His sweetness - had revealed it at the perfect time. The very next day we landed in Namibia, and as we walked the grounds a few days later, hand-in-hand, processing through and releasing the wound of innocence stolen, God brought closure to an incredibly confusing chapter of my life. We stood outside that white door, cried, and let it go.

Upon arriving home in the States, just before Thanksgiving, we discovered we were pregnant with our first child. We did the math and discovered our little lady was conceived in Namibia. How like our God to bring new life out of a chapter of my life that had reeked with decay.

We named our daughter 'Alathea Grace', Alathea being Greek for "truth".

For she, our precious gift, was the new life birthed out of a season drenched in truth, and seasoned heavily with grace.

You intended to harm me, but God intended it
for good to accomplish what is now being done,
the saving of many lives.

Genesis 50:20

RESOURCES

*that have shaped and challenged
me on this journey to wholeness:*

SOUL:

- All Things New by *John Eldredge*
- Waking The Dead by *John Eldredge*
- Healing The Wounded Heart by *Dan Allender*
- Heart Made Whole by *Christa Black Gifford*
- Sacred Rhythms by *Ruth Haley Barton*
- The Art of Letting Go by *Richard Rohr*
- Turn On Your Brain by *Dr. Caroline Leaf*
- Anatomy of the Soul by *Dr. Curt Thompson*
- The Soul of Shame by *Dr. Curt Thompson*
- Rising Strong by *Brené Brown*
- Soul Keeping by *John Ortberg*
- Renovation of the Heart by *Dallas Willard*
- The Gift of Being Yourself by *David Benner*

BODY:

- Every Body Matters by *Gary Thomas*
- The Body Keeps the Score by *Bessel van der Kolk*
- The Wellness Revelation by *Alisa Keeton*
- The Miracle Morning by *Hal Elrod*
- The Power of Habit by *Charles Duhigg*
- The One Thing by *Keller + Papasan*

SPIRIT:

- The Eternal Current by *Aaron Niequist*
- Even In Our Darkness by *Jack Deere*
- Into The Silent Land by *Martin Laird*
- Life of The Beloved by *Henri J. Nouwen*
- Out of Sorts by *Sarah Bessey*
- Blessed Are The Misfits by *Brant Hanson*
- Unoffendable by *Brant Hanson*

- You Are What You Love by *James K. A. Smith*
- Rooted by *Banning Liebscher*
- Chasing Francis by *Ian Morgan Cron*
- Unleashed by *Erwin Raphael McManus*
- The Ragamuffin Gospel by *Brennan Manning*
- Hidden in Christ by *James Bryan Smith*
- Messy Grace by *Caleb Kaltenbach*
- Chase the Lion by *Mark Batterson*
- Whisper by *Mark Batterson*
- The Jesus Manifesto by *Sweet + Viola*
- Abba's Child by *Brennan Manning*
- The Shack by *William P. Young*

ENNEAGRAM RESOURCES:
- The Road Back To You by *Ian Cron + Suzanne Stabile*
- The Enneagram: A Christian Perspective by *Richard Rohr*
- The Sacred Enneagram by *Christopher Heuertz*
- Self To Lose, Self To Find by *Marilyn Vancil*
- The Path Between Us by *Suzanne Stabile*
- Personality Types by *Don Riso + Russ Hudson*
- *Beth McCord* | Coaching + Courses : www.yourenneagramcoach.com
- The Enneagram Institute | Test : www.enneagraminstitute.com
- The Road Back To You Podcast : www.theroadbacktoyou.com)
- Typology Podcast (*Cron*) : www.typologypodcast.com
- The Enneagram Journey Podcast (*Stabile*) : www.theenneagramjourney.org
- *Sleeping At Last* | Musical artist who has written a song for each of the nine types : www.sleepingatlast.com

ABOUT THE AUTHOR

Joy McMillan is the founder of Simply Bloom Co,
a creative little company with a big heart.

A writer, speaker, graphic designer & coach,
she loves helping women embrace their stories and
live out their purpose with passion. Founder of the
#weROARproject and creative whirlwind behind the
Simply Bloom shop, she's the author of XES, Penduka + SOZO.

Originally hailing from Southern Africa, Joy lives and loves in
Michigan with her hubby and their two little loin-fruit.

NOTES

1 check out enneagraminstitute.com for test and type overviews
2 Kintsugi, also known as Kintsukuroi, is the Japanese art of repairing broken pottery with lacquer dusted or mixed with powdered gold or silver. Translated as "golden joinery", this practice treats breakage and repair as part of the history of an object, adding to its beauty, rather than something to discard or disguise.
3 According to legend, early coal mines did not feature ventilation systems, so miners would bring a caged canary into new coal mines. Because canaries are especially sensitive to methane and carbon monoxide, as long as the bird kept singing, the miners knew their air supply was safe. A dead canary meant an immediate evacuation.
4 Genesis 3
5 Matthew 9:20
6 theovernight.org/index.cfm?fuseaction=cms.page&id=1034
7 theovernight.org/index.cfm?fuseaction=cms.page&id=1034
8 relevantmagazine.com/life/why-churches-need-talk-about-suicide
9 Philippians 1:6 + Isaiah 40:28
10 Momology by Shelly Radic, page 67
11 caltech.edu/news/microbes-help-produce-serotonin-gut-46495
12 nydailynews.com/life-style/health/white-poison-danger-sugar-beat-article-1.1605232
13 dx.doi.org/10.1136/bjsports-2017-097971
14 www.nbcnews.com/id/32543288/ns/health-diet_and_nutrition/t/cut-back-way-back-sugar-says-heart-group/
15 newsroom.ucla.edu/releases/this-is-your-brain-on-sugar-ucla-233992
16 sciencedaily.com/releases/2014/11/141118141852.htm
17 cambridge.org/core/journals/the-british-journal-of-psychiatry/article/dietary-pattern-and-depressive-symptoms-in-middle-age/96D634CD33BD7B11F0C731BF73BA9CD3
18 youtu.be/lEXBxijQREo
19 academic.oup.com/ajcn/article-abstract/26/11/1180/4732762
20 psychologytoday.com/us/blog/hide-and-seek/201706/touch-hunger
21 ideas.time.com/2012/06/19/the-problem-with-no-hug-policies-in-schoo
22 growingupwithoutafather.org/learned.html
23 onlinelibrary.wiley.com/doi/full/10.1111/1467-8624.00569
24 solitarywatch.com/2015/07/13/voices-from-solitary-fly-in-the-ointment
25 nytimes.com/1993/11/09/sports/marathon-at-86-years-old-mavis-lindgren-is-a-road-runner.html

Made in the USA
Monee, IL
18 November 2019

17004393R10154